P9-AFD-370

FILMMAKERS SERIES

edited by
ANTHONY SLIDE

1. *James Whale,* by James Curtis. 1982
2. *Cinema Stylists,* by John Belton. 1983
3. *Harry Langdon,* by William Schelly. 1982
4. *William A. Wellman,* by Frank Thompson. 1983
5. *Stanley Donen,* by Joseph Casper. 1983
6. *Brian De Palma,* by Michael Bliss. 1983
7. *J. Stuart Blackton,* by Marian Blackton Trimble. 1985
8. *Martin Scorsese and Michael Cimino,* by Michael Bliss. 1985
9. *Franklin J. Schaffner,* by Erwin Kim. 1985
10. *D.W. Griffith at Biograph,* by Cooper C. Graham, et al. 1985
11. *Some Day We'll Laugh: An Autobiography,* by Esther Ralston. 1985
12. *The Memoirs of Alice Guy Blaché,* trans. by Roberta and Simone Blaché. 1986
13. *Leni Riefenstahl and Olympia,* by Cooper C. Graham. 1986
14. *Robert Florey,* by Brian Taves. 1986

In Preparation

Al Christie, by Sam Gill
Five Cinematographers, by Scott Eyman
Aldous Huxley, by Virginia M. Clark
Martin and Osa Johnson, by Pascal J. and Eleanor M. Imperato

LENI RIEFENSTAHL AND OLYMPIA

by
Cooper C. Graham

Filmmakers, No. 13

THE SCARECROW PRESS, INC.
Metuchen, N.J., & London • 1986

Excerpts from L. Andrew Mannheim's "Leni: Maligned Genius of the Nazis?" Modern Photography (February 1974), pp. 88-95, 112-19, reprinted by permission of the publisher.

Frontispiece: Preparations for the filming. From left: Rolf Lantin, Kurt Neubert, Walter Frentz (pointing), Leni Riefenstahl, Aurelia Friedl, unidentified grip, Hans Ertl (with hat). (Courtesy Leni Riefenstahl)

Library of Congress Cataloging-in-Publication Data

Graham, Cooper C., 1938-
Leni Riefenstahl and Olympia.

(Filmmakers ; no. 13)
Based in part on the author's thesis (Ph. D.)--New York University.
Includes index.
1. Olympic Games (11th : 1936 : Berlin, Germany)
2. Olympische Spiele (Motion picture) 3. Riefenstahl, Leni. 4. Moving pictures--Production and direction.
I. Title. II. Series: Filmmakers series ; no. 13.
GV722 1936.G73 1986 796.4'8 86-6715
ISBN 0-8108-1896-5

Manufactured in the United States of America

• CONTENTS •

• PREFACE •

This book was originally part of a Ph.D. dissertation written for the Department of Cinema Studies of New York University. I had been fascinated by the film Olympia for a long time, and I thought it would be interesting to analyze its relationship to National Socialism. Olympia was particularly significant since it was perhaps the best film produced in Hitler's Germany, and yet its topic is, at least on the surface, an innocent one. In addition, its maker, Leni Riefenstahl, has long maintained that she was not involved with the regime in making the film.

Since the arguments about Olympia have fallen into one of two categories--either the historical one that the film was made without the support of the regime, or the aesthetic one that the film itself is not influenced by National Socialist ideas or aesthetics--I divided the dissertation into two sections: first, a history of the production of the film and second, an aesthetic analysis. I had initially intended to place most of my emphasis on section two, with the historical section almost an expanded introduction. However, in the process of researching the dissertation, I became fascinated by the making of the film. I found a mass of interesting material, with the result that the historical section, in spite of my efforts to contain it, expanded until it assumed a life of its own and threatened to take over the dissertation.

This book is the history of the film's production. The making of Olympia was an epic story in itself, involving a huge cast of characters--some of them villains--and set against the background of a regime that was soon to enter history as one of the bloodiest of all time. I believe that this history also sheds much light on the generation of Germans who either wittingly or unwittingly worked for Adolf Hitler's vision of a new order.

Note to the Reader

The following abbreviations are used for major documentary sources in the chapter notes:

BA	Bundesarchiv, Coblentz, West Germany.
RMVP	Reichsministerium für Volksaufklärung und Propaganda.
RMI	Reichsministerium des Innern.

• ACKNOWLEDGMENTS •

Many people are involved in this work, and there is really no way that I can adequately thank them. First, I would like to thank Leni Riefenstahl in addition to indicating the extent of her cooperation. I began writing Frau Riefenstahl in 1981 and was able to provide her with some information about the Library of Congress holdings of her film. She was cordial and sent me some extremely interesting and useful material. I went to Germany in 1981, staying there almost a year researching this book. During that time, I had high hopes of interviewing Frau Riefenstahl. However, she was starting work on her own memoirs and was undergoing a painful hip operation, so she was unable to see me.

Later, when I returned to Germany to interview Willy Zielke, she agreed to grant me an interview on Whit Monday, May 23, 1983. The interview was friendly at first, but as soon as it became clear that I had seen much information at the Bundesarchiv and had read other material that did not support her interpretation of the financing of the film, the temperature dropped considerably. Frau Riefenstahl did provide me with considerable hard information about the editing of the film and the making of the sound track; for this I am extremely grateful. However, when I telephoned her several days later to see if I could talk to Erna Peters, her head cutter, she told me that she was no longer interested in working with me and if I did not say exactly what she had told me during the interview, she would sue me. We parted in a reasonably amicable manner after further discussion, but neither of us had much desire to renew contact. Nevertheless, I am grateful for the information that Frau Riefenstahl did provide.

I also obtained interviews from Heinz von Jaworsky (now

known as Henry Javorsky) and Willy Zielke. Henry Javorsky strikes me as one of that rare breed, a genuinely happy person. He was apologetic about not remembering more about the Olympic film, but he remembered far more than he thought he would be able to. Willy Zielke, in spite of being in poor health, graciously granted me two days of interviews. One of the great cameramen of the period, Zielke still has many wonderful ideas for films and photographic projects. Also, he has written a set of unpublished memoirs and has translated a biography of Chaliapin from Russian to German. I thank him for his time and trouble, and I hope that when I am his age I have half his vim. I thank Frau Zielke, too, for her extensive hospitality.

This work would not have been written without the help of the Library of Congress, an organization that still manages to awe me with the extensiveness of its holdings. I believe that I have used most divisions of the Library at one time or another; they have all produced wonders.

In the Motion Picture Section, I wish especially to thank the following persons: Patrick Loughney, who took out time from his own projects to help with mine; David Parker, who knew about Hubert Stowitts and read parts of this manuscript, making very useful suggestions; Paul Spehr, who provided me with introductions to most of the major archivists in the German Federal Republic and in the German Democratic Republic; Patrick Sheehan, without whom there would have been no chapter three; Emily Sieger and Barbara Humphrys, who gave me innumerable leads and arranged viewings of the many versions of *Olympia* at the Library; Erik Barnouw, former head of the Motion Picture/Broadcasting/Recorded Sound Division, who recommended me to Frau Riefenstahl; and Joseph Balian, without whom I would have chewed up countless prints of *Olympia* in a Steenbeck viewing machine long ago.

In the Prints and Photographs section, I wish to thank Annette Melville, who steered me to much useful photographed material. In the Recorded Sound section, I wish to thank Sam Brylawski for tips on interviewing techniques and for help in finding sound records of the 1936 Games.

There are also numerous people I wish to thank in the German Federal Republic. First of all, I want to thank the Goethe-Institut, which brought my rusty college German up to a point where I could function effectively in the language. The task of these institutes is far from simple, and they perform it extremely well. There is no way I can adequately thank Heinz and Gisela Heider or their daughters, Sonja and Anja. They took us in when we arrived sick and bedraggled in Coblentz, fed us, took care of us for six months, helped decipher pre-war German handwriting on Propaganda Ministry documents, wrote letters, coped with stubborn authorities both in East and West Germany, babysat for our children, and taught my then three-year-old daughter Margaret a rich Rhineland German. We will be forever in their debt.

Various institutions were extremely helpful. I want to thank Hans Barkhausen and Dr. Friedrich P. Kahlenberg for allowing me to use the extensive and excellent Bundesarchiv in Coblentz; Eberhardt Spiess of the Deutsches Institut für Filmkunde, currently in Frankfurt; die Bibliothek der Universität am Giessberg; die Stuttgarter Landesbibliothek, die Bayerischer Staatsbibliothek, and die Staatsbibliothek Preussischen Kulturbesitz in Berlin. I wish to thank Fred K. Prieberg, author of Musik im N.S. Staat, who gave me much information about Herbert Windt. Konrad Vogelsang generously shared his information about film music in National Socialist Germany.

In the German Democratic Republic, I wish to thank Wolfgang Klaue and Wolfgang Lies of the Archiv für den wissenschaftlichen Film in Potsdam-Babelsberg for letting me see their film material, and especially for providing me with copious written and photographic material about the Olympic film. They have been extremely generous.

In England, I wish to thank the British Film Institute, which was extremely helpful in sending me what it had available on the British history of the film.

In America, there are a number of individuals I wish to thank. First of all, I wish to acknowledge my great debt to my wife, Patricia Sayre Graham, as well as my debt to Barbara English Maris and Judith Lang Zaimont, extremely capable professional musicians all, who helped me avoid major musical gaffes in transcribing and discussing Herbert Windt's music. I also want to thank Brown Benson for making beautiful transcriptions from my chaotic manuscripts, Mary Ellen Crowley for her help in laying out the illustrations, and

Holger Homann and Felice Homann for their help in translation.

I also wish to thank David Crippen, Reference Archivist of the Henry Ford Archives; George Pratt at Eastman House for allowing me to look at Riefenstahl's reconstructed version of Olympia on 35mm film, and granting an interview; Lynn Garafola, who generously shared the results of her extensive research on Hubert Stowitts with me; Jo Ann Udovich, who sent me several articles on the film from Paris; Carolyn Hopkins for her hospitality in Zürich; Chris Horak of the George Eastman House; and Val Almendarez of the Academy of Motion Picture Arts and Sciences, without whom I would not have found out about Ernst Jäger in America; David R. Smith, Archivist of the Walt Disney Archives; Daniel H. Simon, Director of the Berlin Document Center; Jane Armstrong at the Applied Life Studies Library at the University of Illinois, who familiarized me with the Avery Brundage Collection; Charles Silver and Eileen Bowser at the Museum of Modern Art, who provided me with material from the Museum's correspondence file with Leni Riefenstahl.

I also wish to thank the National Archives, the New York Public Library and the excellent Enoch Pratt Free Library in Baltimore, Maryland, my home town, for a number of services performed. As well, I want to thank the Peoria Public Library in Peoria, Illinois. During an extended stay in Peoria, I used the library extensively and was grateful for the amount of useful information it provided.

Thanks are also due my colleagues at New York University, Elaine Mancini and Steven Higgins. Their suggestions for the manuscript have always been to the point and helpful. I am grateful to my dissertation committee--Robert Sklar, Janet Staiger, William K. Everson, and Brian Winston--for their help in guiding this work. To my advisor, Jay Leyda, I can only acknowledge my profound gratitude for his providing a brilliant example of what film scholarship can and should be.

Most of all, I want to thank my wife and children, Margaret and Geoffrey, who spent a year in Germany with me, learning German and coping with a foreign culture the hard way, while I had a comparatively easy time of it in the research libraries and the archives. I also thank them for putting up with me those times I was preoccupied with this book which has been most of the time since 1981.

I wish that I could claim that this work is the last word on the Olympic film of 1936, but it probably is not. There were numerous people I could not find to interview. Hans Ertl was unavailable, although his extremely interesting book, Meine wilden dreissiger Jahre, has filled many gaps. Walter Frentz is living on Lake Constance; Erna Peters is still alive, though unwell; and Leo de Laforgue is living in Berlin. In addition, by all reports, Frau Riefenstahl herself has numerous records and papers that one can only hope will see the light of day eventually; her memoirs promise to be interesting reading.

I was not allowed access to the minutes of Dr. Goebbels' staff meetings, which are at the Deutsches Zentralarchiv in the D.D.R. These minutes would certainly cast more light on the always interesting relationship between Dr. Goebbels and Leni Riefenstahl. However, I do believe that this work provides much useful information for film scholars. If it promotes further research into Riefenstahl's films and into the largely ignored subject of documentary film in the National Socialist period, I will regard the project as a success.

C.C.G.

• EDITOR'S FOREWORD •

Leni Riefenstahl is surely one of the most controversial names in the history of the motion picture. A major portion of the public, both within and outside of the film industry, continue to revile her with accusations of close ties to Hitler and the National Socialist Party. A minority recognize her for what she undoubtedly is, the greatest of all women film directors (past and present) and a major documentary filmmaker.

She made two of the greatest documentary features of all time, Triumph of the Will and Olympia. The first is, unquestionably, a work of political propaganda, illustrating its maker's total understanding of the power and purpose of true documentary. Olympia might in the hands of any other filmmaker have been, like all of the other documentaries on the Olympic Games which were to follow, merely a dull and tedious record of an international event. However, under Leni Riefenstahl's direction, and thanks to her editorial genius, Olympia becomes a paean of praise to physical culture and to the glory of victory on the fields of sport. Not coincidentally, Olympia also becomes very much a filmic appreciation of National Socialism.

Thanks to Dr. Cooper Graham's painstaking research both here and in Germany, this book provides a definitive study of the making of the film and of its critical and popular reception. In analyzing the film's purpose, Dr. Graham brings to light many of the subtle undertones in the production, which might be lost to the casual or uninformed observer. He discusses style and structure, aesthetics and ideology, making of Leni Riefenstahl and Olympia a definitive study of the film and an exhaustive examination of its maker.

Anthony Slide

• CHAPTER I •

THE BACKGROUND AND FINANCING OF THE OLYMPIC FILM

THE POLITICAL BACKGROUND OF THE 1936 OLYMPIC GAMES

In order to understand the full meaning of the Olympic film, it is first necessary to some extent to talk about the Eleventh Olympiad and its importance to Germany. This entails a discussion of the political situation in Germany and abroad during the first years of the National Socialist regime. It is nearly impossible--and almost an immoral action--for a person to approach the period while at the same time suspending familiarity with its well-documented horrors: the terror, the persecution of all non-National Socialist political parties, the extermination of the Jews, the war, the concentration camps and the other testimonies to a gruesome regime. But it must be remembered that in the 1930s, according to the judgment of many people (many of whom were not Germans), the whole system seemed to be working rather well.

The mid-1930s was a period when Germany gave the appearance of having conquered many of the problems plaguing the Western democracies. Due to the unorthodox policies of Hjalmar Schacht, the problem of unemployment seemed to be solved. Prices of goods were kept artificially low, and while there were shortages, at least many products were within the financial reach of the German consumer. Much of the employment came from various massive building programs, such as the construction of the new *Autobahn* system, or the building of new youth hostels, or the draining of the swamps to produce farmland. The regime had founded a workcorps called the Reich Arbeitsdienst (RAD) as well; it was a Hitlerian equivalent (albeit with paramilitary trappings) of the CCC of the New Deal. Using the KdF programs (Kraft durch Freude), the government had devised numerous schemes for providing cheap recreation and holiday travel to workers; the idea of a people's car, the Volkswagen, also stemmed from KdF. The regime provided a list of services that was unknown in the Weimar period.

In spite of the abolition of free labor unions, the terrorism, the ban on all political parties except the NSDAP, and the lack of a free press, there seems to be little doubt that the majority of Germans in those years were enthusiastic about the benefits of National Socialism, and it seems to be true that life was better for many Germans at that time than it had been under the always unstable Weimar Republic--especially to those Germans of a conservative turn of mind. There were no strikes, no other types of labor unrest, no riots in the streets. The inefficient parliamentary system, with all the concomitant political infighting, logrolling, and pork barrel politics, had been abolished. In Germany, there seemed to be only a cohesive, efficient Volkgemeinschaft (under the leadership of its Führer) achieving common, clearly defined goals.[1]

Not only Germans but many foreign observers were impressed. Winston Churchill wrote in 1934 that apart from the anti-Semitism, which he found reprehensible, there were many things to admire about Adolf Hitler. Lloyd George met Hitler and was favorably impressed. The Duke and Duchess of Windsor went to Berlin and met Hitler in 1937 and seemed to have been somewhat pro-German ever after. Various conservative American business circles and commentators appear to have been similarly admiring. Hitler also had many admirers in France, where there had nearly been a Fascist coup in February 1934.

It should also be remembered that Hitler was loudly and convincingly saying to everyone how much he wanted peace. In one of his most famous speeches on this subject, made on May 21, 1935, he said:

> Our racial theory regards every war for the subjection and domination of an alien people as a proceeding which sooner or later changes and weakens the victor internally, and eventually brings about his defeat.... As there is no longer any occupied

> space in Europe, every victory ... can at best result in a quantitative increase in the number of the inhabitants of a country. But if the nations attach so much importance to that, they can achieve it without tears in a simpler and more natural way--[by] a sound social policy, by increasing the readiness of a nation to have children.
>
> No! Nationalist Socialist Germany wants peace because of its fundamental convictions. And it wants peace also owing to the realization of the simple primitive fact that no war would be likely essentially to alter the distress in Europe.... The principal effect of every war is to destroy the flower of the nation....
>
> Germany needs peace and desires peace!

And further:

> Whoever lights the torch of war in Europe can wish for nothing but chaos. We, however, live in the firm conviction that in our time will be fulfilled not the decline but the renaissance of the West. That Germany may make an imperishable contribution to this great work is our proud hope and our unshakable belief.[2]

In this light, the propaganda the National Socialists wanted to convey about themselves to both Germans and non-Germans becomes clearly understandable. First, Germany was a land of peace and order. After the violent incidents in the spring of 1933 (when Hitler was made Reich Chancellor and enemies of the National Socialists were murdered in the street or were tortured to death in the cellars of SA barracks), order had been restored. This was certainly in contrast to the decadent France of the Third Republic now under the leadership of the Front Populaire and "the Jew Léon Blum," where there was constant labor unrest, riots, trouble with the communists, and a notoriously inefficient political system. While Germany might have wanted the readjustment of certain boundaries, it certainly did not want war. On the contrary, Germany wanted to extend the hand of friendship to all the peoples of Europe. Second, because Germany was this "island of peace and order" in the midst of a strife-torn Europe, Germans could produce great things. They were providing full employment and a gigantic public works program, reclaiming land, draining swamps, and modernizing the railways. The National Socialists were no wild men, but a responsible government creating a stable, industrious society for the German people.[3]

This was the Reich that the leaders wished to display to the world. One need hardly point out that their display was a complete sham. By the time of the Olympic Games in August of 1936, this was apparent, or should have been. On March 7, 1936, a month after the Winter Olympic Games in Garmisch-Partenkirchen, Hitler tore up the Treaty of Locarno and re-annexed the Rhineland. Both England and France decided that Hitler's move was not worth fighting about, although it clearly violated several treaties and in the event of another war would have left France's flank completely exposed. And this was only the most recent in a series of aggressive acts taken by the Hitler government against its neighbors. On October 14, 1933, Germany had withdrawn from the League of Nations. On July 25, 1934, the National Socialists had murdered the Austrian Chancellor Engelbert Dollfuss. On March 16, 1935, Hitler had reintroduced universal military service. On July 22, 1936, a week before the opening of the Olympic games, Hitler pledged support to General Francisco Franco in the coming Spanish Civil War. In the summer of 1936, the press was already beating the drum with anti-Austrian and anti-Czech propaganda. A person with any powers of discernment at all would have been able to realize that the claims by the regime that it was promoting peace were already widely divergent from its praxis.

Nevertheless, the National Socialists were remarkably successful with their propaganda, both at home and abroad, and they missed no opportunity to show the world that the New Germany, in an atmosphere of calm, order, and purpose was producing wonders that the rest of the world could well envy.

One can see that the Olympic Games fit these propaganda aims perfectly; they did this in three ways: 1) The Germans could impress the world with the efficiency and size of the Games. They would be the best organized, most extensive and greatest Olympic Games the world had ever seen. 2) The Germans could also impress the world by the accomplishments of their athletes (German athletes had not done especially well at the Games at Los Angeles in 1932). 3) The National Socialists could show that they were full of good will toward the whole world and wished only to be friends.

However, as important as the Games might have been to them, the National Socialists--primarily because of their racial ideology--jeopardized the Games' success. Immediately after the original seizure of power in 1933, Jews had been the subject of a reign of terror. Because of international bad press, the terror had abated, but an increasing number of decrees segregated Jews from non-Jews. This segregation also took place in sports. On June 2, 1933, Jews were excluded from youth, welfare, and gymnastic organizations. Julius Streicher wrote in Der Stürmer:

> We need to waste no words here, Jews are Jews and there is no place for them in German sports. Germany is the fatherland of Germans and not Jews, and the Germans have the right to do what they want in their own country.[4]

By the beginning of 1935, there were no Jews allowed on public or private practice fields in Germany.

In 1932, the National Socialists had used similar language while referring to Black athletes. The Völkischer Beobachter trumpeted:

> There is nothing for Negroes at the Olympics.... The ancient Greeks would turn in their graves if they knew what modern man had made of their holy national games.... [T]he next games take place in Berlin in 1936.... The Blacks must be excluded.[5]

Because of rhetoric like this, but more because the rhetoric was being translated into action, inasmuch as Jews were being systematically excluded from sport in Germany, the United States proposed a boycott of the Olympic Games in Berlin. On June 6, 1933, the International Olympic Committee (IOC) met at Vienna and went even further. The American members of the IOC stated that they would start a campaign to remove the Games from Germany if the Germans maintained their position with regard to Jewish athletes. Dr. Theodor Lewald, President of the Organization Committee of the German Games, part Jewish himself and certainly no National Socialist, announced from Berlin on June 7 that his government had authorized him to say that Jews would not be excluded from the Olympic teams "as a matter of principle." This was well and good, but since Jews could not use practice fields or play regularly in Germany with German teams, they hardly had much of a chance to compete for a berth on an Olympic team. And there were an increasing number of observers who simply felt that the National Socialists could not be trusted to fulfill their promises, no matter what they said. Because of these considerations, the Amateur Athletic Union (AAU) voted at a meeting in the United States on November 21, 1933, to boycott the Games in Germany unless Jewish athletes were allowed to compete freely in all sports. This resolution was vigorously supported by nearly all members, including Avery Brundage, the President of the American Olympic Committee.

(It is unfortunately beyond the scope of this book to investigate thoroughly the activities of Avery Brundage, General Charles Sherrill, and William May Garland of the American Olympic Committee. This writer had relied heavily on Richard Mandell's book <u>The Nazi Olympics</u> for background material on the proposed boycott, but there is a wealth of untapped information touching on American and German efforts to stave off a boycott. [The information may be found at the Avery Brundage Collection at the University of Illinois, as well as at the Bundesarchiv in Coblentz.] Suffice it to say that Avery Brundage was one of the most influential men in American athletics, a stickler for the maintenance of strict amateur standards in Olympic sports, and a man who had always been controversial. His role in the final decision to send an American team to Berlin represented the first time that he gained major prominence.)

Until June 1934, the American Committee refused to accept the German invitation. Then the Germans stated that twenty-one Jewish athletes had been invited to train on German teams for the Olympics. Brundage went to Germany on a fact-finding tour. He was convinced and evidently impressed by what he saw. He recommended American participation in the Olympics, and the American Olympic Committee went along with his recommendation. However, the AAU (under the leadership of Judge Jeremiah T. Mahoney) continued to fight for a boycott of the Olympics, since, contrary to what Brundage was saying, stories of racial and religious persecution had continued to come out of Germany. For instance, none of the twenty-one German Jews invited to train with the German teams actually showed up, for reasons unexplained. The boycott movement continued to grow in America. In a remarkable meeting, General Charles Sherrill met with Hitler on August 24, 1935, to get a firm commitment from him that all Jews would be allowed to compete freely on German teams. Sherrill helpfully explained that he was a friend of the New Germany and the National Socialist Movement, that Hitler would have to do something to avoid the boycott since American media people were firmly in the hands of Jews, and that the Jews were such poor athletes none would probably qualify for a German team anyway.[6] Hitler refused Jewish athletes on German teams on the basis that doing this would be contrary to all that he stood for. In case anyone still misunderstood his position, on September 15, 1935 he proclaimed the Nuremberg Racial Laws. Jews were deprived of German citizenship, and marriage between Jews and Aryans was forbidden. Jews had already been discriminated against, but the new laws made them subjects and completely deprived them of their civil rights in Germany. The quarrel grew in force between the Olympic Committee and the AAU, with Brundage and Sherrill fighting the boycott and Mahoney in favor of it. In the course of the ensuing dialogue, Brundage and Sherrill made comments that were both red-baiting and anti-Semitic. Sherrill stated that America would be far better off if it had a Mussolini to straighten things out, both men called their opponents communists, and Sherrill said in public what he had said privately to Hitler about the dominance of Jews in the American media. Brundage sent telegrams to the Reich Sport Leader Hans von Tschammer und Osten in which he complained of the behavior of the American Jews and stated publicly that American Jews had better not try to strengthen their situation by an Olympic boycott. The behavior of the spokesmen for American sport has never been more biased or unconsidered.

In light of Hitler's comments to Sherrill and the recently enacted Nuremberg Laws, it is difficult to see how Brundage and Sherrill could argue realistically that the Nationalist Socialist Regime had any real intention of abiding by the Vienna Conference or that the Germans were really intending to allow Jews to compete on Olympic teams; but, in fact, that is what they did. Finally, after a major debate held on December 8, 1935, it was decided by the narrow margin of two and one-half votes to send an American team to the Olympics in Berlin.

Other nations besides the United States expressed the wish that the Germans might treat their Jewish sportsmen fairly, in accordance with the spirit of the Olympics. However, only in America was the outrage over the German treatment of Jewish athletes so widespread that a boycott was threatened.

The National Socialists were frightened by the commotion, and they did make concessions. They decided to soft-pedal their more overt racial and religious propaganda. They made no outcry about Black athletes, and, as propaganda gestures, they allowed Rudi Ball, a Jew and one of the best hockey players in Germany, and Helene Mayer, a Jewish fencer, to participate on German teams. Helene Mayer was to win a silver medal for Adolf Hitler. The National Socialists stopped the anti-Church persecution at the special order of Hitler. They took down anti-Semitic signs in Berlin, and made every effort to convince foreigners of their sense of justice and fair play.

Thus the public outcry and threatened American boycott of the Olympic Games forced the Germans into a pretense of upholding the Olympic ideal. The National Socialist reaction to the threatened boycott also shows how quickly the National Socialists were willing--at least temporarily--to suppress not only their ideology in the interests of practical politics but also their immediate propaganda goals. The irony of this hypocritical maintenance of the Olympic ideal, which was more or less forced upon the National Socialists, was that it was later used by apologists for Germany and the 1936 Games (including Avery Brundage, Carl Diem, and Leni Riefenstahl herself) as proof that the 1936 Games were not political and the National Socialists were not the monsters they had been painted as being. The ultimate effect of the international revulsion to the new German ideology was, paradoxically, to end up aiding rather than harming the international standing of the regime by insuring that it held a fair Olympics.

As we will see, the propaganda aims of the regime were to have an effect on the Olympic film. Recognizing this, we must continue to remember that for Hitler and the regime, the Games were an instrument of Nazi propaganda. What we also must remember is the <u>kind</u> of instrument the Games were.

THE ORGANIZATION OF THE GAMES

In order to discuss the production of the Olympic film, it is also necessary to examine to some extent the organization of the Berlin Olympics themselves; several of the chief conflicts that arose in the organization of the Games had significant effects on the making of the film. These conflicts were also to some extent repeated in the conflicts between the film makers and the political producers of the film. In addition, several persons who were prominent in the Olympic movement were later involved in a defense of the film, so it becomes necessary to find out what the functions of these persons were. This is one of the areas in which political decisions involving the organization of the Games themselves had inevitable repercussions on the organization and responsibility for the Olympic film.

Germany was originally granted the Olympic Games by the Olympic Congress in Barcelona in 1931 when Germany was still a republic. After the National Socialists took power in January 1933, there was some talk about removing the Games from Germany, but as we have seen, the talk was ended by the Vienna Conference, and there was no decision to change the location of the Games. The new regime continued the plans started in the Weimar period, and the organization immediately responsible for carrying out the plans was the Organization Committee for the eleventh Olympic Games. This committee was made up of three groups: The first group included the German members of the IOC. It was made up of highly respected Germans whose participation in the Olympic movement went back to Wilhelmine and Weimar Germany. As members of the IOC, they were in principle at least above national considerations. This group included State Secretary Dr. Theodor Lewald, the Duke Adolf Friedrich zu Mecklenburg, and Dr. Karl Ritter von Halt. Dr. Lewald, who has already been mentioned briefly, had been head of the German Olympic Commission since 1924 and had helped to organize the German Olympic teams in 1904 and 1906. Though Lewald was a Christian, his grandmother had been Jewish, which technically made him a *Mischling* and non-Aryan. Dr. Lewald was too prominent to be dismissed, however, so he was kicked upstairs to become head of the Olympic Organization Committee. As we will see, this august title was not going to mean much. Dr. von Halt was responsible for organization of the Winter Olympic Games. He was a National Socialist and a Sturmabteilung (SA) member, but his dedication to sports seems to have been real. He was later to try to help Riefenstahl by bearing witness to Goebbel's actions against her. It could reasonably be said that these German members of the IOC were not particularly close to the regime.

The second group represented on the Organization Committee was the German Olympic Commission (Der deutsche Olympische Auschuss). This group was comprised of many of the prominent National Socialists, and its aims were more openly nationalistic and closer to the regime. As previously stated, Dr. Lewald--once president of this commission--had been ousted. He was replaced by Reich Sport Leader Hans von Tschammer und Osten, a staunch National Socialist who was quite close to Hitler. With von Tschammer und Osten as president, the policy of the regime was sure to be carried out, and even though he had had virtually no sports experience on the level of the Olympic Games, he would get plenty of help from the Organization Committee. Lewald and Ritter von Halt were both members of the German Olympic Commission, but as we will see, they were both very much under the thumb of von Tschammer und Osten, and it was there they would remain.

Also kept subservient to von Tschammer und Osten was perhaps the most famous and prominent spokesman for the Olympic movement (except for Baron Pierre de Coubertin himself), the secretary of the Organization Committee, Dr. Carl Diem. The contribution of Dr. Diem to the Olympic movement and to German sport is overwhelming. Born in 1882, Diem started in sports as a runner and formed his first sporting club when he was seventeen. He was on the board of directors of the German Sport Authorities for Track and Field and, from 1912 to 1933, was the secretary-general for Physical Fitness. In 1920 he was one of the founders of the German School for Physical Fitness (Die Hochschule für Leibesübungen) in Cologne. Dr. Diem was in charge of the German expedition to the Olympic Games in Athens in 1906, in Stockholm in 1912, in Amsterdam in 1928, and in Los Angeles in 1932. (Germany had not been invited to the Games in 1920 and 1924.) He travelled widely and knew many languages. He had been in charge of the planning and scheduling of the sixth Olympic Games to be held in Berlin in 1916, and the cancellation of these Games due to World War I had been a major blow to him. He was instrumental in getting Germany invited to the

Games in Amsterdam in 1928, having the Games held in Berlin in 1936 instead of in Barcelona, and staving off the threatened boycott. He wrote constantly and produced hundreds of articles on sports and the Olympics.[7]

He was also an early believer in the possibilities of sports film. In 1924, Dr. Diem was secretary of the German Commission for Physical Fitness (Deutsche Ausschuss für Leibesübungen), the then official German organization for sport which was later disbanded by the National Socialists. This organization, through Dr. Lewald and Dr. Diem, produced a film about the Olympics of 1920 and 1924 that was directed by A. Holtz and Kurth Seeger. A program accompanied the film, and Dr. Diem wrote the foreword:

> Yes, not once since this war [World War I] had a friendly disposition, such had been present in ancient Greece, developed. The foes had taken petty vengeance on German athletes, and had excluded them from the Games. But ... as Olympic victories will be ours in the future, when we will happily accept them, we should not complain![8]

In 1928, Dr. Diem and Lewald were involved in the production of a film called Der neue Mensch. It in many ways followed the ground broken by the more famous Wege zur Kraft und Schönheit made three years before and is a good example of what Siegfried Kracauer meant by a proto-National-Socialist film. The film stressed that modern man is too cerebral. He may be able to think, but he is totally out of touch with his body and is therefore unhealthly. A new man is therefore needed, one who will not be overly intellectual but who will exercise as man did in the past. The film pointed out that in 1918 (and the date is no accident) there was only one playground for each 15,000 persons in Germany, and it frequently equated the rise of Germany with the rise of German sport. There is an animated sequence of a man having to swim the Baltic to join the rest of his fellow Germans who are exercising on a playing field in Germany (an anti-Versailles and anti-Polish Corridor joke). The film shows quite clearly the climate of revanchisme in Germany--as it existed even among those who were not National Socialists--but it also shows that Diem and Lewald were acutely aware of the uses of the sports film at a time when the Anglo-Saxons had not done much with the idea.

It is clear that in a democratic society Dr. Diem would have had far more authority than he actually possessed. In fact, he performed much of the actual work in making the Berlin Olympics a success. As we shall see, however, he was not in a position to make many decisions.

Bureaucrats made up the third group involved in the Organization Committee. Members included State Secretary Pfundtner of the Reich Ministry of the Interior who was responsible for the building program, Doctor Berndt of the Propaganda Ministry who would be responsible for many of the propaganda aspects of the Games, and Captain Fürstner who would be responsible for getting the work done on the Olympic Village. As most of them were members of the armed forces, or of the regime of the Berlin city government, they were hardly in a position to take an independent line. For the most part, authority was in the hands of a few very important persons who were members of the Organization Committee or of the German Olympic Commission and who had widely divergent ideas about how to conduct the Games.

This hierarchy was to become the foundation for conflict between Dr. Lewald, who headed the Organization Committee, and the German Olympic Commission, under the leadership of von Tschammer und Osten. However, members of the International Olympic Committee were not necessarily inimical to the National Socialists, and there were some National Socialists who cooperated with Diem or Lewald. But, to a large extent, Diem and Lewald were nuisances to the National Socialists. They were tolerated only because of their very long and very public struggle on behalf of the Olympic movement and because getting rid of them would cause much unfavorable publicity from all over the world. If it seemed that Diem and Lewald were in a precarious position, future events were to worsen that position.

At the first meetings of the Organization Committee, it was decided that only the Reich could finance the Games (although the Reich had by no means taken on this responsibility). Then, on October 5, 1933, Adolf Hitler reviewed all the plans for the sports complex. Hitler decided to enlarge the plans, to build a stadium capable of holding 100,000 persons. He also decided to build a swimming stadium and a riding complex, as well as a large open air arena to the northwest. In addition, a huge sports complex called the Sport Forum (later called the House of German Sport) would be built. Hitler specifically said that the Reich would finance the building.

> The Chancellor [Hitler] explained that the stadium should be constructed by the Reich, it is to be an undertaking of the Reich; if one has invited the world to be one's guest, something great and beautiful should be built.[9]

So with Hitler taking a personal interest in the Games--and the Reich holding the purse strings--the autonomy of the Organization Committee was lessened. In a letter to Dr. Lewald dated December 21, 1933, State Secretary Pfundtner wrote pointedly that in a discussion on December 14, Hitler had approved of the revised plans of the architect Werner March for the Olympic complex, and that in the future, Dr. Pfundtner would be responsible to Hitler as well as to the Reich Sport Leader. (There is no mention of the fact that, theoretically, as president of the Organization Committee Pfundtner should be solely responsible to Dr. Lewald). Pfundtner goes on to issue the following order:

> I ask also that all special information going to the press having anything to do with the building program should only be announced by the Reich Sport Leader, who is in the closest contact with me.[10]

The Reich Ministry of the Interior also sent a note to the press. The note stated that <u>all notices about the architectural--as well as sport--preparations</u> concerning the Olympic games were to come only from the Reich Sport Leader.

This pronouncement effectively removed the President of the Organization Committee as spokesman for the Games. On January 18, Dr. Lewald wrote a letter to Pfundtner complaining about the decision to give the ultimate authority to the Reich Sport Leader, saying that this decision made it especially hard for him [Lewald] to carry out his job outside of Germany.[11] Dr. Lewald made a special point of stating that Dr. Diem could provide considerable expertise and experience in the preparations for the Games. The Reich Sport Leader replied that there had been attempts to make Dr. Diem his chief of staff, but, "Diem cannot be used because of his strong involvement with the former political system."[12] The latter ended with the rejection of any larger sphere of influence for Dr. Diem. In March of 1934, Dr. Diem again asked to have something to do with the preparation of the Olympic Games in his capacity as secretary of the Organization Committee. He said that he felt he was intruding when he spoke to the Reich Sport Leader and that he was ready to put himself at the Reich Sport Leader's disposition. He again pleaded that he had a sufficient amount of expertise and knowledge to be of considerable use to the regime. If an answer was sent to Diem, it is not recorded.[13]

The whole situation came to a head in October 1934. It had been decided to have a competition to select the words to be used for the Olympic hymn. Dr. Lewald, in conjunction with the poet Börries Freiherr von Münchhausen, selected the winner without consulting either Dr. Goebbels (in his capacity as Minister of People's Enlightenment and Propaganda), the Reich Sport Leader (von Tschammer und Osten), or the Minister of the Interior (Wilhelm Frick); then he issued his decision to the press. He also personally invited Baron Pierre de Coubertin, the founder of the modern Olympic Games, to Berlin. The Party leaders were made sufficiently angry by these independent actions that they spelled out the areas of responsibility of the various groups involved. The main conflict existed between the Organization Committee of the eleventh Olympic Games (the president of which was Dr. Lewald) and the German Olympic Commission (the president of which was the Reich Sport Leader). The Reich Ministry of the Interior issued the following memorandum to settle the controversy.[14] It first quoted from the Jahrbuch des Leibesübungen 1930, p. 194ff.:

> The IOC entrusts the national committee of each land with the carrying through of the Olympics in which the chosen city lies. This committee can further assign tasks to a special committee which is specially chosen for this purpose, and whose leader then works through the IOC. The commission of the special committee is dissolved with the ending of the games.[15]

The Organization Committee was just such a special committee. The memorandum then further quotes:

> The Organization Committee of the chosen land to which the games have been entrusted is responsible for the games and must to this end have all possible powers.

The memorandum implied that the Organization Committee's powers were quite broad, indeed, and that the German Olympic Commission could not supersede the authority of the Committee. The memorandum also specifically stated that the Organization Committee took precedence over any national commissions, because the Organization Committee had been established by a decision of the German Olympic Commission on November 11, 1932. A withdrawal of the powers given to the Committee was not now possible, and an attempt to withdraw them would, "No doubt by those circles unfriendly to Germany, be misused to maintain that the independent accomplishment of the Olympic Games was not possible in Germany."

So the ministry made the following decision. The Olympic Organization Committee had full powers externally, outside of Germany. However, the German Olympic Commission had full powers over the preparation for the games internally, over all those preparations that fell within the administrative province (verwaltungsmässige Vorbereitung), and the Reich Minister of the Interior had to be consulted with reference to all important questions having to do with the general preparation for the Games.

As a serious attempt to solve the problem, the decision is patently absurd. What is external and what is internal? For instance, it sounds as if Dr. Lewald had power to issue invitations to persons abroad, and that he was therefore within his powers in issuing an invitation to Pierre de Coubertin. On the other hand it is possible to argue that the preparation of a guest list and the issuance of invitations is an important enough question to require the attention and approval of the Reich Minister of the Interior. It is evident that whatever distinctions the decision seemed to imply, in reality the Organization Committee no longer had the power to act and that the real power lay with the German Olympic Commission, i.e., the regime. This was clearly the understanding of State Secretary Pfundtner, who went even further in his interpretation of the memorandum. On October 15, 1934, he wrote Dr. Lewald the following letter:

> In all internal matters is the Organization Committee therefore the trustee of the German Olympic Commission and therefore compelled to obtain the agreement of its empowerer in all important matters.[16]

Furthermore, the Reich Minister of the Interior must be consulted about all decisions in the general preparations for the Games, internal or external.

So by the end of 1934, the Organization Committee of the eleventh Olympic Games had been reduced to a rubber stamp. The real power lay elsewhere. From then on, the production of the Olympic Games would be a National Socialist responsibility. This is important because Riefenstahl has stressed that it was the Organization Committee--and Dr. Diem and Dr. Lewald in particular--who commissioned her to make the Olympic film. But by 1935, the Organization Committee and its members, including Dr. Diem and Lewald, were firmly gleichgeschaltet into a National Socialist framework. The subsequent history of the Olympic film must be understood in this context.

THE REGIME AND THE OLYMPIC FILM

It is in light of the propaganda aims of the regime and its increasing control over the administrative machinery of the Games that the contradictory statements of Leni Riefenstahl should be discussed. Riefenstahl has always maintained that she made the Olympic film free of government interference. Relative to many other enterprises in this period in Germany, she did retain a large measure of control. Certainly she had already established her trustworthiness with Triumph des Willens. But by this time, there was virtually no entity that could really claim to be independent of the regime.

As has been already discussed, at least two--and possibly more--groups were involved in planning the Olympic Games. As was typical of structures of this nature in National Socialist Germany, they were to some extent working at cross purposes and in competition with each other. On the one hand, there were the relatively nonpolitical Olympic types, such as Dr. Carl Diem, and on the other, the hard core Party figures such as von Tschammer und Osten. Riefenstahl has understandably tended to emphasize her relations with the first group and to deemphasize her relationships with the latter.

In recent years, Riefenstahl has maintained that Dr. Carl Diem asked her to make the Olympic film. She told me this personally,[17] and she has maintained the same position with other interviewers, such as L. Andrew Mannheim.[18] Riefenstahl told Mannheim that Diem was quite taken with her after he saw her training for a sports diploma in 1935, and he asked her to make the Olympic film. According to Riefenstahl, Diem also persuaded the IOC to accept her as director of the Olympic film.

On the other hand, Riefenstahl has repeatedly stated since the war that Adolf Hitler commissioned her to make the Olympic film. She even said it in her own "Report on the Production of the Olympic Films" (see Appendix C). She also told this to U.S. Army Intelligence after the war, and she told it to the New York Times in 1972, adding that Hitler promised her complete independence from Dr. Goebbels.[19] Hitler told her that she must make the film because the Party functionaries did not know anything about art. Since Riefenstahl has herself admitted that she could go to Hitler when she was encountering problems with his underlings,[20] and Hitler stated to his intimates that Riefenstahl was one of the few women to whom he had given real responsibility,[21] it does not make much sense at this late date for her to deny Hitler's sponsorship.

And yet Dr. Diem also later maintained that the Organization Committee was the body that commissioned Riefenstahl to make the Olympic film. It is necessary here to jump ahead of chronological events to 1958, when Riefenstahl was trying to obtain permission to show Olympia publicly for the first time since the war. At that time the film was banned, and she was trying to make the case that the film was in no way a National Socialist production. In a letter written on behalf of Riefenstahl, Dr. Diem stated that:

> 6. Among the tasks allotted to the Organization Committee belonged the reporting of the Games in every form that was not granted to the Propaganda Ministry. In accordance with this power Frau Riefenstahl was commissioned to do the documentary film. The Propaganda Ministry had nothing to do with this decision, also its later opposition has not been taken into consideration.[22]

This statement of Dr. Diem's was paraphrased in Riefenstahl's statement to the Filmbewertungsstelle, which was later translated and printed in Film Culture.

> Among the duties of the organization committee was reportage applicable to the games in every form, which was at no time under the supervision of the Propaganda Ministry. In this competence Mrs. Leni Riefenstahl (sic) was given the order for the production of the documentary film. The Propaganda Ministry had nothing to do with this decision and also its later protests remained without consideration. Mrs. Leni Riefenstahl obtained from the organization-committee the right for the production of the film, and held herself obligatory to the given conditions without question [emphasis in the original].[23]

This may have been Riefenstahl's belief, and it may well have been that of Dr. Diem as well, but it was not the official position of the Third Reich. On July 10, 1936, less than three weeks before the beginning of the Olympic Games, the Minister of the Interior Dr. Wilhelm Frick announced the following with regard to the Olympic Games:

> 3. The concentration of all efforts in the area of advertising, press, radio and film and artistic performances is the task of Herr Funk, the State Secretary of the Reich Ministry for People's Enlightenment and Propaganda.[24]

There is evidence that Dr. Diem was quite interested and involved in an Olympic film. As we have seen, Dr. Diem was interested in film about sport, and Riefenstahl was both a lover of sports and an accomplished director. It is quite possible that Riefenstahl was Diem's choice. However, in light of what has already been said about Dr. Diem's being kept subservient to von Tschammer und Osten in the 1936 Games, his statement that the Olympic Film was commissioned by the Organization Committee is extremely misleading. It is obvious that the Organization Committee did not have the power to make any major decision without the review of the German Olympic Commission.

It would appear that Riefenstahl was the choice both of Carl Diem and Adolf Hitler, with Hitler obviously having final say in the matter. This interpretation of the facts tends to be verified by an explanation Riefenstahl gave to Dr. Gert Sudholt in the magazine Klüter Blätter. According to what she said in that article, Dr. Diem wanted her for the Olympic film, but she was involved in her preparations for her film Penthesilea, and she refused. Diem then went to the Party leadership, as well as to Hitler. When Hitler asked Riefenstahl, she could not refuse, but she demanded, and claims to have gotten, artistic control of the film, a rare happening in National Socialist Germany.[25]

This control put her in direct contact with chief of the Propaganda Ministry and head of the German film industry, Dr. Paul J. Goebbels. Much has been said and written about the feud between Riefenstahl and Dr. Goebbels (even by people who have--or had--little love for Riefenstahl). Riefenstahl herself has emphasized the enmity between them as proof that she was no National Socialist. Yet Dr. Goebbel's diary reflects that at first, at least, relations were cordial. The diaries also seem to put the lie to Riefenstahl's claim that she was completely independent; on at least several different occasions, she had to report directly to Dr. Goebbels on her preparations for the film. Later on, Dr. Goebbels would be furious at her, and as we will see, he would try to get rid of her as director of the Olympic film; in 1935, however, there seemed to be a guarded respect existing between them.

Adolf Hitler appointed Riefenstahl as director as early as August of 1935, and he also appears to have decided to fund the film through the Propaganda Ministry. On August 17, 1935, Dr. Goebbels wrote, "Frl. Riefenstahl reported on the preparations for the Olympic film. She is a clever thing!" Hitler even designated how much funding the Olympic film was to receive. On August 21, 1935, Dr. Goebbels wrote, "Monday: to the Führer. Conference.... For the Olympic film one and one-half million granted." Relations between Riefenstahl and Dr. Goebbels continued to be at least polite. On October 5, 1935, Goebbels wrote, "Discussed thoroughly her Olympic film with Leni Riefenstahl. A woman who knows what she wants!" Later on the same day, "At home. Film matters with L. Riefenstahl prepared. Still much to work out. Till late in the evenings." On October 9, he wrote, "At home much work. Evenings with Riefenstahl and Ullrich looking at films..."[26]

In October the contract with Riefenstahl was finally worked out. On October 13, Dr. Goebbels wrote, "Contract with Leni Riefenstahl with reference to the Olympic Games approved. Moreover agreeing with all my viewpoints. I am very happy about this. Now I can again work with full vigor. Funk is also happy."[27] Also on October 13, the Reich Finance Ministry reported that 1.5 million RM had been requested for the Olympic film. This fund was not part of the normal Propaganda Ministry monies, but was to be a special allocation. Dr. Goebbels specifically wished Reich funding for the project. A memorandum of the Reich Finance Ministry made it clear that Dr. Goebbels wanted Reich funding of the film although the Reich Finance Ministry tried to shift the burden:

> The Propaganda Ministry has presented the draft of a contract for the production of an Olympic film, by which the production of a Summer Olympic film would be conferred on Leni Riefenstahl. The costs are estimated at 1.5 million RM. I have advised on this that the film will bring certain income so that it would be no problem to finance the film privately, for example through the Film-Kredit-Bank. The use of Reich funds in this way would be avoided. M. R. Ott added, that Herr Minister Goebbels wished the financing through Reich funds.[28]

The draft of a contract appears as Appendix A. This draft has been identified as the contract that Riefenstahl signed, but there is no evidence of this. The document is entitled a draft only (Entwurf) and is not an executed copy. Furthermore, we know that the final contract was between the Propaganda Ministry and The Olympia-Film Gmbh., not with Frau Riefenstahl personally. In addition, we know from Dr. Goebbels' diary that a contract was not signed until November 7. However, a translation of the draft is included because it is the contract Dr. Goebbels wanted. The draft was approved (although we do not know by whom), and from the evidence from the financial records and news reports, the final signed contract was not greatly different (see Appendix B).[29] In fact, it was remarkably casual, considering that it was designed to cover such a major undertaking.

Except to provide some sort of film and to account for funds, there were no duties at all assigned to Riefenstahl. In addition to her personal remuneration of quarter of a million Reichmarks, she had complete artistic and organizational control. The property rights to the film were not spelled out, (a factor which would cause Dr. Goebbels considerable headaches in the future). Was Olympia a property of the Reich, or did it still belong to Olympia-Film GmbH? Were the 1.5

million Reichmarks to be paid back? If so, how and when? The only clause that goes into any detail is clause 6, which imposes duties on the newsreel companies who are not even parties to the contract and would not be bound legally by the agreement. It is hard to avoid the conclusion that the vagueness of the document was entirely to Riefenstahl's benefit, but whether this result was due to legal inexpertise or was deliberately planned is hard to say. Also true of course is the reality that Dr. Goebbels could send almost anyone to a concentration camp, so usually he was scarcely in need of airtight clauses in his employment contracts. However, since Riefenstahl was a personal friend of Hitler, Goebbels would have needed a far more sophisticated contract than this in order to clarify the legal status of the film, and later on he must have regretted not having it.

Also useful, perhaps, would be a discussion of Dr. Goebbels' insistence on the use of Reich funds; such a discussion provides an interesting analogy to Hitler's insistence on the use of Reich funds for the Olympic building program. No doubt, Hitler and Goebbels realized that when an individual controls the purse strings, that person also has power over an enterprise. On the other hand, Hitler also realized that ample funds were important for the success of the Games, and he was insistent that the plans be generously funded. The same motivation seems to be true in part in Dr. Goebbels' allocation of Reich funds for Olympia. He seemed to a large degree interested in helping Riefenstahl. According to M. R. Dr. Ott, the Film-Kredit-Bank turned down private financing for the Olympic film because it only financed films made by private companies; the bank did not finance films sponsored by the Reich. However, on October 18, 1935, another financial institution, the Reichs-Kredit-Anstalt, stated that it was willing to finance the Olympic film privately, which meant that the use of Reich funds would not be necessary.[30] However, the private financers felt that the film had a much better chance of being a commercial success if it were released as soon as possible after the Games, and so they pressed for an early release as part of the deal. This news was passed on to the Propaganda Ministry, which responded on December 18, 1935.

> To the Reich Minister of Finance:
>
> To your letter of October 31, 1935-Pro. 3200-75-IC--I take the liberty of imparting to you that due to extent of material and the hugeness of the work

> involved, it will not be possible to finish the film on the Summer Olympics before 1937. Under these conditions it is not possible to finance the film privately without recourse to the Reich. I will therefore in accordance with your agreement, ask that the required amount up to 1,500,000 RM be placed in my budget account for the fiscal year 1936....
>
> (s) Walther Funk[31]

To some extent, therefore, the Propaganda Ministry's decision to turn down private financing took a certain amount of pressure off Riefenstahl. She would not have to try to get the film out to compete with newsreels. This decision seems to indicate that relations at this time between Dr. Goebbels and Riefenstahl were not yet strained.

On December 10, 1935, the German press carried the story that Dr. Goebbels had given Riefenstahl the job of directing the film of the Summer Olympics. The *Völkischer Beobachter*, the official Party newspaper, stated, "The idea of an Olympic Games among the nations in the framework of the New Germany must be made visible. This is the basic concept behind the plan for the content of the film...."[32] The notice also stated that Hans Weidemann, the vice-president of the Reich Film Chamber, was in charge of the Winter Olympic film, and that this assignment had been turned down by Riefenstahl.

> For Leni Riefenstahl it was impossible to accept this work as well, since the creation of the film of the Winter Games in accordance with her artistic methods would have made her preparations for the Summer Olympics impossible.

Whether the notice was accurate in stating that Riefenstahl turned down the Winter Olympic Film is not known. Interestingly, however, the announcement that Weidemann was to direct the film of the Winter Olympics was made the same day, thus suggesting that the decision was Riefenstahl's.

It is well known that this present account does not agree with Riefenstahl's recollection of the facts. In 1958, when *Olympia* was to be given its first public showing since the war, Riefenstahl wrote a defense of the film and stated, among other things:

> ... Leni Riefenstahl secured the financing of the Olympia-Films by a distribution contract with Tobis-Filmkunst. Because of this distribution contract--which contained a guarantee amount of RM 750,000--the, at the time, production-chief of Tobis, director Mainz, had later to justify this contract before the officials of the Propaganda Ministry. The Propaganda Ministry charged him that by allowing such a guarantee he damaged Tobis.[33]

Riefenstahl also told Gordon Hitchens on October 11, 1971:

> ... so I asked Tobis, and the director, Main [sic], he make it [Olympia] immediately, guaranteed for 1 1/2 million marks [sic]. I told him that I will make two films. He knows that the government is against, yes? But he was very strong, he has made a lot of big things.... After he made this agreement with me, he got into a lot of trouble with Goebbels and the Ministerium, yes?[34]

As we shall see, Friedrich A. Mainz was fired from the post of director of Tobis-Tonbild-Syndikat AG in the spring of 1937. Part of the reason was the distribution contract he signed with Olympia Film GmbH. To this extent, Riefenstahl's statements are accurate. What does not seem to be accurate is the allegation that Mainz financed the film. The weight of evidence in the Bundesarchiv in Coblentz seems to show overwhelmingly that the Olympic film was totally financed by the Propaganda Ministry.

When I brought this matter up to Frau Riefenstahl in May 1983, she stated that she had every intention of viewing the material at Coblentz and that she intended to rebut this material in her memoirs. Whether she can remains to be seen.

We have seen that the National Socialist regime had certain clear propaganda goals. In part, the 1936 Olympic Games were designed to further these goals, and as we will see in the course of further discussion, these goals would also affect the Olympic film. We have also seen that, in 1934, the non-National Socialist members of the Organization Committee were becoming increasingly dominated by the largely National Socialist German Olympic Commission and were following the general incorporation pattern of all civil institutions into the

National Socialist government apparatus during this period (known as Gleichschaltung). The existence of this power shift made it highly unlikely that Riefenstahl reported to any authority--Olympic or otherwise--other than Adolf Hitler and Dr. Goebbels.

By the end of 1935 Riefenstahl had an extremely favorable contract. The Propaganda Ministry approved the contract and it also had Hitler's support. Therefore the resources of the Third Reich were at Riefenstahl's disposal. On November 7, 1935, Dr. Goebbels wrote in his diary: "Fräulein Riefenstahl has her contract ... Olympic film. A 1 1/2 million transaction. She is entirely happy."[35] She should have been.

NOTES

1. Frank Grube and Gerhard Richter, Alltag in Dritten Reich (Hamburg: Hoffman und Campe, 1982), p. 7; William L. Shirer, The Rise and Fall of the Third Reich (New York: Simon and Schuster, 1960), pp. 231-32.

2. Shirer, pp. 286-87, citing Norman H. Baynes, ed. The Speeches of Adolf Hitler, 2 vols. (London and New York: Oxford University Press, 1942), and Count Raoul de Roussy de Sales, My New Order (New York: Reynal and Hitchcock, 1941), pp. 309-34.

3. There is wealth of material from the period that displays these propaganda aims. The film Gebt mir vier Jahre Zeit, released in connection with the propaganda exhibition of the same name in the Spring of 1937, celebrates these achievements, as does the film Jahre der Entscheidung, which was produced in 1936 for the Propaganda Ministry. Many books display the same propaganda aims and boast of the Olympic achievement as well, such as M. Stanley McClatchie, Sieh, das Herz Europas (Berlin: Verlag Henrich Hoffman, 1937) and Die Olympischen Spiele 1936, 2 vols. (Hamburg-Bahrenfeld: Cigaretten-Bilderdienst).

4. I have extensively used Richard D. Mandell, The Nazi Olympics (New York: Macmillan Co., 1971), for the sections of this chapter dealing with the segregation of Jewish athletes from German teams, and the resulting boycott movement. Streicher's quote is from pp. 58-59, citing the Committee on Fair Play in Sports, Preserve the Olympic Ideal: A Statement of the Case Against American Participation in the Olympic Games in Berlin (New York: 20 Vesey Street, [1935]), p. 51.

5. Arnd Krüger, Die Olympischen Spiele 1936 und die Weltmeinung (Berlin, Munich and Frankfurt am Main: Verlag Bartels und Wernitz KG, 1973), p. 33, citing the Völkischer Beobachter, 19 August 1932.

6. "Aufzeichnung über den Empfang des amerikanischen Botschafters a. D. S. H. Sherrill durch den Führer und Reichkanzler in München, am 24 August 1935," BA, R 18, vol. 5614, pp. 39-55.

7. Mandell, Nazi Olympics, pp. 84-87.

8. "Das Olympische Filmwerk in den ersten Vorbereitungen," Film-Kurier (Berlin), 27 April 1936.

9. "Aufzeichnung," 5 October 1933, BA, R 18, vol. 5608, p. 171.

10. BA, Hauptarchiv Staatssecretär Pfundtner, BA, R 18, vol. 5609, pp. 131-32.

11. RMI III 4150b/6.1, BA, R 18, vol. 5609.

12. "Abschrift, RMI: III 4150b/18.1, BA, R 18, vol. 5609, p. 155.

13. Abscrift, RMI, III 4211/20.2, BA, R 18, vol. 5609, pp. 321-35.

14. BA, R 18, vol. 5611, pp. 107-110.

15. Ibid., p. 107-8.

16. BA, R 18, vol. 5611, pp. 111-113.

17. Leni Riefenstahl, interview with author held at Munich on 23 May 1983.

18. L. Andrew Mannheim, "Leni," Modern Photography, February 1974, p. 118.

19. Headquarters, Seventh Army Interrogation of Leni Riefenstahl, Ref. no. PWB/SALC/3, 30 May 1945, Berlin Documents Center, Riefenstahl File; Hans Stueck, "Leni Riefenstahl returns to the Olympics," New York Times, 23 August 1972, p. 31.

20. See Appendix C, pp. 276-277.

21. Adolf Hitler, Hitlers Tischgespräche im Führerhauptquartier. third edition, Ed. Dr. Henry Picker (Stuttgart: Seewald Verlag, 1976), p. 91.

22. Letter of Dr. Diem to the Filmbewertungsstelle, 5 March 1958, Deutsches Institut für Filmkunde, Wiesbaden.

23. Leni Riefenstahl, "The Production of the Olympia Films, Incorrect Statements, and Their Refutation." Film Culture, no. 56-57, Spring 1973, trans. from "Über die Herstellung der Olympia-Filme," a statement prepared by Riefenstahl in 1958. The author has translated this manuscript, since the original document contains additional material not in Film Culture, and it is included as Appendix C.

24. Film-Kurier, 10 July 1936.

25. Charles Ford, Leni Riefenstahl, trans. Antoinette Gittinger (Munich: Wilhelm Heyne Verlag, 1982), p. 88, citing Klüter Blätter (Munich), 9 (September 1977).

26. "Goebbels Tagebuch," 1935, Bundesarchiv, Nachlass Goebbels, NL 118/72, pp. 43, 45, 76 and 78. For background on the financing of the Olympic film, I am grateful to Hans Barkhausen, who in his fine article, "Footnote to the History of Riefenstahl's Olympia, "Film Quarterly, 28 (Fall, 1974): 8-17, not only definitely established the financing of the Olympic film, but indicated the wealth of material that exists at the Bundesarchiv concerning the film.

27. Ibid., p. 81. Walther Funk was then vice-president of the Reich Chamber of Culture and was an extremely capable bureaucrat.

28. "Reichsfinanzministerium," Abt. 1, R 2, vol. 4788, pp. 429-430, BA.

29. Ibid., pp. 433-435.

30. Ibid., p. 439.

31. Ibid., p. 447.

32. "Gestaltung des Olympia-films," Völkischer Beobachter (Berlin), 10 December 1935.

33. Riefenstahl, "The Production of the Olympia Films," p. 171.

34. Gordon Hitchens, "Leni Riefenstahl Interviewed by Gordon Hitchens," Film Culture, 56-57 (Spring 1973): 104.

35. "Goebbels Tagebuch," 1935, p. 98.

• CHAPTER II •

ORGANIZATION AND PLANNING

After Riefenstahl received notice that she was to be in charge of the Olympic film, she still had other projects to wind up before she could start full time on Olympia. On August 24, 1935, Triumph des Willens was shown at the Venice Film Festival, and on September 9 Riefenstahl was notified that she had received the Luce Institute Cup, one of the highest awards given at the festival. In September, she was busy preparing her short Wehrmacht film, Tag der Freiheit, which would be shot on September 16 during the 1935 Nuremberg rallies. The cameramen involved were Hans Ertl, Walter Frentz, Albert Kling, Kurt Neubert, Guzzi Lantschner and Willy Zielke--all men who would be very important to the Olympic film.[1] By mid-October, she had finished cutting the film, so she must have worked on it quite quickly. In September, she took time out to appear--along with Unity and Diana Mitford as well as with Frau Troost--as guest of honor with Julius Streicher at the Congress of Nazi Groups Abroad held at Erlangen.[2]

But it should not be assumed that she hadn't begun working on the Olympic film. She was already discussing her plans with Dr. Goebbels, so she must have worked out quite a lot of her preliminary ideas. In addition, much of her socializing--as well as the production of the Wehrmacht film--was for the purpose of preserving political friendships. As is widely known, Hitler was anxious for a political rapprochement with the army in 1934--this was one of the major reasons for the Röhm purge on June 30, 1934--and it was a major source of embarrassment for him when there were no shots of the army in Triumph des Willens. It appears that Riefenstahl shot the Wehrmacht film largely to keep Hitler and the army happy.[3] The appearance at the rally at Erlangen with Streicher may also have been to preserve a friendship. Streicher had placed a large building that he owned in Nuremberg at her disposal during the filming of Triumph des Willens. In forty-eight hours, he had provided her crew with a kitchen, a dining hall, and a telephone switchboard; also available were darkrooms and conference rooms.[4] Nothing was possible in National Socialist Germany without the establishment of a firm power base among the ever-shifting alliances and enmities of the system. And it was evident that Riefenstahl was adept at establishing, as well as exploiting, these personal relationships.

On February 26, 1936, she was even sent to Rome to be received by Benito Mussolini, who was an admirer of Triumph des Willens. It would be interesting to know precisely why she was dispatched to Italy. One possible explanation: It had been reported in the trade journals that the Italians, too, were keenly interested in making an Olympic film. If so, sending Riefenstahl to see Mussolini was a masterful stroke. The Italian leader was ever susceptible to an attractive woman, and in reports of their meeting, plans for an Italian Olympic film were officially denied.[5]

By February, however, it appeared that Riefenstahl was devoting a considerable amount of time to the Olympic film. She was interviewed by Film-Kurier as she was on her way to the Winter Olympics at Garmisch-Partenkirchen. She had many old friends working on the Winter Olympics film for Hans Weidemann; indeed, she had recommended most of them to Weidemann.[6] She stated that as a result of her thinking about Penthesilea, she was especially interested in the use of sound in film.

> In her last work she experienced such extraordinary connections between the music and the image that she says, "Today I would like to first compose films myself. We see and hear especially in the music of old films how much further in filmic seeing and hearing we have come."[7]

She went on to say that she had a basic idea about the style of the film, but she did not describe that idea. It would appear from her comments about music, however, that she was already interested in making at least a partly stylized documentary.

But the first major problem confronting her was the considerable one of how to film the Olympic Games. Most of the difficulties were far from aesthetic ones; they involved questions of logistics, weather, conferences with national Olympics committees, and other related headaches. The majority of the track-and-field events were to be held in the Reich Sport Field, but in addition, numerous other events were taking place, some in areas quite far from Berlin. These included Kiel (yachting), Grünau (rowing), Dietrich-Eckart open air theater (gymnastics), Döberitz (pentathlon and Olympic Village), and Deutschlandhalle (boxing, wrestling, and fencing). In addition, the 100-kilometer bicycle race, the marathon, the pentathlon and the long-distance riding events would cover a large amount of ground, and would demand the presence of numerous cameramen at various strategic locations. Riefenstahl would later write:

> Every member of the staff would have to be thoroughly acquainted with the sites of the contests. They were all inspected in detail: the Lustgarten, where the torchbearer arrived, the streets on which the Fuehrer would approach, the Olympic Village, the main stadium, the swimming stadium, the polo field, the sea, the Spree, the Deutschland Hall, the fencing halls, the courses of the Marathon race and the cycling races. No spot within the range of the Olympic events should be unknown to the camera-men.[8]

Adding to the difficulty was the fact that many of these events would be taking place simultaneously, so the possibility existed that Riefenstahl might have to cover many events simultaneously. She would also have to keep people on hand for back-up in cases of unforeseen events--and other people, as well, for human interest and reaction material. She said, "The programme of 16 days had to be visualized beforehand by a kind of an imaginative camera. All its details had to be critically analyzed and thoroughly investigated, keeping in mind the requirements of filming."[9]

It should be pointed out that Riefenstahl's assignment was not simply to record enough highlights of the Olympics to make a feature-length film. She was to record all the events in order to compile a sport film archive of the 1936 Olympic Games. In addition to the Olympic film itself, the Olympia-Film Company was to release some twenty short films on Olympic subjects, so Riefenstahl's assignment was especially far-reaching.[10]

In an interview that Riefenstahl gave on July 14, 1936, she described the four stages of production she had planned for the Olympic film: organizing, planning the manuscript or basic shooting script, shooting the film, and tackling the final cutting, which was expected to last some eighteen months.[11] The basic plan was not very sophisticated--and obviously the four phases could not always follow each other in an orderly fashion--but it is perhaps a useful table of organization for the following chapters. This chapter will deal with the establishment of the organization for the film and then the basic planning and preparations for the Games themselves.

ORGANIZATION

In November of 1935, the Olympia-Film GmbH was established, with capital stock of 20,000 Reichmarks. Riefenstahl put up 18,000 and her brother, Heinz Riefenstahl, paid in the other 2,000.[12] Walter Traut and Walter Groskopf were listed as officers of the corporation. This is significant because Traut was to be in charge of production and Groskopf was to be financial manager. Traut had been an expert skier and a protégé of Arnold Fanck. He was also an old friend of Riefenstahl and had worked with her before as production manager on _Das blaue Licht_ and _Triumph des Willens_.

Working for Traut were also three assistant production managers. They would be responsible for the smooth functioning of men and machines at various locations. The assistant managers would also carry through supply and maintenance functions. These men were Arthur Kiekebusch, Rudolf Fichtner, and Konstantin Boenisch.

It was important for Riefenstahl to get the nucleus of people she was to need--especially cameramen--as soon as possible. Equipment had to be checked, ideas worked out, shots set up and rehearsed.

> The way in which the camera was to be focused was tried out more than once. One of the most important matters, the difficult wheeling round of the apparatus, in order to accompany the proceedings, was repeated

> over and over again, during every kind of weather, with all light conditions and under all thinkable circumstances. It was sometimes tried out under apparently impossible conditions. All experiences were written down immediately and later used for the Olympic Games. Naturally all the cameramen finally employed could not take part in the extensive study. A group including Hans Ertl, Walter Frentz and Guzzi Lantschner formed this preparative committee.[13]

At the beginning of May, Riefenstahl began work on her manuscript and started hiring the cameramen who were to become the nucleus of the *Olympia* film crew. As a rule, the men she chose were young South German sportsmen, either from The Black Forest or Bavaria; many had worked with Arnold Fanck. The first hired were Walter Frentz, Hans Ertl, Gustav (Guzzi) Lantschner, and Heinz von Jaworsky.[14] Frentz, Ertl, and Lantschner were to be among the most important cameramen on the film.

Walter Frentz, who was to be extremely useful to Riefenstahl in the stadium and who was in charge of the yachting events in Kiel, was in many ways quite typical. Frentz was born in Stuttgart and attended the Technical High School in Munich. He was extremely interested in the kayak and was the head of the High School Association of German Kayakers. During one student holiday, he and some friends made a short film called *Wildwasserparadies in Oesterreich und Jugoslawien*. The film was shown at a 16mm-film exhibit and became a great success in spite of its technical shortcomings. The industry saw it and in 1931 hired Frentz as technical assistant to the film *Wasserteufel von Hieslau*, where he got some valuable lessons about what not to do.

In 1931, Frentz shot *Wildwasserfahrt* and then was hired by Ufa to go to America to work on the film *Wasser hat Balken*. Subsequently, he worked on many Kulturfilme, including *Die Wildwasser der Trave*, which, according to a reporter at *Film-Kurier*, was a minor masterpiece. After Hitler's seizure of power Frentz was discovered by Leni Riefenstahl, and he worked on *Sieg des Glaubens*, the film involving the 1933 party rally. In *Triumph des Willens*, he had a great triumph of his own: he photographed the close-ups of Hitler during his journey by car through Nuremberg, obtaining footage "so thrilling it was as if Frentz had caught the current of life instead of celluloid and forced it in his camera."[15] He also made the film Hände am Werk on the occasion of the Reich Mayday, Winterspiele in Braunlage und Berchtesgaden, as well as did newsreel work; his last work before the Olympics was Fahrtenbuch Albanien. Frentz had also worked on Riefenstahl's Wehrmacht film. He was later to become Hitler's personal cameraman.

Hans Ertl was a thirty-two-year-old native Bavarian who had grown up in the mountains. His father had wanted him to be a wholesale dealer in Munich, but the mountains had held too great an attraction. Although he was enrolled in the business school in Munich, Ertl spent most of his time doing extremely advanced climbing. He was also something of a proselytizer, writing essays and giving lectures, but he had no interest in film.

One day, however, Arnold Fanck called and asked Ertl to go to Greenland to work on S.O.S. Eisberg. Originally, he was hired to carve steps in icebergs, but as a mountain specialist, he quickly rose from the ranks. He had time enough to develop a deep interest in film and its uses and to record the beauty of his mountains. He bought a book on film techniques and started to study. Fanck then asked him to work on Stürme über dem Montblanc, where, as "Sprengmeister," he had the interesting work of starting avalanches. Ertl was also allowed to do still photography work for the film. He then got his first 35-millimeter camera and, in the winter of 1933-1934, worked on Olympic preparation films. Then in April of 1934 he was asked to accompany Dyrenfurth on his expedition to the Himalayas, the fulfillment of a dream for Ertl. Ertl reached the height of 7,775 meters, well over 23,000 feet and established a German mountain-climbing record.

He returned to Germany in October of 1934 and was hired to work on the Olympic publicity film, Die Glocke ruft. He also worked on the final preparations films for the Olympic Games, as well as on the film Jugend erlebt Heimat. His first work for Riefenstahl was on the Wehrmacht film. She took one look at the material that he shot in the Himalayas and was so impressed that she hired him on the spot. On her recommendation, he also worked for Hans Weidemann on the Winter Olympics film.[16] In the Summer Olympics film, he would have responsibility for the running events, for swimming, and for diving.

Heinz von Jaworsky was also known as Heinz Jaworsky (and later as Henry Javorsky). Seeing Arnold Fanck's Die weisse Hölle von Piz Palu when he was in school, he went film crazy. He went to the Alps looking for Dr. Fanck, ran into him, Sepp Allgeier, and Riefenstahl by accident and was immediately hired to work on Stürme über dem Montblanc.

Jaworsky later wrote a book about his experiences and mailed it to Riefenstahl. Riefenstahl was just forming the Leni Riefenstahl Studios and telephoned Jaworsky to ask him if he wanted a job. Jaworsky accepted and worked on Das blaue Licht for ten dollars a month plus expenses. He became friends with Richard Angst, Hans Schneeberger, and Harald Reinl--then a student and an expert skier. He also worked on S.O.S. Eisberg for Fanck (although he did not go to Greenland) and became an assistant to Hans Schneeberger. As second cameraman, he worked on the Ernst Udet film Wunder des Fliegens; this marked the beginning of a long relationship with Udet. Jaworsky also worked for Luis Trenker on Der Kaiser von Kalifornien. He refused to work on Triumph des Willens, claiming that it was too political, but during the war he would work as an aerial photographer on such films as Kameraden, D III 88, Feuertaufe, Kampfgeschwader Lutzow, and Pour le Merité.[17] On the Olympic film, he was assisted by his brother Gerd von Jaworsky.

Gustav (Guzzi) Lantschner and his brother, Otto, were Bavarians and expert skiers as well as mountaineers. They had been hired by Arnold Fanck to work in different films as actors; both acted in Stürme über dem Montblanc with Riefenstahl. Guzzi also acted with her in Der weisse Rausch. Evidently they were lovers for a time.[18] Guzzi had acting credits for Abenteuer im Engadin, Nordpol-ahoi!, and Rivalen der Luft. He had joined the NSDAP in 1929, and according to Ernst Jäger, both he and Otto were active in the Nazification of Bavaria. (They got their skiing friends to distribute pamphlets at ski resorts.)[19]

Guzzi Lantschner was expert enough at skiing to win the silver medal for the men's combined slalom-downhill event in the Winter Olympics at Garmisch-Partenkirchen (1936). Riefenstahl used him and Otto as her assistants on Triumph des Willens and as a cameraman on Tag der Freiheit. During the Olympic Games, Guzzi would photograph high diving, gymnastics, and riding events. Otto Lantschner's main job was to shoot a film about the filming of the Olympics.

Two other cameramen were not in Riefenstahl's inner circle but were highly important to the film. Both Kurt Neubert and Hans Scheib were men with interesting specialities.

Kurt Neubert was an expert with the slow-motion camera. Riefenstahl thought so much of him that she hired him for the Olympic film a year in advance. (He was one of the best-known slow-motion experts in Germany and in Europe.) Neubert had been given his start by Arnold Fanck in Freiburg (1922). His first camera had weighed about three hundred pounds, and he had been required to haul it all over the mountains for Fanck's films. Later, he became known as a specialist with DeBrie cameras. He had shot Riefenstahl's dancing scenes in Der Heilige Berg and was a cameraman on Fanck's Der grosse Sprung and Der weisse Rausch. He shot many ski films as well as biographical films for Ufa. He also spent twenty-three months in Tierra del Fuego with Gunther Plüschow, an association which resulted in the film Silberkondor über Feuerland. In addition, Neubert spent a year in the African wilderness. He had worked with Riefenstahl before on the Wehrmacht film, Tag der Freiheit. His assistant would be Eberhard von der Heyden, who was also to shoot slow-motion footage.[20]

Hans Scheib was an expert with the telescopic lens. He would be especially important in situations where a cameraman was forbidden to be too close to an athlete. Since Riefenstahl wanted to stress the personal emotions of the athletes, to subjectify as many of the athletic events as much as possible, Scheib's work was bound to be crucial. It was also planned for him to film many of the reaction shots of spectators, since, as he put it, he was in an ideal position to photograph an onlooker eating a bockwurst without the spectator realizing that he was being photographed. Scheib had worked on Der Insel der Dämonen and Palos Brautfahrt.[21] According to Heinz von Jaworsky, he was half-Jewish; eventually, he emigrated to Spain.[22]

The headquarters of the film company was to be the Haus Ruhwald (roughly translated as "peaceful woods"), a castle located on the Spandauer Berg in the middle of a lovely park. From this location in western Berlin, the staff could be transported to the Reich Sport Field (and other locations) within a matter of minutes. The crew would live in the castle before and during the filming, unless they were assigned to Kiel or Grünau. One hundred twenty beds were placed in the halls in the castle, and a large cafeteria was established in the basement of the building. The breakfasts served in this cafeteria evidently became quite famous, and the Propaganda Ministry was later to object that the film company was far too generous in the feeding of its staff.

In the large rooms overhead, a film storehouse was established under the management of Johannes Häussler. It was expected that about 400,000 meters of film would be shot by the company in making the Olympic film, and, at 15,000 meters a day during the Games, about half of this would be shot from August 1 to August 16 alone. In addition, tests were to show that at least two-dozen types of film would be needed, depending upon the nature of the scene, the camera position, the light and so on. Most fictional films shot during these times did not use more than three types of film. A catastrophe of major proportions would have resulted had any kind of film run out in the midst of shooting. In addition, subsidiary film storehouses had to be established at Grünau, at Kiel, and at the Reich Sport Field. The supplying of film was accomplished with trailers and extra automobiles that acted as mobile film storehouses; Haus Ruhwald was at the operations' center.

Next to the Haus Ruhwald was another building. This structure housed Walter Groskopf (the financial head), Walter Traut (the chief of production), and Ernst Jäger (the press chief), along with their respective staffs. Kiekebusch and Konstantin Boenisch were also in this building. Boenisch would have responsibility for all apparatus used in the course of the filming (e.g., apparatus for travelling shots, camera towers, rubber boats, fire department ladders); Kiekebusch was to be responsible for all cameras (including the underwater and slow-motion cameras).[23]

At this point, it seems appropriate to introduce Ernst Jäger. He is as close to being Riefenstahl's Boswell during this period as anyone we are likely to find. Ernst Jäger, whose full name was Ernst Jäger-Ejott, was a friend of Riefenstahl, their friendship extending back to the twenties in Berlin. Jäger was also the editor of Film-Kurier, one of the best film trade journals in Germany. He had ghostwritten Leni Riefenstahl's book on the making of Triumph des Willens, entitled Hinter den Kulissen des Reichsparteitagfilms.[24]

Riefenstahl engaged Jäger as press chief for the Olympic film while he was still editor of Film-Kurier; this meant his reporting was hardly unbiased.[25] Germans generally were not as upset about possible conflicts of interest as the English or as Americans were. It also must be pointed out that since Riefenstahl and the film both had official sanction, Jäger probably would not have reported the making of the film differently--even if Riefenstahl had not been paying him a salary. Nevertheless, his reportage has to be taken with a grain of salt, especially when he is eulogizing Riefenstahl's genius, which he does quite often. Jäger, however, was not incompetent. His position insured the Olympic film's getting extensive and more than adequate coverage in the trade magazines--Film-Kurier, Licht Bild Bühne, as well as the other newspapers and magazines in Germany.

In 1937, Dr. Goebbels fired him from his position on Film-Kurier because, according to Jäger, he had a Jewish wife and had been a Social Democrat. Jäger reported, too, that Dr. Goebbels was not happy that he had given good reviews to George Gershwin, Max Reinhardt, and Reuben Mamoulian (1935).[26]

Jäger did indeed have a Jewish wife, but whether he was a Social Democrat or that he wrote good reviews about Gershwin, Mamoulian, or Reinhardt is harder to verify. He is known to have been pretty snide about America in the pages of Film-Kurier and he could certainly produce National Socialist prose when the occasion called for it. In any case, he was fired by Dr. Goebbels and expelled from the Schrifttumskammer. According to Riefenstahl, Jäger then fell into debt. She had to support him on several occasions. Finally, she succeeded in persuading Dr. Goebbels into readmitting Jäger to the Schrifttumskammer.[27] When Riefenstahl later travelled to America to sell the Olympic film there, she chose Jäger to accompany her. Among other things, Jäger seems to have made some connections in Hollywood while working with Film-Kurier. As we shall see later, Riefenstahl and Jäger had a falling out while they were in Hollywood. Jäger defected to America and wrote a series of articles for the Hollywood Tribune entitled "How Leni Riefenstahl Became Hitler's Girlfriend." When she was interrogated by the U.S. Seventh Army after the war, Riefenstahl said there was no truth whatsoever in any of these stories.[28] After his defection, Jäger worked in Hollywood under a pen name. He went into early television with Frank Wysbar, another German émigré to Hollywood, and became Wysbar's press chief. In 1952, he severed relations with Wysbar and again accepted a job with Riefenstahl to negotiate for her in America, England, and Germany, all this an indication of the way in which Riefenstahl seemed to have been able to reconcile herself to former enemies.[29]

The reconciliation, however, would take place in the future. This was the spring of 1936 and we will return later to Herr Jäger. For the time, it is enough to say that, in his way, he was as important to the success of the Olympic film as was any cameraman.

By mid-April, Riefenstahl had hired the people who were going to be the closest and most important to her. She had set up a headquarters, a financial and administrative section, and a powerful publicity department, which clearly was not going to rely on the Propaganda Ministry for publicity. In many ways, Olympia-Film GmbH was a typical product of the National Socialist regime. It cut across several tables of organization: Exactly who was responsible for the Olympia Company--Hitler, Goebbels, Diem, or all of them--is unclear. The company was dynamic. It had a great capacity for further growth; yet at the same time, it was rather informal. National Socialist Germany was constantly producing new organizations whose functions paralleled existing organizations and produced inevitable conflict. The growing Olympia-Film GmbH was in itself a good example of this.

Obviously, the organizational phase was not finished. As planning progressed, and as more and more persons were hired, there would be additional organizational problems, but with this basic organization, Riefenstahl was able to start the planning phase of her production.

PLANNING

In May, Riefenstahl started visiting locations of various events and having conferences with the members of her staff who were more or less in the inner circle: Ertl, Lantschner, and Frentz. She would travel with them to the Harz Mountains or elsewhere to work on her notes and ideas for the film (called by all "The Manuscript"); she also wanted new ideas. It was probably a welcome relief for her to get away from the telephone and other interruptions. The Harz Mountains was the site where her basic plan for the film was worked out, or at least articulated.

Three thematic circles formed the structure of the film: 1) the struggle for victory in the Games, 2) the beauty that this struggle brings about, and 3) the idea of the Olympic Games.[30] Riefenstahl seems to have stuck to this basic approach quite closely. Of course, not all the preliminary work was so theoretical. Much of it dealt with the nuts and bolts problems of how to film individual events; for this no substitute existed for visiting the various sites.

On May 13, 1936, Riefenstahl and an entourage of film workers visited the Olympic village in Döberitz. She was greeted by the administrator of the Village, Captain Fürstner, who was to escort the party. Walter March, the brother of Werner March, the chief architect for the Reich Sport Field, was also on hand. During the tour, Riefenstahl constantly jotted notes to herself in the large book (*The Manuscript*) that was full of other notes, memos, sketches, etc. From this mass of material, she would later tell her cameramen what she wanted photographed. Her notes contained various impressions, like "Horses' heads next to one another" or "Girls in the grandstand." A glimpse of the bell tower inspired the thought that later they would have to mix the sound of bells over the basic motif of Richard Strauss' "Olympic Hymn," this plan an indication that Riefenstahl was already thinking in sound.

After the first part of the tour, she started asking questions: "Can we make travelling shots here?" or "Here we must use a special wagon to go along the lake so that we can cut into the branches in the birch forest" or "How is it going with the light cables?" The sauna commanded Riefenstahl's interest as well as everyone else's, and it was predicted that the sauna would become the *dernier cri* in Berlin after the Games. "The film people saw the light here as well. For the portrayal of the 'morning mood,' the bathhouse gets an A." In the sauna and shower, Rolf Lantin, Riefenstahl's still photographer, started taking photographs, and a hand-film camera was used to test light levels. The side walls were removed to let in more light. "Good opportunity for travelling shots here, when the men go to shower."

Riefenstahl also was interested in the various animals to be found in the park surrounding the Village. Some groups of foreign athletes had specifically asked for a stork, which was supposed to be a symbol of good luck, and Riefenstahl was particularly taken by the animal. There followed a short conference about the best way to get the needed shots.

Although it was decided that the photographing of the Olympic Village would not be particularly tricky (unlike the photographing of the stadium or Grünau), the question was raised regarding how best to get master shots. Should they use a small airplane, powered glider, free balloon, or a fixed balloon? Riefenstahl voted for the free balloon.

> Yes, quite low over the trees, I have already done that myself. And how much damage that little bit of gravel could do if someone found it necessary to throw it out. And that little gondola won't kill anybody.

The choice of materials was communicated to March, who realized that the architecture of the Olympic Village was not to be much in evidence at all. He said disconsolately, "And only fifty meters of Village will be shown in the main film." Riefenstahl consoled him by saying that doubtless the Village would be well covered in newsreels.[31]

What is interesting in all this is how clearly the prologue to Fest der Schönheit follows Riefenstahl's preliminary ideas set forth in May. There are travelling nature shots along the lake. Shots of trees, the stork, and other animals are very much in evidence in the finished film; so is the use of the sauna in the "morning mood" sequence requested by Riefenstahl.

No attempt was made to show the Olympic Village either as an architectural or organizational feat in the final film. This suggests that, at least in certain areas, Riefenstahl had, by May of 1936, a very clear idea of what she wanted. It is not known, however, whether the free balloon shots were a success or not. Like most of these bravura shots, they were not used, and there are no establishing shots of the Olympic Village in the final film.

As the discussion of plans above indicates, Riefenstahl

and her staff had planned the use of various devices for the film. Riefenstahl described them as follows:

> All available technical devices had to be used in preparing for this task. From the beginning it was obvious that cameramen should enter the inner field of the Stadium as little as possible in order not to disturb the contests. On the other hand, the most important pictures had to be taken here, where seconds decided dramatic contests. On this field more than any other place, the fever, the excitement, the expectation and the interest of the public found expression. Each single phase had to be caught in the lens. Therefore, towers were constructed for the cameramen, and pits were dug for them at the 100 metre track and at the grounds for the high jump and the broad jump. Anything the technical imagination could possibly create was tried out with the aim of obtaining photography of a variety never attained yet. A catapult camera was utilized. It consisted of a camera that moves on rails, automatically following the runner. Hereby the attention of public, as well as that of the runner, was no longer being diverted by other human beings in the field. There were cameramen placed in aeroplanes circling the field. One worked from an observation balloon. At the regatta course at Grünau, a special section was reserved for the boats of the camera people. The number of technical experiments undertaken by the preparative committee, the new attachments tried out on the cameras, surpassed anything ever attempted before. A camera was installed in an 8-oar boat for accompanying the rowing contestants. Another one was fixed on the back of a horse to discover how far the gallopping [*sic*] horse and the camera could be co-ordinated.[32]

Riefenstahl was proud of the technical ideas developed for the film. Moreover, devices like the catapults and balloons made for good publicity. Much discussion of them, therefore, appeared in the trade journals. But some of the devices would be banned by the International Olympic Committee as too disturbing to the athletes, and other ideas would simply not work out. Most of the balloon shots, for instance, were not steady enough to be used. In the finished film, the shots from the towers and the pits were to be extremely important, but there is not much evidence that footage shot from many of the other devices was particularly useful.

In May, Riefenstahl had sent Walter Frentz, her water film expert, to Kiel to start preliminary plans for the yachting events, which were to run from August 4 to August 14. On June 6 and 7, she went to Kiel herself. Her guide in Kiel was Lieutenant-Commander Hauck, who showed her many of the differences between the events, as well as discussed with her problems that might arise in both the inner and outer harbor at Kiel, both of which are long and narrow. Admiral Francois and Rear-Admiral Götting, who were on board the start ship Undine, promised the complete support of the Navy for the filming. Riefenstahl was then received by the chairman of the German Sailing Association, Lieutenant General von Kemisch, who took her around the courses on the yacht Maria and helped her with organizational problems as well as providing additional ideas for The Manuscript. Various test shots were also made, in spite of bad weather. Riefenstahl wanted to cover the Star, six-meter and eight-meter classes.[33]

By mid-June, Frentz was sending test footage back to the Geyer laboratories that was of excellent quality. Much of this footage, shot during training, was used in the final film, especially those shots taken from the boats (no cameraman would have been allowed on the boats during an actual Olympic race).

On June 7, 1936, Riefenstahl took time out from the film to attend a reception at the invitation of Italian Ambassador and Mrs. Bernardo Attolico. Bella Fromm reported:

> Leni Riefenstahl was there, though nobody knew in whose honor she was invited. Goebbels snubbed her. Neither Hitler nor Streicher was present.
>
> "So pale!" I said to Leni. "And no lipstick."
>
> "The Fuehrer detests make-up," she shrugged. "You never can tell when he's going to show up, so I've quit using the stuff altogether."[34]

Early in June, Riefenstahl hired Willy Otto Zielke. Zielke is one of the most interesting and enigmatic figures in German film, and one is tempted to say that in another time and place, he might have become one of the recognized masters of German cinema. Riefenstahl later described him as a genius.[35] He was first a photographer, and studied at the Bayerische Staatlehranstalt in Munich. At the studio exhibition in Stuttgart in 1929, he showed his work with glass objects. At that time, he was interested in glass as a photographic material. He was curious about the way it collected, broke, and refracted light.

Zielke was influenced by Moholy-Nagy and Albert Renger-Patzsch and started working in the _Neue Sachlichkeit_ movement in Germany.[36] In the thirties, he turned to film, and in 1935, directed _Das Stahltier_ for the German railroads. It was a brilliant, nearly surreal work, and in spite of the _Neue Sachlichkeit_ style of its montage, the film portrayed the remaining influence of expressionism.

The locomotive was portrayed as a steel beast or mechanical Caligari, as much a destroyer as it was a savior. The motion picture was a brilliant piece of work, but it portrayed the history of railroads largely as a cycle of train wrecks, which was not the message that the German railroad officials wished to leave with its public. In addition, the film depicted the history of rail travel in terms of English and French inventions. While this interpretation may have been historically accurate, Dr. Goebbels judged that Zielke was guilty of the crime called the "Damaging of German Reputation" (Shädigung des deutschen Ansehens), a crime that could have gotten him in serious trouble. The film was shelved, and Zielke was sent to an insane asylum, an action that probably saved his life.

Riefenstahl wanted Zielke very much for the prologue. She was able to pull enough strings to get him out of the asylum. Then she had had him driven to Berlin by Walter Frentz. Zielke describes his first meeting with Frau Riefenstahl as follows:

> And then I was confronted with Frau Riefenstahl, and she explained to me the way she envisioned the prologue for her Olympic film. She wanted to have it so that a very short but lively drama would develop, in which the dancers around the altar upon which the holy fire burned, the so-called Olympic flame, would first have arisen out of the sea. And for that end, the Aegean Sea was very beautiful, picturesque, wonderfully surrounded by cypresses, pines and

> bright yellow sand. And that is the way that Böcklin painted it in his pictures. And it would develop a conception of the beauty of the sea, Romanticism. Above all in [Böcklin's] Isle of the Dead, many motives were contained that should have been contained in my film. But since we were working with a very large staff in men and material, and it cost so much money every day, thousands and thousands, we could not afford the luxury of travelling to where Böcklin had painted his Isle of the Dead. That would have devoured twice as much money just to get an adornment. That would have been insane, irresponsible, financially excessive. So Frau Riefenstahl changed the plans, in that I would make use of the themes of ancient Greece, especially the temples.[37]

It was also decided to drop the idea of Naiads emerging from the water, and simply use temple dancers, who by means of their dance lit the fire at the holy altar.

With this rough concept, on or about June 9, 1936, Zielke went to Greece (along with assistant manager Rudolf Fichtner and a crew) to start shooting the prologue. He shot material at the Poseidon Temple, at the Acropolis, at Cape Sunion, at Corinth, and at other historic areas of Greece.

Although the Greek government and the assistants on location were quite helpful, shooting in Greece on location was not easy. At the Acropolis, where Zielke wanted to get a series of tracking shots, as well as a complete tracking shot around the whole complex, the crew could only shoot between 4:00 and 11:00 in the morning and 4:00 to 9:00 in the evening because of the murderous heat. They had only the bare essentials for their work, a couple of tracks and a small amount of scaffolding, which made shooting this footage in the rolling hills around the buildings quite difficult. It might be worthwhile to quote a description of Zielke's filming around the Acropolis:

> Zielke is no waster of material, he places everything correctly and carefully before he starts shooting. The fog and clouds are to obey his direction. Fog and clouds play a special role in Riefenstahl's shooting script. She loves the nuances in mood. We know it from her masterpiece Das blaue Licht, in the way she

> employed clouds, shadows and the fog from the waterfall as a painterly animated element, as opposed to making kitsch out of the shot--In a work photo that is at hand, one can see the travelling apparatus at the foot of the Acropolis--the fog rises, the fog falls, the pyrotechnician Schmidt, a prized expert in German film, will have mixed his smoke powder so well, that the desired effect will be attained. If one only knew what a large amount of organization and assistance is necessary until the Greek lads swing the smoke pots while the wind peaceably and in accordance with the script, spreads the "clouds" over the Acropolis. Later, in the finished film, it will only be a light haze, scarcely noticeable, a nuance between light and shade, but it had to be included in the total plan technically as well as artistically beforehand in order for it to have its time and place.[38]

The use of this haze is quite important throughout the prologue, and Zielke used a lot of smoke. Fichtner was back in Berlin by June 26, reporting that the group in Greece had used up fifty kilograms of smoke powder and needed some more.[39] These travelling shots and the use of the smoke were to be highly effective because they added to the sense of mystery that hangs over the prologue. For the same reason, Zielke shot the material in soft focus:

> ...Certainly you could not shoot such things as you do today, with a tiny aperture, everything hair sharp, so that you can see the sandstone, all the pores and everything. Then the illusion is kaputt, it is no dream, but rather a scholarly photograph, no way dreamlike.[40]

To get the soft focus effect, Zielke used all sorts of devices including veiling the lens with crèpe de Chine. Zielke explains the effect of this veiling as follows:

> When it comes through this veil, by the beams that are interrupted, the contour of any object does not come as one line, but as two lines; a sharp line and an unsharp line. Through the superimposition of the unsharp line, which is thicker, over the sharp line of reality, a so-called aureole is produced, thus a heavenly glow. And this aureole gives to the whole

> film a dreamlike appearance, the unsharp appearance that comes to one who dreams, a vision.[41]

Zielke shot at the Acropolis extensively. After doing the complex tracking shots at the Parthenon, he recorded single details; the great heads of the gods and the goddesses as well as some extremely beautiful heads of women that were represented on the Erechtheion, the smaller temple in the Acropolis. He also went to the National Museum in Athens, where he shot the statues that later appeared in the prologue. The material that Zielke shot in Athens was what ultimately was used in the film. Although he travelled to the other locations, he was not enthusiastic about what he saw. For instance, he looked at the temple of Apollo above Corinth and found it basically uninteresting, but he was ordered to film the temple anyway:

> "Telegram from Frau Riefenstahl, I should shoot the columns; they were uninteresting.... She did only what she had thought out at the editing table, theoretical. She left the practical filming to me, it was my prologue. I told her on the telephone that it was just throwing away money, it was not usable. 'No, shoot it,' she said, 'since you're there. We'll see later if it can be used.' And so on, if you please."[42]

Zielke then went to Cape Sunion, and again he felt that shooting was a waste of time.

> "At Cape Sunion there were three columns and a very high column in between, and a great many clouds. It was also nothing, there was nothing interesting for the film, nothing. But I shot this too, _tout égal_, the main thing was that I fulfill my contract. It became like the military, shoot to the right, shoot to the left, and then go home, all done. So I shot the film. _C'est fini_."[43]

Perhaps, as Zielke maintains, the shooting was mechanical, but there is no doubt that his footage was very beautiful. When the rushes were seen by the rest of the crew, they elicited nothing but admiration; Zielke's Greek footage is still the most beautiful in the film. In Greece, his contribution to the film was enormous.

As has already been discussed, the Olympic Games were designed, in part, to persuade the world that the National Socialist regime wanted only peace with the world. In accordance with this propaganda aim, the film was designed to show Hitler and the Nazis as nonthreatening figures. According to Ernst Jäger, Riefenstahl had shown Hitler as a hero in Triumph des Willens. In Olympia, she wanted to show Hitler as:

> ... the private man, the spectator who modestly stepped back before the heroes of the hour, the athletes. At the important victories, he was to applaud: his pleasure would signify more than an Olympic victory. A whole string of cameramen was specially trained to take candid shots of his most natural poses.[44]

Especially assigned to photographing Hitler was the cameraman Leo de Laforgue, a man who almost always was present when Hitler was attending the Games. Having joined the NSDAP in April of 1933, after Hitler had attained power, de Laforgue was what the Germans called a "March Violet."[45] It would probably be best to quote Herr de Laforgue himself regarding the extent of his duties. On November 3, 1936, he wrote Reichsminister Dr. Wilhelm Frick, asking especially for the Olympic honor award, and gave as grounds the following:

> (1) As appears from the attached clippings I was assigned officially as sole film artist to film the complete close-ups and long shots of the Führer, the Reich Minister and the Guests of Honor as well as the King of Bulgaria and the Crown Prince of Italy and Sweden. In spite of all difficulties, according to the estimates of the finished film materials, quite exceptional results were obtained. These showed not only overjoyed and enthusiastic moments of the Führer, but also all other personalities were captured for the film documentary during the most dramatic points of the Olympic Games. But irrespective of the documentary value of the unique shots were their greater meaningfulness for the coming Olympic film in artistic as well as politic-propagandistic considerations.... In the joyous hope for the granting of my request, that is so understandable, since I stood daily eye

> to eye with my Führer, I sign with the German Greeting
>
> Heil Hitler
> /s/ Leo de Laforgue[45]

In June and July, many of the other cameramen were hired who were to work on _Olympia_. They represent almost a _Who's Who_ of German documentary and culture film makers, and many were hired with specific purposes in mind.

Helmuth von Stwolinski had made a name for himself as a photographer of expeditions. Riefenstahl was to use him for the rowing events in Grünau.

Edmund Epkens, from Cologne, had his own company. He was chief of the studio section in the famous Düsseldorf exhibition, _Film und Foto_. He had made an industrial film on a conference of mirror glass manufacturers, and he was known for culture films. He had shot the sections of _Drei tolle Tage_ and _Arena humsti-bumsti_ that took place in Cologne. He was to operate seven different pieces of camera equipment in the Olympic film.

Wilhelm Siem had gone to Pathé Frères directly from school in 1911. He had worked for four years both in South America and in North America for Fox, Universal, United Artists and R.C.A. In Germany, he had worked on the strange and unsuccessful _Ewiger Wald_, a film that tried to show that Germany's fate was closely intermeshed with the continued flourishing of the Teutonic forest. Evidently Riefenstahl was impressed with Siem's work, because it was on the basis of this film that he was hired. He was a specialist on sea photography, so he was to be used in Kiel, especially.

Joseph (Sepp) Ketterer had met Allgeier when he was a skier; he worked as Allgeier's assistant for a long time. He also worked on Trenker's _Berge in Flammen_, _Der Rebell_, and on Riefenstahl's _Sieg des Glaubens_.

Friedrich (Fritz) von Friedl was, for a long while, assistant to Richard Angst. Before Riefenstahl engaged him, von Friedl was becoming known for a series of very good short films that he had made.

Hasso Hartnagel (or simply Hasso) was the husband of

the famous Swedish actress Signe Hasso and quite famous in his own right for excellent crane shots. He was extremely well known in Germany, Sweden, and Switzerland.

Andor von Barsy was hired to do most of the shooting in and around the city of Berlin. He was one of the best-known members of the Dutch avant-garde and had originally come from Hungary. He had co-produced the film Totes Wasser.

Wilfried Basse had gained a reputation as a film maker for his long documentary film, Deutschland zwischen Gestern and Heute; his short study, Wittembergplatz, also received acclaim.

Alfred Siegert was a film maker from Chemnitz who specialized in industrial and culture films, including Kunstlerisches Kranzleinschaffen (a film about the making of Christmas wreathes), Ein Wunderwerk der Präzision (a film about a pocket watch glass works), and Im Reiche der Klingenden Taler (a film whose title is a play on words on the Klingenthal or Klingen Valley). He had been hired by Riefenstahl to do especially large and complicated traversing and travelling shots during the most important events.

H. O. Schulze was one of the best cameramen Riefenstahl had working for her. Hans Weidemann had chosen him as first cameraman for the Winter Olympic film. Schulze had also taken part in one of the best-known British expeditions to Africa for Rhodesian film and was under contract with Tobis. In addition, he was a transfocator specialist--a transfocator being an early type of zoom lens.

Albert Kling had been a film camera mechanic. He had fixed an old camera that he then used, in his free time, for making films. Kling got his first filming job through a photography store. Later he made some culture and industrial films and earned enough money to buy a printer from Dr. Fanck in Freiburg. He developed into an expert aerial photographer and shot the first footage ever taken from a zeppelin. Riefenstahl had hired him for aerial shots for Triumph des Willens, and he had worked closely with her since that time. He was to take shots from the airship Hindenburg and from planes--as well as from the free balloon.[47]

Perhaps the most complex assignment of the whole Olympic film was that which was shot at Grünau. Due to the nature of rowing, it was impossible to get a camera close to the contestants, and the sport did not lend itself to lyrical treatment, as did gymnastics or sailing. Therefore, at the same time that Riefenstahl was trying to document the races, she wanted to get the camera sufficiently close to the contestants so as to capture the--as one reporter put it--" ... struggle, despair, victory, exhaustion, surrender, endurance." But how to capture these emotions (in those days before the modern long lens) was unclear to everyone. In addition, the weather was a problem. The rain was falling in sheets as Riefenstahl inspected the area on June 12, and it showed no signs of improving. Fortunately, the Great Berlin Regatta was being held on June 26, and the German Championships were to be held on July 18, so there would be lots of chances for test runs in various kinds of weather.

But still there was the problem of how to bring the camera closer to the sculls. Riefenstahl thought she might be able to build a bridge in front of the grandstand. She had long conferences with the experts. The water was nine feet deep and the bottom was a quagmire, so pilings would have to be driven another fifteen feet into it. The cost would be 160,000 Reichmarks. Then someone had the idea of constructing a narrow wooden path along the finish line on the Grünau side. The camera would be fitted with an appropriate lens and could then travel along with the sculls to the goal. The idea was a helpful one, but it did not really get the camera out where Riefenstahl wanted it.

There were other problems, too. There were to be seventeen events at Grünau. To cover them all would have taken a complete evening. What should be shown? Riefenstahl evidently had her heart set on the eight-man sculls, but she was not sure what other footage to use. She took a motorboat ride along the canoe course. There was supposed to have been a mass start in the canoe doubles, and Riefenstahl was enthusiastic about including it in the film. She and her staff were also busy trying to decide how many towers would be needed on the course--radio and film personnel would have to share them. She seems not to have given much thought to the fact that she might distract the athletes with her filming. The company had hired some motorboats with built-in cameras that they were able to use for test shots of training events. They also bought a motorboat, which they certainly would not be able to use in the course of Olympic rowing events. (This purchase would later annoy the Propaganda Ministry.) Riefenstahl even mused over the possibility that Ernst Udet could photograph the races from an airplane, this thought suggesting that she had an unrealistic idea of what the Olympic Committee and the referee would stand for.[48]

Riefenstahl returned to Grünau on June 26 for the Berlin Regatta. She wanted to shoot the starts and finishes, as well as to test slow motion shots, panning shots, and tracking shots. Further tests were scheduled for the German championships on the fifteenth of July. This was the date when the international Olympic teams were going to begin training at Grünau, and Riefenstahl had planned to do a large amount of training footage of the sculls. In spite of a lot of ingenuity, the film team had not really solved the problem of how to get closer to the racers; this would remain the major problem for Riefenstahl at Grünau.[49]

As it had turned out at Kiel, the ultimate solution to the problem of making the races at Grünau immediate and exciting was the use of footage taken during training. This was especially true in the preparation for the eight-man scull sequence. After the international crews started training at Grünau, some of the footage that Heinz von Jaworsky obtained was invaluable. He recalls:

> And we did things like this, of course. You are sitting where the first rower sits, facing the coxswain, and the seat goes back and forth, right. It's on kind of roller bearings, right? So I remember I sat on that thing with the camera and did the rowing movement which shows what the man, the first rower would see--the coxswain, who was wearing a little megaphone, shouting at them, right? So I did this with the camera, rolling on my seat.... Since I had done lots of rowing myself on that type, it was not unfamiliar to me.[50]

Jaworsky obtained this footage with a hand-held, spring-wound Bell and Howell Eyemo. (A Debrie was much too heavy to be placed in a rowing scull.) The footage obtained from the position of the coxswain and the first rowers in the eight man sculls added much excitement to the sequence of the eight-man sculls in the film, especially since the sequence depended heavily on the effect of rhythm, both on the sound track and in the image, and the rowing movements captured in this footage added immeasurably to this effect. The other races, which were shot from the stands or from the wooden platform, do not have the immediacy of the eight-man event.

The camera and film testing went apace. Riefenstahl went through some quite interesting tests of film stock. She had various objects shot with Agfa, Kodak, Perutz--and perhaps Gevaert--film, and she used various kinds of filters. With these films and three filters, she first shot a man's head frontally lit and in the open air. Then she did the same with architectural motifs, such as the stone of the stadium with sun and shadows against the sky. The same experiments were finally done with a bouquet of flowers that was placed both against the background of a wood and a meadow. All the shots were then assembled for screening and nobody was told which piece was on which film.

> The result was rather curious. At that time, Perutz film was practically unknown and had hardly ever been used for motion pictures. Well, we found that Perutz material invariably gave the best results with subjects such as trees and greenery. The emulsion seemed to have a strong green sensitivity and produced really artistic effects. Faces and people came out best on Kodak film, and Agfa was the most impressive for buildings, sculptures and stonework. We were absolutely unanimous about it. So we bought a stock of all three makes and the production manager in charge of the film simply issued it to the cameramen according to what they would be filming.[51]

According to Riefenstahl, the film speeds were equivalent to twenty to twenty-five to thirty-two ASA, which was considered quite fast. These film stocks were also tested for mixes and each test was shot twice. One of each test was sent to the Geyer Laboratories so that Geyer would have a complete run of all tests. The second set was developed at another special developing establishment.[52]

> Apart from big cameras in fixed locations or on dollies (mainly French Debrie and German Askania models with high-framing rates for slow-motion effects), Leni aimed for compact mobile models which could be hand held. They included a couple of Sinclairs, several from Bell & Howell with lens turrets, and a miniaturized item called the Kinamo. This held just 16 1/2 ft. of film--35mm, of course; practically nothing was shot on 16mm at the Olympics--and was not much bigger than a present-day amateur movie camera. The Kinamo served mainly for single-take close-ups of athletes at starts and the like, and also for the captive balloon attempts.
>
> Close-ups of athletes were also shot with a tele lens on one of the larger cameras, a 600mm unit which, in those days, was the longest one Leni's cameramen had. She ordered the latest lenses from all leading optic manufacturers--from Zeiss, Astro and from Cooke in England. The majority were Cooke and Astro lenses, and many were (up to then, ultra fast) f/1.8. But the fastest was an f/0.95 she got for night shots. On the whole, technical specifications were fairly modest by today's standards; she had neither coated lenses nor zooms.[53]

A camera that got quite a bit of publicity and shows up in a considerable number of photographs of the Olympic cameramen was the new Askania shoulder camera. Holding sixty meters of film, it sat on the cameraman's shoulder, leaving both hands free for focussing, positioning, and changing film. Unlike hand cameras, the picture was not jiggled by the cameraman's breathing and was generally far more stable. The Askania shoulder camera was first used in the Olympic Games.[54]

As has already been mentioned, one of Riefenstahl's major aims in many of the athletic events was to get close to the athletes and to subjectify their efforts. To do this, she had to insure that the process of filming disturbed them as little as possible. This meant many tests to make the cameras as soundproof as possible. Evidently, quite good results were obtained, even with slow motion cameras which, because of their high number of revolutions per second, make a terrible racket.[55]

If there were problems to be worked out with the film and cameras, there were also problems with some of the cameramen. Riefenstahl was not always pleased with the work of some of the people she had hired--especially the most trained and experienced--because they refused to take chances.

> Often the cameramen are too fearful. They never dare to get the most, either from the idea, or the material, or with the filters. They say that by weak evening light it's no longer possible to shoot, that's it!
>
> And it's precisely there that for the artistic cameramen the twilight hour is the most productive. In Das blaue Licht, Hans Schneeberger and I worked in this late mild sunlight that was already changing to yellow light. Of course, you must know how to handle it, it doesn't depend only on luck or feeling.
>
> However, how much sooner I would take such a groping team, always trying, in preference to the exact computation of light and shadow in a studio. For nature, you have to be a thousand times more talented.[56]

Much later, Riefenstahl would again recollect that she preferred her nucleus of Ertl, Lantschner, and Frentz (men who were fresh, and willing to try anything) to the professionals she had hired who were far too conventional.[57]

She was extremely interested in detail and visited sports events to get a better idea of the film problems involved. In the third week of June, for instance, she spent a whole day at the Gau championships for Brandenburg, held at the Allianz Sportsplatz in Mariendorf. The German champion, Erwin Huber, who was to be in the decathlon, was in these games, and Riefenstahl was extremely interested in studying him as well as reviewing all the athletic events.[58]

On Sunday, the twenty-first of June, she and a crew were at the sports stadium taking test shots of the soccer championships. They were especially interested in taking unobserved reaction shots of the spectators, both with telescopic lens and without.

> ...Two of her collaborators shot along with the newsreel operators in the oppressive heat.... Herr de

> Laforgue crept with a Kinamo through the area and struggled with the courage of a lion against the wall of spectators that refused to waver or budge--"Mensch, you should have taken our pictures before!" called the public as soon as he ... had put his camera into position. A worthy man, who was sitting in the area of the entry onto the field and who had not taken his eye off of the cameraman, grumbled at each attempted goal or other eleventh-hour moment, "Why are they filming the public the whole time? They should be filming the game once in a while!"[59]

On this same Sunday, Ertl was making studies for the marathon, and Walter Frentz had finished his test shots in Kiel. Riefenstahl was worried that when her crew in Kiel photographed the monument to the fallen in the battle of Jutland, which was located at Laboe and was originally to have been part of her coverage of the yacht races, they would omit the gulls wheeling about. She was also worried that the photographers would not photograph the goldfish at the Olympic Village.[60]

Not only was Riefenstahl doing her homework on athletic events; she was also learning as much as she could about ancient Greece, especially in regards to its history and its architecture. This was to be important because Riefenstahl would quite soon be going to Greece for the torchbearing. To help her, as well as to get another cameraman for the film, she hired an extremely interesting man, Dr. Walter Hege. Dr. Hege was an expert on the architecture of ancient Greece and had been working (along with Walter Frentz) on the film Die Glocke ruft, the propaganda film for the up-and-coming Olympic Games. Mostly Hege had been filming the ancient sites of the Games in Greece. He was also to produce a culture film to be distributed in connection with the Olympic Games. Riefenstahl hired him, and he gave nightly lectures at the Haus Ruhwald on Greek architecture and history. He was also hired especially to photograph the stadium and the other Olympic architecture, as well as the sculpture produced for the Games. Hege was the only photographer whose assistant was not merely a woman but a baroness, Ursula von und zu Loewenstein. According to Heinz von Jaworsky, the baroness was big and as strong as a horse; she carried all of Dr. Hege's equipment for him. Hege was quite small, and the sight of him and the baroness together was quite humorous.[61]

In the Geyer Works, the processing laboratory for the Olympic film, plans were being made for the coming film deluge. Geyer had promised that all film shot on any particular day of the Olympics would be returned to the film company on the next day. This was crucial, for if a cameraman were shooting bad film, he must know as soon as possible so he could take steps to correct his error. In addition, while extra covering shots were taken of most of the athletic events in any case for insurance, in the event that certain shots were defective it would be necessary to know as soon as possible before the athletes involved left Berlin, so that retakes could be made. Geyer's promise put a heavy burden on it. The planners were thinking in terms of about fifteen thousand meters of film a day.

To deal with this monstrous amount of film, the Geyer laboratory developed a new copy machine called the rekord NK 18, which could develop and copy 1200 meters of film an hour. Two special cars were used to transport the material shot between the sites of the competitions and the Geyer Laboratory. The negative would immediately be put into the developing tanks and finished by late that evening. Each roll of film was inscribed with the cameraman's name, his number, and a description of the material shot. The date the material was shot also was included, as well as the name of the camera assistant. Following these precautions, the incoming exposed material would immediately be registered and classified according to the event and the cameraman. In this manner, by the next day one could get a good overview of the quality of the film that had been shot.

The Olympia film company had hired two supervising editors, Max Michel, who had come from Bavaria-Film, and Heinz Schwarzmann, who had worked at Paramount and was also writing his Ph.D. thesis. The two men ran the developed film for the first time and judged the film on its pictorial value. Any problems with the film were recorded, and these written reports were then transferred to the Haus Ruhwald so that each camera operator was informed exactly as to the quality of the film he had shot the day before. Besides the two head cutters, there were ten assistants who sorted the materials and classified them according to the event and date. The actual cutting would come only after the Games were over, when all material had been sorted and the film company knew exactly what it had to work with.

Complete technical plans for the eventual cutting had also been worked out. Special viewing and sound rooms had been prepared. Long shelves had been built with special clamps attached; the shelves were backlit so that when the shots were stretched between the clamps, the cutter could recognize the contents of each shot without difficulty.

Even before the Games, the footage was beginning to pile up. By June 30, the cameramen were running tests of equipment all over Germany. Frentz had just finished camera placements for the yachting in Kiel. Guzzi Lantschner was filming the riders in Hannover and he would be in Hamburg by July 4 to start test filming the German gymnasts. Ertl was working in Grünau on the rowing events as well as on the swimming events in Berlin. Already at the Geyer Laboratories, the film cans were arriving with their red covers that said, "Olympia-Film--Probeaufnahmen--." Geyer would have to develop 16mm film and blow it up to 35; all newsreel material dealing with the Olympics would go through the *Olympia* cutting rooms at Geyer.[62]

THE TORCHBEARING

I have chosen to go into the seven-country expedition and Riefenstahl's trip to Greece, although in retrospect the trip may seem like more of a publicity event than an example of real filming.

Only an extremely small amount of what was shot by the cameramen was ever, in fact, used in the final film: so in some ways the trip was a waste of time--but in other ways it was important. First, it is an example, par excellence, of the way in which Riefenstahl herself was a media event. For a short time, in the various countries through which she passed, she was treated as though she were the official emissary of the Reich. Second, it was during the course of filming the torchbearing from Mount Olympus that she evolved the scheme of passing the torch not only from Greece to Berlin but from ancient times to modern ones.

The trip was planned as follows: A group of cameramen was to drive from Berlin to Athens, studying shots and looking for themes in the various locations through which the torch was to be carried from Olympus to Berlin. The countries to be thus traversed were Germany, Czechoslovakia, Austria, Hungary, Yugoslavia, Bulgaria, and Greece. Riefenstahl and another group were to fly to Athens via Belgrade. Then the two groups were to rejoin, proceed to Mount Olympus, and cover the torchbearing as far as Athens. Riefenstahl and her party would then fly back to Berlin, and the cameramen would cover the torchbearing back to Berlin by car. The automobiles would naturally have to leave first, so early on July 6, 1936, three Mercedes bedecked with Olympic flags left the Haus Ruhwald in the Spandauer Chaussee. The group was led by Carl Friedrich Fischer and included Albert Otto Kling, Heinz von Jaworsky and his assistant Wolfgang Hart, as well as Josef Ketterer. Adam Samstag, Friedrich Schmidt, and Adolf Jung were the drivers. Riefenstahl wanted ideas from the cameramen, and in her instructions to them, her basic idea of two Olympic films seems remarkably clear:

> I want you to shoot the torchbearing in two styles: one realistic, the other stylized. From every country bring me three or four effective themes of the course!

The cameramen would have to travel more than eighteen hundred miles over extremely bad roads between the sixth and eighteenth of July. Riefenstahl was to leave some two weeks later, on July 17, and the torchbearing was scheduled to begin on July 21.

On July 17, Riefenstahl and her entourage left Berlin to meet her cameramen in Greece and to begin the filming of the torchbearing back to Berlin. Ernst Jäger accompanied Riefenstahl on her trip to Greece, and I will be relying heavily on his long account of the voyage.[63]

The airplane, a Junker-52 flown by Gaim, carried the following people: Riefenstahl, Jäger, the Baron von Weyssenhoff, Erna Peters, Rolf Lantin, Walter Frentz, Otto Lantschner, Harald Reinl, Franz Gronatz, and Jürgen Ascherfeld.

Harald Reinl was a friend of Riefenstahl. He had acted in Stürme über dem Montblanc and would co-author the script for Tiefland. Erna Peters was Riefenstahl's cutting assistant. Lantin was her photographer. Frentz and Lantschner were two of the cameramen for the film who were especially close to Riefenstahl. Ascherfeld was the delegate for the torchbearers and the legal representative for the torchbearing through the seven countries. He was also the sport representative in the Reichs Post Ministry and co-editor of the Ernest Curtius volume, Olympia.[64] The Baron von Weyssenhoff was the government councillor in the Propaganda Ministry who took care of the trip arrangements.

As previously stated, it is clear from the makeup of this group that Riefenstahl was representing the Reich in addition to making a film. There is no very clear distinction within this group between the people who were headed to Greece on official business (such as Ascherfeld) and the film makers. Riefenstahl was news. She had a plane at her disposal. She had her own writer and photographer accompanying her, and as we will see, her itinerary was more like that of a visiting head of state than like that of a film director.

The plane first stopped at Belgrade, where Riefenstahl was interviewed by the press. She handed out memoranda about preparations for the film, the torchbearing, and her trip to Greece. The group then drank tea with the daughter of the Yugoslavian press minister and talked about the daughter's marriage and forthcoming trip to Berlin. Following this encounter came a tour of the city, after which they all took a rest to get away from the 95-degree heat. Riefenstahl took this opportunity to work on her manuscript with Walter Frentz.

> The section that she takes up consists of a chaos of notes that only her hand and eye can make sense of. Her frightening tempo appears to be caused by the awful heat of the hotel.... After an hour she has transferred her memos with many critical comments into her manuscript, has dictated letters, what Kebelmann, what Neubert should take shots of in Berlin, has selected photos that have been collected from German and foreign papers in order to preserve original sports shots, pictures of the Reich Sport Field, of the Olympic training; has had more and more new ideas, notions, perceptions, which are transferred into the manuscript.[65]

The group then visited the tomb of the unknown soldier and met the press chief of the Yugoslavian government, Dr. Kosta M. Louketitch along with other diplomats and press people. That evening Riefenstahl was the guest of the Kreisleiter of the NSDAP Neuhausen, and his wife, where she met some more of the press, athletes, and politicians.

The next day, the Riefenstahl entourage flew to Greece. Riefenstahl again worked on her manuscript, concentrating on the quarter mile. The plane stopped in Saloniki, where Riefenstahl gave another short interview. It then flew on to Athens where the group met the cameramen who had driven the three Mercedes from Berlin to Athens.

They had had troubles of their own. Starting with Prague, the seven-country expedition was often the target of government suspicion. Through Austria, it was accompanied by two officials from the criminal office (it could be argued that, in light of what was to happen to Austria and Czechoslovakia a certain amount of suspicion of semiofficial groups from Germany was far from inappropriate). In Greece, the priests in different villages were unhelpful if not hostile, and the villagers tended to take their cues from the priests. Bedbugs and customs officials were the worst enemies of the expedition. Jaworsky remembers one incident in Yugoslavia involving the bedbugs especially:

> It was a very funny incident.... Kling was sleeping with me--or Fischer, one of the two, we shared the room together, and he started screaming. It was so hot that we slept naked with just a bedsheet, and he screamed. I hit the light, and his bed was full of bedbugs. At first I had to laugh, then I shouted and rang the bell, and a kind of male maid came who didn't understand a word of German. But he came like an old Spitzweg picture, you know, with a night-cap and a candle in his hand, and in his left hand what we call a <u>Flitspritze</u>, a spray gun, so he knew without understanding a word of German what we were screaming about. And I'll never forget that he uncovered Kling, I think it was, who was naked in his bed and started to spray him with insecticide. Before he came to me, we got up, we went outside to the Gypsies who were still playing, and stayed all night with the Gypsies.[66]

At one border, the photographers were told by the customs agent that their papers would have to be translated into Greek, so they played billiards for thirty-six hours until their translated papers arrived. When one car developed an oil leak, they glued liquid cement on the point of fracture, put adhesive tape over the break, and went on. The dust was so bad in Hungary and Yugoslavia that the Mercedes had to stay half a kilometer apart. But almost three weeks after it left, the expedition finally made it to Athens.

In Athens, there was an official reception, after which the group went to stay in the Grande Bretagne. To welcome the group, Dr. Wrede, the Landesleiter of the NSDAP, who was an archeologist by profession, ran an article in the Neue Athener Zeitung, a German newspaper printed in Athens. The article is a splendid example of pompous National Socialist prose:

> Greeting the Germans in Greece
>
> Tomorrow morning the Olympic Flame will be lit in the stadium and at noon the torch takes up the flame and in the hand of the first runner begins its journey from Volk to Volk. When it reaches the Olympic Stadium in Berlin with the last runner and after the flame blazes up on the tower, then the peaceful competition of nations, the German Olympics will begin....
>
> We greet, however, above all the German comrades that the homeland has sent to us, in order to pass on the event of the preliminary festivities with which the Greek people begins its celebration with word, picture and text. We especially greet the artist, Leni Riefenstahl. Her work is known to us and in Greece.
>
> May the Olympic torch take our greetings to Germany and our wishes for all who compete there that the eleventh Olympiad have the success in the ultimate, deepest sense that the Fuehrer has envisioned.
>
> Wrede[67]

On Saturday, July 18, the group watched the outtakes that Willy Zielke shot of the Acropolis and reviewed other material as well. The group was quite enthusiastic about the quality of the footage. That evening there was a reception given by the German Chargé d' Affaires Pistor. At the reception, Riefenstahl was interested in locating people who could be of use to her during the torchbearing, even considering the interesting face of minister Luvaris. She was interviewed by Der Angriff, DNB, and other papers.

On Sunday morning early, the group left Athens for

Mount Olympus. Riefenstahl had at this point two aims. Both were very much in keeping with her notion of reportage of the Games versus her view of stylization of the Olympic idea. She wanted to document the running of the athletes with their magnesium torches. But, for the prologue, she wished to make a stylized version of the running in the cities of ancient Greece.

The crew left at six in the morning. With them were the three Mercedes as well as three trucks, all carrying German flags. They went through Corinth and stopped in Tripolis. Dr. Wrede accompanied the convoy and provided a guide to the countryside. After seeing Tripolis, the crew climbed to 2,000 meters and reached the village of Vytina. There the villagers treated the visitors to a chorus of "Germania." Finally, they reached Mount Olympus.

Following a brief flurry concerning the magnesium torches (which were to be used for outdoor photography and had been misplaced), the camera group first shot a general camera test of a Greek dance group which, under the leadership of Coula Pratsica, was part of the torch-lighting ceremonies. Riefenstahl was not at all pleased with the altar to be used for the torch-lighting ceremony. To her it seemed prosaic, as did the official ceremonies in general. She decided to compose her own shot.

On the lowest round altar, she lit a fire. The first torchbearer emerged from behind a column while the maidens greeted him. He lit his torch and then started his run from the altar. All this was improvised. Riefenstahl told Jaworsky to place his camera in a depression in the earth before the steps to the altar while Kling took up another position at a normal height in relation to the altar steps. The Greek runner was wearing modern gym shorts, a detail that displeased Riefenstahl.

Magnesium torch number one was lit. It flared up, emitting sparks that started little fires all around Jaworsky in his pit. Reporters jumped up and put the fires out with handkerchiefs, feet, and stones. They decided to try a second take, and the runner was sent back, but again there were too many sparks. Riefenstahl was becoming more and more upset. "It doesn't work with the gym shorts, it destroys the whole mood." She wanted a classical loincloth, but no one could find one.

Arthur Grimm suggested one could be made from towels and went to get some from the hotel. From these, a loincloth was made, but the Greek runner refused to wear it. So Jürgen Ascherfeld, the German sport advisor to the Post Ministry, volunteered to put on the loincloth, and they made the shot, causing a certain amount of resentment among the spectators. Some thought that a German had been chosen over a Greek to be the first Olympic runner.

As time for the real torchbearing came nearer, Riefenstahl raced from position to position, moving hand cameras around and motivating her people to look for themes and ideas. Her energy was remarkable, and every German on Mount Olympus was drafted, or had volunteered, to help her.

Jäger found himself putting out magnesium fires and mumbling that the woman was certainly some sort of monster. Finally, it was time to depart from the festival place, but there were problems still to be solved. How could the photographers get around the runners when the runners left the sacred grove? The cars were all marked with a pass on the windshields; however, this did not stop the police from preventing the cars from going around or even following the runners. The road was completely blocked off, and the group watched forlornly as the first runner disappeared down the road. Riefenstahl became extremely angry. Along with Rolf Lantin, she jumped from her car and began arguing with the police. Her arguments had no effect, and she broke into tears. The police must have been moved, because she was allowed to follow and photograph the torchbearers. Ten minutes later she was laughing. "In all cases it is always useful to have a few tears on hand."

The crew followed the runners, photographing as they went. It was during this stretch that Riefenstahl saw Anatol Dobriansky, the handsome runner who was featured in the prologue. Heinz von Jaworsky reports:

> At one point--I would say he was within the first twenty--a young Greek was running and taking the torch and he was extremely handsome, tan-like bronze, beautiful curly hair, well-built. And she said--shoot more of him, shoot more of him! Shoot everywhere more of him, he is beautiful![68]

Immediately, Riefenstahl made arrangements to take Anatol with her to Berlin for more shooting; later she had an affair with him. One of the items on her expense account that the Propaganda Ministry was not too pleased about was a transfer of some 200 Reichsmarks to Anatol's parents from the Olympia Company. According to Herr Groskopf, the business manager of the company, this was the only payment that Anatol ever received. The entry also confirms that Anatol, later, was part of the shooting for the prologue at the Kurischer Nehrung.[69]

As they rode along, the crew photographed the jubilation in various Greek towns. One of the major problems for the camera crew was the boundless hospitality of the Greeks. Heinz von Jaworsky remembers:

> In every little village, they stopped us and then the Mayor or whatever, they had a big tray--or trays--full of glasses of retsina, resin wine, and this resin that was in there, and that really puts your stomach and intestines together after the first, and all day long you had to drink that, we had a hard job remaining polite, to make believe you drink it and try to get rid of it and not to drink it, it made us sick. It pulls all your parts together. Every little village, there was a delegation to greet the Olympic Committee, and here they stood with a big tray of this horrible wine.[70]

One moment that seems to have made a deep impression on Riefenstahl and Jäger, both, occurred when a train came along on a track that paralleled the road on which the torchbearer was running. The train braked and steamed alongside the torchbearer as the people on the train pressed to the windows and doors. It accompanied the runner to the next station.

The camera crew went back through Vytina. By four the next morning they were in the bathing area of Lukati. They were then to film the celebration in Corinth, after which they had to leave the torchbearers for a while to go to Athens. Everyone was exhausted by the barrage of impressions.

In Athens, the sun was too bright to film except between five and six in the morning. The crew had much to do.

They were first to visit and photograph the Acropolis. Walter Frentz, who had been in Athens the year before for the Olympic film Die Glocke Ruft, stood by the same passage he had stood by the year before. Professor N. Balanos, the famous conservator and restorer, shortly before had ordered the whole foundation of the Acropolis ripped up in order to lay a new base. The professor was extremely helpful to Frentz, who was looking for a new altar for a certain scene in which the torch would be carried (by an actor from Athens) through the Acropolis. Mr. Balanos evidently borrowed an altar from a local church--but without telling the priest. The priest was shocked when he found his altar missing. Frentz filmed the torchbearer as he swiftly ran through the propyläen.

Riefenstahl had gone with most of the camera equipment to the Olympic stadium (the stadium had been built in 1896 for the first modern Olympic Games). At the stadium, the torch was brought to light the old Olympic altar. George II, the king of Greece, was there, as was the minister of war and other dignitaries. Jäger later reported that Riefenstahl offended the king by waving her handkerchief at him; he was so shocked that he refused to see her.[71]

The next morning, July 22, the whole entourage left for Delphi. They were accompanied by Dr. Wrede and his wife. At first, the party was so overwhelmed by the ruins and the landscape that they had trouble dragging themselves from the view to shoot.

Riefenstahl gained wide publicity coverage for an event that happened in Delphi. In the stadium, a Greek torchbearer invited her to dance the Greek national dance with him. There was no way to decline. So to the rousing applause of the entire stadium, Riefenstahl found herself being swept in great circles by the young Greek. At the end of the dance, the Greek athletes carried her around the stadium on their shoulders, an act for which they garnered added applause. After the torch dedication, Riefenstahl was so impressed that she declared that she had found the location to shoot her Penthesilea film. She held her whole crew and Anatol Dobriansky there and let the torchbearing go on without them. They spent the whole day in Delphi, until eight in the evening staging shots with good angles and good lighting.

Much of the footage of Anatol lighting the Olympic torch

and starting his run appears to have been shot at Delphi. In addition, many of the evening shots, including the one in which Anatol passes the torch to the next runner, were also taken at Delphi, probably at the ancient amphitheater. Much of the material was shot in the evening, the so-called "golden hour," when there was still some light, but the film gives the effect of having been shot at night.[72] Riefenstahl and the crew were inspired by Delphi, and more footage from this day was used in the final film than from all other footage shot during the trip to Greece.

This filming wound up the trip. There were closing ceremonies in Athens. Riefenstahl sent an enthusiastic telegram to Dr. Diem describing the torchbearers in their ancient setting (for the concept had been an old dream of his). The next morning, July 23, she was back in Berlin.

The interesting thing about the trip to Greece is this: Virtually none of the documentary footage shot of the torchbearing was used. What the trip does show is that Riefenstahl was still grasping for an approach and more than willing to shoot film while the ideas clarified in her mind. Her approach was probably intuitive rather than totally planned beforehand. She did her homework, but she was not frightened to improvise when it was necessary. Because she adopted this approach, and because she was receptive to new stimuli, Riefenstahl not only started shooting film of Anatol but conceived how she could use him as an ideal of ancient Greece. One can see how far Riefenstahl had already moved from a purely documentary approach to the film. If, truly, she were trying to establish a balance between documentary material and idea, how quickly the documentary approach gave way. What the trip to Greece really accomplished was to give Riefenstahl insight into how she might work out many of the problems inherent in the prologue.

On July 27, she received the guidelines from the International Amateur Athletic Federation. The guidelines covered what the film company could and could not do in the course of the Games. The IAAF was not unhelpful, and indeed Riefenstahl was working under far fewer restrictions than the cameramen had at Los Angeles in 1932, but the instructions clearly held that the Olympic Games were for the purposes of sport, not of film making. Its letter of July 27 read in part as follows:

The IAAF has carefully studied the filming of the track and field week during the Olympic Games. We took into consideration the fact that all has to be done to produce a model sport film of the Olympic Games of 1936. Therefore, we (the directing officials for athletics in the Organizing Committee for the XIth Olympiad), are glad to inform you, in the name of the IAAF, that:

1. You may use 2 pits for the camera-men taking pictures of the high jump at the high-jumping site, and another pit, 5 metres from the starting line of the 100 metre dash. One at the side of the finishing tape. One at the end of the 100 metre course. One at the southern side of the southern jumping course.
2. The following towers will be permitted: 3 towers in the center of the field during the longer races. One tower behind the start of the 100 metre course. A sliding rail behind the protecting grid for throwing the hammer during the qualifying tests. The towers must be removed immediately after use.
3. The following are forbidden on principle: the taking of motion pictures directly in front of the contestants in the races as well as in the throwing and jumping contests. All cameramen must operate sitting or prone. North of the northern jumping course and south of the southern jumping course, pictures may be taken from the lowered passageway only with the exception of the pits on the southern side.
4. In the throwing contests, the broad jump, and the hop, step and jump, only the first attempt (in the qualifying test, preliminary and final) may be photographed. In the men's high jump, photographs may be taken of the qualifying test only up to a height of 1.80 metres, of the final up to a height of 1.85 metres, in the women's high jump, up to a height of 1.40 metres in the qualifying test, and to 1.50 metres in the final. In the pole vault, up to a height of 3.60 metres in the qualifying test, and up to 3.80 metres in the final.
5. Immediately after the try-outs the camera-men must return to the lowered passageway. From there pictures may be taken without restrictions.

The boundaries are the same as for photographing:
a) Pictures may be taken only from outside the running course. Boundary: grass.
b) Throwing and jumping boundary at least 3 metres on each side, marked by a yellow line.

6. The number of camera-men should not exceed 3 for throwing and jumping. The use of noiseless cameras is desirable.
7. If a competitor does not desire to have his picture taken, his wishes must be complied with immediately.
8. After the finals, the winners and those placing in the field events can be filmed during one trial each provided that this does not disturb other contests.
9. The number of the daily identification cards for the Olympic Film and News Reel camera-men will be fixed at
   6 for the inner field
   9 for the sunken passageway

Cameramen taking each other's place must exchange their arm-bands behind the enclosure of the Marathon entrance.
The use of a catapult camera on sliding rails cannot be allowed on the 100 metre track, since that would not comply with the Regulations of the International Amateur Athletic Federation. Permission cannot be given for the use of a special camera car for the Marathon Race. However, reverting to the desire of your company, formerly expressed, we should gladly admit one of your camera operators with a portable moving picture camera into the third car of the judges for filming the competitors in the race. Along the course we shall make all possible provisions for assisting the filming, especially near the control stations and the canteens.
The IAAF calls your attention to the fact that competitors in the Olympic Games may not take part in any public performance for filming purposes. The IAAF is convinced that the agreement made yesterday and this letter cover all the possibilities for filming the track and field events in a manner not possible at former Games.

Very respectfully yours,
(signed) S. Stankovits, Bo Ekelund
IAAF.[73]

The company was disappointed when many ideas it had conceived of for coverage of Olympic events were vetoed. Especially disappointing was the ban on the use of the catapult, a device the film makers were extremely proud of.

> All at once the catapult, which had been the sensation of all the film devices, was forbidden. The green cast-iron beams had sat forlornly on the lawn of Haus Ruhwald. It appeared that the clever construction work of Fischer and Lebeau would remain unused.[74]

But Riefenstahl was not finished with the catapult; it was to have its moment in the Games.

Paragraph 4 of the IAAF letter is also especially interesting because the throwing contests, the broad jump, the high jump, and the hop, skip and jump were all featured prominently in the film. Perhaps Riefenstahl can shed light on the matter, but it appears that the film contains many more shots of preliminary heats than it does of actual events. If Riefenstahl had been able to have the rules in the letter changed (and she herself has cited the letter), she does not mention it.

In the last week of July, the German and foreign newsreel companies received the detailed conditions under which they would be allowed to make newsreels of the Olympics (<u>see</u> Appendix B).[75] Although these conditions were at least in part due to the conditions imposed on Riefenstahl by the IAAF, the cry of outrage, at least from the American companies, could probably have reached Berlin from Hollywood without benefit of radio. The <u>Motion Picture Herald</u> reviewed the contract as if it were tantamount to an act of war and started its story by saying, "Adolph [<u>sic</u>] Hitler decrees that American newsreels must advertise Germany at the Olympic Games, and on his terms. All else is <u>streng verboten</u>."[76] In fact, Hitler had not decreed this, although it could have been an intent of the Propaganda Ministry to censor materials going out of Germany. But the main purpose of the contract was, of course, to insure that Riefenstahl kept control of Olympic material so that no other entity could make an Olympic film. The <u>Herald</u> understood this, but it did not like it. The paper complained that American cameramen could shoot only when and where authorized, that they must place all positive and negative film at Riefenstahl's disposal, as well as one "lavender" print of each finished Olympic newsreel subject. Furthermore, the Herald alleged, the contract required the American newsreel companies to use German cameramen, although no such clause is present in the contract. The Herald was quite upset about the proviso that no footage could be used except for newsreel purposes, and they were not happy with the possibility that the personnel of the newsreel companies might be commandeered:

> The American newsreel managements cannot even be certain that their staffs will not be conscripted by the Hitlerites, for a clause buried midway in the contract provides that the newsreel companies, if so requested, have to put at the disposal of the G.m.b.H. ... any of their cameramen who are not busy.[77]

The American companies were also far from pleased about the limitations on the amount of film they could screen--although the 250 meter figure represents a compromise by Riefenstahl. Originally, she had only allowed 125 meters.[78] American newsreel companies, the Herald thundered, were not even able to shoot American athletes in training at the Olympic Village.

But what incensed the Herald even more than the contract was a series of "working rules" devised by Riefenstahl: One, every cameraman had to wear the "official Hitler-prescribed Nazi Olympic uniform." Two, each cameraman had to be accompanied by a German agent who would act as an on-the-spot censor. Three, the American companies had to use German sound equipment. If the Americans insisted on using American equipment, they had to leave the equipment in Germany for a year at the disposal of the German government.

It is hard to avoid the conclusion that the matter of the contract was not terribly well handled by the Germans. Although there may have been good reasons for some of the provisions, Riefenstahl's actions caused resentment among the American companies, and these resentments would be remembered later.

By the end of July, all that could be done had been done. On July 31, Riefenstahl was at the stadium, inspecting the tracks that had been erected for a special travelling shot.

The tracks had been prepared on the great open-air steps between the marathon towers, and when Hitler strode down the steps, the camera was to travel along with him. For the last time before the Games started, Riefenstahl checked the various positions with Ertl and Frentz. She talked with von Barsy, who was making special atmosphere shots, and there was still something to work out with Neubert as he checked his slow-motion camera for the last time. As much as was humanly possible, everything had been prepared. The terrible responsibility of recording the Olympics must have weighed on Riefenstahl very heavily. At the opening ceremonies alone, sixty-five cameramen were expected to be shooting.[79] Weather problems could erupt--or difficulties with a crucial camera at a crucial moment. There could be a major incident with the authorities caused if an athlete was disturbed. Despite all the careful preparation, a million other things could go wrong.

Everything depended on what the film crews could record during the next sixteen days.

NOTES

1. Film-Kurier, 17 October 1935.

2. David Pryce-Jones, Unity Mitford (New York: The Dial Press, 1977), pp. 132-135. Riefenstahl has denied that she was with Streicher, although the documentation is extensive.

3. Charles Ford, Leni Riefenstahl, p. 81.

4. Erik Barnouw, Documentary (New York: Oxford University Press, 1974), citing Leni Riefenstahl [Ernst Jäger], Hinter den Kulissen des Reichsparteitagfilms (Munich: Zentraverlag der NSDAP, 1935), p. 17.

5. "Leni Riefenstahls Rombesuch: Mussolinis Interesse am Dokumentfilm," Film-Kurier, 27 February 1936, pp. 1-2.

6. Hans Weidemann file. Captured German Documents. Propaganda Ministry, Serial 125, Item RFK 12. National Archives, Washington, D.C.

7. "Vom Olympia--Winter zum Olympia-Filmwerk," Film-Kurier, 1 February 1936.

8. [Leni Riefenstahl], "The Creation of the Olympic Film," The Olympic Games, Berlin 1936: Official Report (translation), (Berlin: Wilhelm Limpert, 1936), p. 329. Frau Riefenstahl provided me with a carbon copy of the original typewritten manuscript in German with the words "von Leni Riefen-

stahl" added, so she is evidently the author.

9. Ibid., p. 329.

10. Ibid., p. 329: "500000 Meter Olympia film." Nachtausgabe (Berlin), 8 July 1936.

11. "Vor Leni Riefenstahls Olympia-Film-Schlacht," 8 Ufa Abendblatt (Berlin), 14 July 1936.

12. "Gesellschaftversammlung der Olympia-Film G.m.b.H.," RMVP, Bundesarchiv, R55/503, pp. 109-110.

13. [Riefenstahl], "The Creation of the Olympic Film," Official Report, pp. 329-330.

14. "Das Olympische Filmwerk in den ersten Vorbereitungen," Film-Kurier, 27 April 1936, p. 1.

15. "Rund um Leni Riefenstahls Olympiafilm: Walter Frentz," Film-Kurier, 10 July 1936, p. 3.

16. "Rund um Leni Riefenstahls Olympiafilm: Hans Ertl," Film-Kurier, 11 June 1936, p. 3; Mannheim, "Leni," p. 115.

17. Gordon Hitchens, Kirk Bond and John Hanhardt, "Henry Jaworsky, Cameraman for Leni Riefenstahl, interviewed by Gordon Hitchens, Kirk Bond and John Hanhardt," Film Culture, 56-57 (Spring 1973): 122-161.

18. Ibid., p. 129.

19. Ernst Jäger, "How Leni Riefenstahl Became Hitler's Girlfriend," Hollywood Tribune, Part 1, 28 April 1939. Berlin, Berlin Document Center, Gustav Lantschner file.

20. "Kurt Neubert--mit dem Zeitlupen 'Tank,'" Film-Kurier, 18 August 1936, p. 3; "Olympiade in der Zeitlupe: Kurt Neubert bei Leni Riefenstahl," Licht Bild Bühne (Berlin), 12 June 1936, p. 1.

21. "Hans Scheib--der Mann mit der langen Brennweite," Film-Kurier, 19 August 1936, p. 3.

22. Hitchens, "Interview with Henry Jaworsky," p. 128.

23. "Haus Ruhwald, Hauptquartier des Olympia--Filmstabs; Leni Riefenstahl und 300 Mitarbeiter startbereit," Film-Kurier, 1 August 1936, p. 7.

24. Charles Ford, Leni Riefenstahl, p. 73.

25. "Haus Ruhwald, Hauptquartier des Olympia--Filmstabs," p. 7.

26. Jäger, "How Leni Riefenstahl Became Hitler's Girlfriend," Part 1.

27. Seventh Army Interrogation, p. 3.

28. Ibid., p. 3.

29. "Leni Riefenstahl haut auf," Film Woche, 5 April 1952, p. 14.

30. "Vor Leni Riefenstahls Olympia-Film-Schlacht."

31. "Leni Riefenstahl sammelt Motive," Film-Kurier, 13 May 1936, p. 3; "Der Olympia Film wird angekurbelt," 12 Uhr (Berlin), 14 May 1936.

32. [Riefenstahl], "The Creation of the Olympic Film," Official Report, p. 330.

33. "Filmvorbereitungen für Olympia-Kiel," 12 Uhr, 12 June 1936; "Kiel im Olympia-Film," Film-Kurier, 8 June 1936; "Leni Riefenstahl bei der Olympia-Auswahl der Segler in Kiel," Licht Bild Bühne, 9 June 1936.

34. Bella Fromm, Blood and Banquets (New York and London: Harper and Brothers, 1942), pp. 222.

35. "Photographie von Willy Zielke," Der Spiegel, 33, (16 August 1982), p. 141.

36. Ibid., p. 141.

37. Willy Zielke, Interview with author at Bad Pyrmont (Germany) on 18 May 1983.

38. "Vom Werden des Olympiafilms: Schnappschusse," Licht Bild Bühne, 26 June 1936, pp. 1-2.

39. Ibid., pp. 1-2. Zielke feels the amount of smoke powder is exaggerated.

40. Willy Zielke, interview with author.

41. Ibid.

42. Ibid.

43. Ibid.

44. "How Leni Riefenstahl Became Hitler's Girlfriend," Hollywood Tribune, Part 4, 19 May 1939, p. 13.

45. Berlin Document Center, Leo de Laforgue file.

46. RMI. BA, R55/105 (Fol. 1), pp. 297-300.

47. Most of this information on cameramen was taken from [Ernst Jäger] "Die Kamera kämpft mit," Part II, Film-Kurier, 14 August 1936. I have also filled out information on credits with the use of various encyclopedias.

48. "Filmgeographie von Grünau," Film-Kurier, 5 June 1936, pp. 1-2.

49. "Nah genug herankommen: das Problem der Olympia-Operateure," Film-Kurier, 30 June 1936.

50. Henry Javorsky, Interview with author at Hollis-wood, New York, on 7 July 1983.

51. Mannheim, "Leni," p. 116.

52. "Nah genug herankommen," pp. 1-2.

53. Mannheim, "Leni," p. 116.

54. "Immer Schussbereit: Eine Schulter-Filmkamera--keine verwackelten Bilder." Deutsche Allgemeine Zeitung, 1 August 1936.

55. "Nah genug herankommen," p. 1.

56. "Drei Filmautos begleiten den Fackellauf der Olympiade," Der Film, 4 July 1936.

57. Mannheim, "Leni."

58. "Nah genug herankommen," p. 1.

59. "Vom Werden des Olympia-Films: Schnappschusse," p. 1.

60. "Vor Leni Riefenstahls Olympia-Film-Schlacht."

61. "Olympia-Film vor der Vollendung," Licht Bild Bühne, 26 September 1935; "Kultur-Auftrag in Olympia," Film-Kurier, 2 June 1936, p. 3; "Das 'Riefenstahl Filmheer' steht bereit," Licht Bild Bühne, 1 August 1936, p. 4; [Jäger], "Und die Kamera kämpft mit," Part 3, 5 August 1936, p. 3; Hitchens, "Interview with Henry Jaworsky," p. 128.

62. "Geyer konstruiert neue Kopiermaschine für Bild und Ton," Film-Kurier, 1 August 1936, pp. 5-6; "Grosskampf bei Geyer," Film-Kurier, 8 August 1936, pp. 1-2; "Nah genug herankommen," pp. 1-2.

63. [Ernst Jäger] "Leni Riefenstahls Olympiade-Film, Berlin 1936. Fackellauf durch Griechenland. Sonderdruck aus dem Film-Kurier." This special edition is a compilation of the articles that ran in Film-Kurier in the third week of July 1936. BA, R56/IV/18.

64. Olympia, von Ernst Curtius, mit ausgewählten Texten von Pindar, Pausinas, Lukian. Photos von Martin Hürlimann. Erläuterungen über den Sport und die Kampfarten der Griechen von Jürgen Ascherfeld. Berlin: Atlantis Verlag, 1935.

65. [Jäger], "Fackellauf," p. 2.

66. Javorsky, interview with author.

67. [Jäger], "Fackellauf", p. 3.

68. Javorsky, Interview with Gordon Hitchens, p. 126.

69. BA, R55/503, p. 118.

70. Javorsky, interview with author.

71. Jäger, "How Leni Riefenstahl Became Hitler's Girlfriend," Part 4, 19 May 1939, p. 13.

72. Javorsky, interview with author.

73. [Riefenstahl], "The Creation of the Olympic Film," Official Report, pp. 331-332.

74. [Jäger], "Die Kamera kämpft mit," Part 6, 8 August 1936, p. 3.

75. James P. Cunningham, "Hitler Makes U.S. Olympics Films Advertise Germany," Motion Picture Herald, 8 August 1936, pp. 13-15.

76. Ibid., p. 13.

77. Ibid., p. 14.

78. "Reels Get Wider Latitude in Shooting the Olympics," Motion Picture Herald, 4 August 1936, pp. 1-2.

79. "Das Riefenstahl Filmheer steht bereit," p. 4.

• CHAPTER III •

THE FILMING OF THE OLYMPIC GAMES

SATURDAY, AUGUST 1, 1936[1]

This date marked the opening ceremonies of the Games. The athletic events were not to commence until the next day. A five-mile Olympic Way had been prepared through Berlin from the Lustgarten, through Unter den Linden, beneath the Brandenburg Gate, along the Charlottenburger Chaussee, and then through the Tiergarten and up the Heerstrasse. Olympic and Swastika banners were everywhere, and the crowd was so thick that it was expected that a million people would watch Hitler's ride along the Olympic way to the Stadium. For those who could not see, loudspeakers were placed all along the way to tell the spectators what was happening. Berlin was ready for the festivities, and the town burned with Olympic fever.

The program for the day officially opened at eight in the morning as German youth groups assembled at all the sports grounds in Berlin. The IOC was supposed to visit one group. At half-past ten (perhaps to give the lie to the anti-church campaign), services were held at the Protestant Cathedral and at St. Hedwig's Catholic Cathedral. At half-past eleven, a ceremony was held at the grave of the unknown soldier. At quarter after twelve, the real Olympic ceremonies began. At the Lustgarten, a large body of Hitler Youth stood at attention and heard speeches by Dr. Goebbels and Baldur von Schirach, the Hitler Youth leader. Members of the IOC and Reich Air Minister Hermann Goering were also present. At half-past twelve, the Olympic torch arrived at the Lustgarten, where it was presented to the Hitler Youth. The flame also lit an altar that had been especially constructed for the occasion. The flame would be guarded by the Hitler Youth until four in the afternoon, when it would then be carried to the stadium.

Meanwhile, Hitler was giving a reception for the IOC. The reception started at half-past one. Moved by the Olympic spirit himself, he promised the IOC that a new German archeological expedition would be sent to do work at Mount Olympus. At four o'clock, he proceeded with the members of the IOC by car to the stadium. As he entered the stadium along with the IOC members, the crowd roared an ovation, and the massed bands broke into the two national anthems, the Horst Wessel song and "Deutschland über Alles." Hitler was presented with a bouquet by a little blonde girl, after which the group proceeded to the tribune of honor.

When Hitler and the IOC contingent were seated, the athletes began to march past. The reception given some countries was friendly; the reception given others was not. The French team was warmly received by the largely German crowd because it had given what appeared to be a fascist salute to Hitler. The French later explained that it was only giving the Olympic salute, but the French team must have realized that the salute was bound to have been misconstrued. The Americans, following the tradition laid down at the London Games in 1908, refused to dip their flag to Hitler and made a simple "eyes right" gesture. This caused whistles and catcalls from the crowd, and Hitler told Goering that he felt that he had been personally insulted.[2] The German team, appearing last because it was the host nation, made a grand entrance. The team was dressed all in white and was extremely impressive to watch. It was led by von Tschammer und Osten.

After the march past, Dr. Lewald made a long, dull speech crammed with National Socialist ideology:

> In a few moments, the torch bearer will appear to light the Olympic fire on his tripod, when it will rise, flaming to heaven, for the weeks of this festival. It creates a real and spiritual bond of fire between our German fatherland and the sacred places of Greece founded 4,000 years ago by our nordic immigrants....[3]

In comparison, Hitler, limited to the short statement prescribed by the IOC, was far more effective. He stepped to the microphone and announced, "I proclaim open the Olympic Games of Berlin, celebrating the Eleventh Olympiad of the modern era."

Following this, sailors raised the great Olympic flag while Paul Winter's Olympic fanfare was being played. The smaller national flags were also raised on the walls of the stadium. Three thousand pigeons were released while a huge chorus, dressed in white, began to sing the "Olympic Hymn" of Richard Strauss. When this was over, a slim blonde runner, holding the Olympic flame, appeared at the entrance of the stadium. He ran down the steps, across the arena--his torch trailing blue smoke--and up the great marathon steps on the other side of the stadium. He dipped his torch to the brazier and a great flame leaped up. The Olympic Games had begun.

Other festivities followed. Rudolf Ismayr, a weight lifter and the deputy of von Tschammer und Osten, took the Olympic Oath while holding the German flag. Then the Olympic scoreboard flashed the words of the founder of the modern Olympic Games, Baron Pierre de Coubertin:

> The important thing is not to win but to take part.
> The essential thing is not to have conquered
> but to have fought to win.

A delegation from Greece was then presented to Hitler. This group included Spiridon Loues, the winner of the marathon in the first modern Olympic Games of 1896, who was now an old shepherd. Loues, wearing the traditional Greek costume, presented Hitler with an olive branch from the sacred grove on Mount Olympus. Hitler, quite moved, thanked him. The opening ceremonies ended with a performance of Handel's "Hallelujah Chorus."

That evening at nine, a huge pageant written by Dr. Diem and involving ten thousand actors and dancers was held. Among others the dancers of the Mary Wigman Company (Wigman was Leni Riefenstahl's old teacher) performed. Harold Kreuzberg and Werner Stammer did a sword dance symbolizing the futility of all wars. It was a stunning show.

All in all, the pageantry and organization of the opening ceremonies seemed to have had a deep effect on most of the onlookers. Moreover, the emphasis on peace and understanding between nations made it hard not to have doubts that perhaps the New Germany had been misunderstood. As the opening ceremonies started, the German Press Service burbled:

> ... The Olympic flame will enter the arena of peaceful combat exactly on that day when twenty-two years ago the torch of war was destined to afflict the world for four years. The entire German people read in this coincidence a happy omen of good will and the readiness of the nations to dedicate all of their forces and faculties to the friendly combat for the benefit of mankind.
>
> They are determined that these Olympic Games shall resolve into something more than a mere breathing spell in the struggle for potential interests. We demand they strive to win the understanding of one nation for another, thus preparing the ground for universal understanding among the world's peoples.[4]

And the New York Times commented:

> These Olympic Games have had an opening notable even beyond expectations, high as these were. They seem likely to accomplish what the rulers of Germany have frankly desired from them, that is, to give the world a new viewpoint from which to regard the Third Reich....[5]

Germany had been successful in its chief propaganda aim. The first day had been a stunning coup d'estime.

The film makers, after having received much publicity and acclaim, were in a state of shock at the size of the task that they were required to accomplish. First of all, the weather on Saturday was absolutely awful and was to remain that way for the next week. It was cold, cloudy and rainy, and Berliners described the conditions as April in August. The cameramen could contend with the cold and rain, but the lack of sunshine would cause technical problems for many of them. Also, they were subdued by their comparative smallness. Only six cameramen were allowed on the field, and they felt lost in the enormousness of the Olympic Stadium. They were also bothered by the discrepancy between the enormous artistic inspiration they'd felt during the opening ceremonies and the limitations imposed on them by their photographic equipment. According to Jäger, the artist and technician in them struggled with each other. So much was happening around them that they simply could not seize on film. They drifted back to the Haus Ruhwald at the end of the opening ceremonies, dead tired and subdued. Because of the awful weather, no one was sure what he had succeeded in photographing.[6]

Riefenstahl held a conference on Saturday night. Although nobody was terribly coherent, a few impressions stood out. Alexander von Lagorio, guest cameraman for the day, had been shooting in the Lustgarten and was quite satisfied with the results. De Laforgue was quite pleased with the method he had evolved for filming Hitler and his guests.

> A whole string of cameramen was especially trained to take "candid" shots of his most natural poses. The moment a certain cameraman, de Laforgue, appeared in the box, Hitler began to show "reactions" to the sporting events. Goebbels shouted at Riefenstahl--he didn't like the arrangement. But the camera kept grinding on and the Fuehrer kept on "acting"....[7]

De Laforgue was pleased because he had obtained five good shots of Hitler. Hasso had been shooting with his crane at the Brandenburg Gate. Hege, Frentz, Ertl, and the Lantschners were so excited they were barely comprehensible.

An announcement was made that the tracking shot of Hitler descending the steps between the marathon gates into the stadium (which had been set up on Friday) had been forbidden.

The conferences continued while Riefenstahl turned to the details of Sunday's shooting. She had already worked out a final timetable, a schedule to show where personnel would be located and a list of camera positions that had been entered in her Manuscript under "Track and Field." Next to her sat Aurelia ("Relly") Friedl, who had worked for Ritter von Halt of the Organization Committee from Garmisch-Partenkirchen.[8] As Riefenstahl dictated, she entered the relevant information into the workbook that each cameraman possessed. In addition to this workbook, the cameraman had a bundle of portfolio-sized papers, which listed the names, subjects and the sport program of each day; this was an idea of Walter Traut. Before each cameraman went on location he was to consult the directions so he would know exactly what he was to shoot; he then was to indicate that the shot had been made.

The cameramen listened, but they were all dead tired. It was now eleven. The men had been averaging about three hours sleep a night. Kiekebusch collapsed at the conference table and fell asleep. Riefenstahl sent everybody to bed except a few cameramen, and she continued the conference with them in her room until half-past three in the morning. She assigned positions according to who was good at tracking shots, who was better in a fixed position, and who tended to let the focus go soft. She knew the problems with the film apparatus and she knew what film stock she wanted to use.

She also had to decide whether to use the cameramen (von Jaworsky, Hart, Ketterer, etc.) who had just returned from Greece, on Sunday. They were filthy, exhausted, and, quite likely, infested with lice. Traut told them they should strike but, failing that, at least go home and rest up. Riefenstahl assigned Kebelmann to the bicycling to do training shots. Hege was removed from architecture to cover the pentathlon riding event, and Scheib would do some special work with the wide angle lens. Von Barsy would cover weight-lifting training, and Tietgens would take shots of the public. It was also announced that, in the event the weather improved, other photographers would take shots of the public in the stadium.

SUNDAY, AUGUST 2, 1936

This was the first day of the actual athletic competition. Once again the weather was quite bad. It was an extremely successful day for Germany, however, as German athletes won several gold medals in track and field, a real coup, as Germany had never before won anything in that division. The events on Sunday were as follows:

Track and Field

Shot Put (Finals)--Won by Hans Wöllke, Germany
Women's Javelin (Finals)--Won by Hilde (Tilly) Fleischer, Germany

10,000-meter Run (Finals)--Won by Ilmari Salminen, Finland; second, Arvo Askola, Finland; third, Volmari Iso-Hollo, Finland

Men's High Jump (Finals)--Won by Cornelius Johnson, United States; second, Dave Albritton, United States; third, Delos Thurber, United States

Men's 100-meter Run (Trials)--Jesse Owens won both his heats and unofficially broke the Olympic and world record in his semifinal heat. The record was not allowed to stand because of a following wind

800-meter Run (Trials)

Modern Pentathlon

5,000-meter Cross-country--Won by Abba, Italy; second, Mollet, Belgium; third, Handrick, Germany.

Hitler was in attendance, and he publicly congratulated Wöllke and Fleischer.

That Sunday morning started early for the film crew. At the Geyer Works, every attempt was being made to get the previous day's film developed. There were two projection rooms in operation, Michel in one and Schwarzmann in another. They were both checking the previous day's shots, with secretaries by their sides taking notes. The material was immediately examined and appraised. Outside, a group of women ran off; they prepared and packed the first prints of the film into cans. Herr Groskopf, the financial head of the Company, arrived with the first of many payments to Geyer. Riefenstahl sent lemonade and rolls to the projection rooms. Michel and Schwarzmann had 8,000 meters apiece to reckon with, but by twelve noon they had developed all of Saturday's film, and they would finish Sunday's film by eight that night.

At Döberitz, where the modern pentathlon riding event was taking place, things were going well. Edi Wieser was the production manager, and Guzzi Lantschner was filming at the jumps.

> The riders are fantastic after five kilometers of this devil's course. A Hungarian has just finished. At the start he took off in a highly elegant manner, now the rider and the horse are gasping through the finish, filthy, both with foam coming from the mouth

> --a terrific shot. Our cameramen are extended across the wide terrain. Field Marshal von Blomberg amiably watches the busy bees in their smart film uniforms.[9]

Things were also going well at the stadium. The sun even came out as the flag was being raised to announce Germany's first victory of the Games. In the midst of Owens' 100-meter heat, Riefenstahl suddenly yelled, "I've got to chuck my Manuscript, I'll need all the 100-meter heats for cutting, this is totally crazy!" Owens had just unofficially broken the world record in his heat. Ertl was standing on his green tower in the middle of the field, panning to catch the 10,000-meter run. Frentz was squatting in a pit, shooting the high jump. De Laforgue took shots of the victors. When Wöllke was summoned to Hitler's box, Riefenstahl also joined them. She was approached and greeted by Hitler as well as Goering, after which she went back to work.

One problem arose which was going to get worse. The whole crew was beginning to have difficulties with the referees. On this day, they even expelled Riefenstahl, but everyone was having problems:

> No word against the sport authorities so long as the Olympic cameras are in action, but the battle over credentials, if recorded by each incident, could easily fill a page of this newspaper. Sometimes a cameraman is thrown off the field, sometimes warned. The newsreel people are crying because they can hardly move.[10]

To combat the problem, Traut spent his Sunday evening having new armbands cut and printed; he hoped that these new bands would be declared valid on Monday. After the evening conference the crew got to bed relatively early--before two in the morning.

MONDAY, AUGUST 3, 1936

The overwhelming dramatic event of the day was the winning of the 100-meter sprint by Jesse Owens in the marvelous time of 0:10:03; Owens beat Ralph Metcalfe by one yard. The Germans were quite happy about the gold medal won by

Karl Hein in the hammer throw and the silver medal won by Erwin Blask in the same event.

Track and Field

Men's 100-meter Sprint (Semifinals and Finals)--Won by Jesse Owens, United States
Hammer Throw (Finals)--Won by Karl Hein, Germany
Women's 100-meter Sprint (Trials)--Fastest time was by Helen Stephens, United States
800-meter Run (Semifinals)--Won by John Woodruff, United States
3,000-meter Steeplechase
400-meter Hurdles (Trials)

Weight Lifting

Light Heavyweight Class

Soccer

Italy v. United States; Norway v. Mexico

Polo

Great Britain v. Mexico

No events were slated at the stadium before half-past ten so the morning was slow. The film crew was busy, however. A lot of important material would be coming up in the afternoon, including the 100-meter sprint, which promised to be one of the most dramatic events of the Games. Riefenstahl took this opportunity to talk to all thirty-four of her cameramen. She spoke to them at some length in the morning and at midday. She allocated five camera assignments to each, taking about five minutes per cameraman. Then she spent ten minutes more with each, discussing camera movements, use of filters, and mixes. At fifteen minutes per cameraman, she spent eight and a half hours working out afternoon scheduling.

Owens' 100-meter sprint was a dramatic event for the camera crew. They were definitely aware that this promised to be a big moment in the Games. Jäger described the race from the camera position as the starting gun fired.

> We were sitting five meters away from the start. Grimm, our artist-photographer, has stuck a Leica in my hand, explaining sympathetically, "You can't miss, shoot away when you see the first leg move." Over at the stadium cellar stands Rolf Lantin, who is supposed to make a panning shot with a simple hand camera. Frentz ordered him to do it. And when even we headquarters types take up camera arms, there must be a real panic.
>
> During the moments of running, we glance over the field--what a fantastic distribution of cameras! There standing high above on the broadcasting roof is Hans Ertl, who pans with a huge telescopic lens. Hans Scheib has also installed his longest telescopic lens and is trying to get the precise start. Behind him the newsreel people are in the covered entrance. On the green tower platform by the marathon gate is Alfred Siegert. In the pit at the finish, Frentz, there also Leni, Guzzi--they are all at their places. It's a matter of seizing a great moment on film.
>
> Only the sun is not at its post. It lets itself be overpowered by evil inky-blue clouds. What will happen to the slow motion shots of Kurt Neubert and Josef Dietze? Won't the long telescopic lens get only dark grey impressions?
>
> Owens dissipated all these questions ... one blink later and Owens is nearing the finish line.
>
> 10:03 seconds. Exactly as much time as one needs to gulp with amazement.
>
> No written sentence can reproduce such a brief moment. Only the immediate event can deeply penetrate us, and the film will bring this about![11]

The film company began to have more and more problems with the referees and the police. One can understand the problems that filming must have caused--Jäger elsewhere reported that the film people were sufficiently disruptive to get beer bottles thrown at them by the crowd--but it was difficult in some cases to see why filming had been forbidden.

During the enormous reactions of the crowd after a German victory, Otto Lantschner wanted to film the stands from the edge of the playing field; he was ejected. Kurt Neubert was told by a policeman to "Get that thing out of here right away," "that thing" being a slow-motion camera weighing one hundred and eighty pounds. Guzzi Lantschner had already been thrown off the field six times in three days. Lantschner told Jäger in despair, "I've scarcely been able to make one of the special shots or camera movements that I have previously planned!"[12]

In this situation, a new proposal was made regarding credentials; this proposal appears to have been the last straw. What it entailed was this: All the film people allowed in the stadium were to wear two different arm bands, one to show that they were accredited film people and the other to show that they were allowed within the stadium itself. The pronouncement caused a minor revolution among the cameramen. The reasoning behind the proposal could be understood, but there was a feeling among the cameramen, equally correct, that the cameramen with armbands would turn into some kind of VIPs. Already jealousy existed both within and without the company, and it was felt that these armbands might make the situation worse. In addition, it was not at all clear whether the cameramen who wore these armbands might be permanently assigned to the stadium and might be stopped from filming events outside the stadium. They would lose their freedom of movement, and as Jäger put it, the armband might become a chain. Riefenstahl was quite angry about the idea that her cameramen might lose their freedom of movement, and the idea was quashed. The cameramen were already nervous and exhausted from fighting the weather and the referees, and they were ground down by lack of sleep.

The sound chief, Siegfried (Sigi) Schultz, had an interesting and eventful time trying to record the sounds in the stadium. The sounds of the Games were fascinating, and Riefenstahl well understood their importance. One of the more interesting aspects of the Games was the claques of various nations yelling out comments to their various champions. After Gerhard Stoeck won the Javelin, Riefenstahl went up to him to congratulate him. The crowd yelled:

> Leni, gebt ihm einen Kuss
> Dass der Stoeck sich freuen muss.

Or after Karl Hein won the hammer throw:

> Bra-vo--Hein
> Das--war--fein.

Or to Käthe Krauss, after she had won her heat in the women's 100-meter sprint, with somewhat less creativity:

> Krauss, das hast du gut gemacht.

The French were recorded yelling to their runner, Perrou, "Perrou, allez, allez." The Scandinavians were also quite noisy, but Schultz had the worst time with the Finns. Since nobody knew what they were saying he could not tell whether he had made a good recording or not. As Jäger said, pompously, "The national (volkstümlich) drama of the games has its strongest reaction-effect precisely in the speaking chorus." It was certainly true that one of the secrets of the effectiveness of the Olympic film is sound. The roars of the crowd have an emotional bite that it would be hard for any image to equal. The final contribution of Schultz to the film would be enormous.

As this day progressed, it became clearer to all what methods and problems were involved in photographing the Games.

TUESDAY, AUGUST 4, 1936

The sports highlight of the day was the duel between Jesse Owens and Luz Long of Germany for the gold medal in the broad jump. Long first jumped a distance of 7.54 meters. Owens came back with a distance of 7.74 meters. Then it was Long's turn again. He beat Owens with a jump of 7.87 meters. Then it was Owens' last jump. Owens reached the amazing distance of 8.06 meters to win the gold medal. Long had established a new German record; he won the silver medal.

Track and Field

Broad Jump (Finals)--Won by Jesse Owens, United States; second, Luz Long, Germany
400-meter Hurdles (Finals)--Won by Glenn Hardin, United States
200-meter Sprint (Trials and Quarter Finals)--Owens won his heat
Women's Discus Throw--Won by Gisela Mauermeyer, Germany

5,000-meter Run (Trials)
Women's 100-meter Dash (Finals)--Won by Helen Stephens, United States

Wrestling

Catch as Catch Can

Modern Pentathlon

Pistol Shooting--Won by Leonard, United States

Yachting

Six-meter Class
Eight-meter Class
Star Class
Monotype Class

Field Hockey

Polo

Soccer

Generally, it was a good day for the film crew. Walter Traut was beaming: he had sixteen armbands for his people. Everyone was polite this day--a major achievement.

But the weather was again uncooperative. During the polo game between Hungary and Germany, the sun came out, but in the afternoon the sky was again covered with dark blue clouds, and in addition, the wind came up. The wind caused problems because it blew a fine, grainy dust into the cameras that could scratch the film surface. Not all the crew complained about the weather, however. Riefenstahl just laughed and said, "If we hold on, we will have made the greatest sports film of all time.... We will prove that you can take good shots even in the worst weather." Hans Scheib, who was shooting "heads in concentration" with his telephoto lens (in accordance with Riefenstahl's Manuscript) also felt that the weather problems had been overrated. He said later, "If it did not go against the whole enterprise, I would say that this light was just perfect for me! Because, just as any amateur photographer knows that he can make a portrait by subdued light, so it is with my shots...."[13]

Jäger saw Professor Hege and his female assistant in a film pit. They were no longer photographing architecture and had been added to the film crew as full-time sports photographers; Hege was happy enough to help out. Behind Jäger, the crowd broke out in the cheer, "Ra, ra, ra, Gisela!" Mauermayer had just won the women's discus for Germany. Riefenstahl came over, exclaiming astonishedly that when Owens had reenacted his winning broad jump for the camera, on later measurement it was found that the reenacted jump surpassed his own winning jump and unofficially measured 8:08 meters.[14]

In a maze of tunnels underneath the stadium, the shuttling of film between the Olympic stadium and the Geyer Laboratories was being carried out. Though not as dramatic as the filming, the service was important. Two Olympic trucks were in constant operation bringing negative material to the stadium, and two special Opel trucks had been converted into "darkroom vans." The people under Kiekebusch responsible for this shuttle of negative stock and developed film were Häussler, Boenisch the production manager, Herr Coelius, and Herr Ruhl. The arrangements seemed to be going well.

The technical preparations that Ertl had masterminded for the swimming event achieved a large amount of publicity. Many of the illustrated magazines had contained pictures of the rubber boat that was to be used, and had included accounts of Ertl's underwater camera. Now he was amassing footage of the training events, and his results were excellent. This was a good omen, although the swimming events were not to start until the eighth.

Hans Scheib got some excellent material on this date. In the pistol-shooting event of the pentathlon, the camera was forbidden in the vicinity of the firing line. Scheib saved the day by setting up his camera some eighty meters distant and making medium close-ups of the contestants shooting.[15] In the final film, the shots of Leonard of the United States, Kettunen of Finland, and Catramby of Brazil seem to be from these series of telephoto shots made by Scheib.

WEDNESDAY, AUGUST 5, 1936

Once again the weather was cold and rainy. The dramatic event of the day was the exciting duel in the pole vault between the Japanese and the Americans. It went on all day with no clear winner, so the event had to be continued in the darkness. Finally, the Americans won all three medals in the following order: Earl Meadows the gold, William Graber the silver, and William Sefton the bronze. The original event could not be filmed since the referees ruled that the rigging of powerful lights would have distracted the athletes. But it was too dramatic an event not to be in the film, and Riefenstahl decided later to reenact the event with the Japanese and American athletes.

Track and Field

200-meter Sprints (Heats and Final)--Won by Jesse Owens, United States
1500-meter Run (Trials)
110-meter Hurdles (Trials)
Pole Vault (Final)--Won by Earl Meadows, William Sefton, and William Graber, United States
50,000-meter Walk (Final)--Won by Harold Whitlock, Great Britain
Men's Discus (Final)--Won by Kenneth Carpenter, United States
Women's 80-meter Hurdle (Trials and Semifinals)

Modern Pentathlon

300-meter swim

Weight Lifting

Middleweight Class
Heavyweight Class

Fencing

Women's Foils

Soccer

Field Hockey

Polo

It was another busy day for Riefenstahl. She spent the first part of it establishing what each cameraman would be doing. Then she personally checked to make sure that there had been no misunderstandings. Riefenstahl had managed to spend an hour or so at Geyer looking at the first footage, and this preview evidently had caused a sharp rise in her esteem for some of her cameramen. She was especially impressed by what she had seen of Epken's work. She also was pleased with Siegert, who showed himself to be not only an expert at smooth panning shots but quite precise in his focusing. Holski, Gottschalk, and Dietze were singled out as well. The footage of Heinz von Jaworsky also gratified her. Even in the flat, grey dimness of those first sunless days, he had managed to get wonderful nuances of light into his film.[16]

The film company was having mixed luck with the authorities. Some of the officials had been very helpful--one policeman had stopped a company member who was groaning under the weight of a tripod sack and carried part of the load for the grateful assistant. However, Ursula von und zu Loewenstein, Hege's excellent assistant, was forbidden to work within the stadium or the surroundings because of her sex. This decision was, according to Jäger, made at the highest level.[17] In addition, one of Riefenstahl's people was ejected from the rostrum of honor, which was in the vicinity of Hitler's box. In later years, Riefenstahl was to complain about Dr. Goebbel's interference with her personnel, but it is unknown who instigated these acts, or indeed whether they might not have come from the IOC or security people. There was also a general tightening of security all through the stadium which affected the press as much as the film company.

In the Berliner Zeitung, there was a caricature of Owens in the broad jump, showing that if Owens had jumped a meter further, he would have landed in Riefenstahl's pit. On this day Riefenstahl opened her pit only a slit so no one could fall in. She was trying to think of a way to make the 200-meter dash the sensation that the discus throwing had been the day before. She had received word from Geyer that the slow-motion material Neubert had taken that morning had been superb, but, according to Jäger, she felt only extremely tired.

De Laforgue was extremely happy with the footage he

was shooting of Hitler and of the dignitaries in Hitler's box. In the morning, Hitler had watched Lieutenant Lemp of Germany win the 300-meter swimming event of the pentathlon in the swimming stadium. De Laforgue was evidently a tough customer and had a thick skin. At one point while shooting, a fat spectator called to him. "Mensch, go into town if you want to shoot film." De Laforgue answered calmly, "I'll push my lens into your brains."[18] Of course, a bit more diplomacy was called for in Hitler's box; photographing Hitler and his guests took a certain amount of nerve. One young avant-garde cameraman who had been given the same assignment stood trembling, then was banished in the corner until he was relieved.

> De Laforgue does not give an inch. He shoots little footage, but it hits the mark.
>
> Hitler is surprised by a sudden rainstorm, someone passes him his raincoat, he puts it around himself without taking his eyes off the playing field. Dr. Goebbels, Minister President Goering do the same next to him--a picture that a moment ago was in sun suddenly becomes a rain study.
>
> Only the concentration in the faces of the guests in the rostrum of honor remains the same.
>
> We pray to the god of sun and the demon of rain that these shots of de Laforgue have come off.[19]

The spring of de Laforgue's hand camera broke. "I am lost, kaputt, destroyed!" he screamed. Someone from the radio took this unfortunate moment to interview him, and stuck a microphone into his hand. He was asked, "Please tell our listeners whether you're pleased to be working on this film of Leni Riefenstahl," whereupon he answered "No!!"[20]

De Laforgue's broken camera, as well as all other broken ones, went to the cellar of the Haus Ruhwald, where the Askania Company had established a repair shop. On this particular day, there were two broken film loaders there and Hans Scheib's tripod head as well. A Debrie camera needed some work, so the repair shop was not limited to Askanias (although the shop was under the leadership of Section Leader Linke of the Askania Company).

Even at Haus Ruhwald, the cheers from the stadium could be heard as the pole vault continued into the night to its spectacular finish, which provided quite a climax to the fifth day of the Games.

THURSDAY, AUGUST 6, 1936

This was to be an extremely eventful day for Riefenstahl --personally as well as on the playing field. The athletic highlight of the day proved to be the beautifully run 1500-meter race that was won by Jack Lovelock of New Zealand.

Track and Field

Men's 100-meter Hurdles (Semifinals and Finals)--Won by Forrest Towns, United States
1500-meter run--Won by Jack Lovelock, New Zealand
Hop, Step and Jump--Won by Naoto Tajima, Japan
Men's Javelin (Finals)--Won by Gerhard Stoeck, Germany
400-meter Run (Trials)
Women's 80-meter Hurdles--Won by Trebisonda Valla, Italy

Modern Pentathlon

400-meter Cross-country Run
Final standing: Gotthardt Handrick, Germany, Silvano Abba, Italy; Charles Leonard, United States

Pistol Shooting

Rapid Fire

Fencing

Individual Foils

Polo

Field Hockey

Soccer

Field Handball

This appears to have been the day when Dr. Goebbels

very nearly removed Riefenstahl as director of the Olympic film because of an incident with a referee that happened some time during the first week. According to Ernst Jäger, during one of the jumping events, just as he was about to film a record-breaking jump, Guzzi Lantschner had once again been ordered from the field. Riefenstahl had pleaded with the referee to allow Lantschner to remain. The referee remained adamant. Riefenstahl screamed, "If you dare to order my cameraman off the field, I will drag you by your ears to the Führer's box, you swine!"[21] The referee, being a high-ranking officer, filed, through official channels, an official complaint of slander, which eventually went to von Tschammer und Osten. The Reich Sport Leader felt that Riefenstahl was incapable of finishing the Olympic film. He hinted to Goebbels that this time he would help to get rid of her.

> Goebbels saw that this incident had played into his hands, but he restrained his eagerness, hoping that once the film was in the can he could get it out of Leni's hands before she started cutting. He already had a successor picked out for the job.[22]

Riefenstahl herself reported the event as follows:

> On the fifth day of the Games in the stadium it came to an open scandal between Dr. Goebbels and L.R. The origin was that L.R. had had a quarrel with a German referee because, in spite of previous agreement by the Olympic contestants, he wanted to remove her camera personnel by force from the interior of the stadium. This was a violation of the agreement and seriously detrimental to the work, since the athletic events were not repeatable and so irretrievably lost for the film. As L.R. vehemently fought for the positions of her camera personnel, the referee complained to Dr. Goebbels. Upon this matter later, Riefenstahl was immediately recalled from her work. Goebbels made such a violent scene with her in the stadium that it caused a sensation. Goebbels tried to provoke a scandal to prove that a woman was unsuitable for such work (a witness to this scene was among others Herr Ritter von Halt).
>
> L.R. was forced to ask the referee's pardon. In any case, the important shots of the hammer throwing on this day were totally lost.[23]

In his diary on this date, Dr. Goebbels did allude to Riefenstahl's actions during the incident. She was quite accurate about Dr. Goebbels' feeling about women:

> August 6, 1936 (Thursday)
> Afternoon stadium. Running and jumping. We are not winning much. I give Riefenstahl a dressing down, she has behaved herself indescribably. Certainly no man![24]

Goebbel's comments obviously are quite sexist, but they do not reflect the maliciousness toward Riefenstahl that is described by Jäger, and there is certainly no evidence of his hand in the other actions that evidently were taking place against her. As previously stated, this does not mean that Dr. Goebbels was not behind these actions. It is always a mistake to believe that diaries are necessarily frank, especially when the writer has pretensions to being an author and the possibility exists that the diaries will be published later.

Ritter von Halt did in fact testify to the incident. In an undated letter to the Filmbewertungsstelle he said that Riefenstahl was independent of the Propaganda Ministry and also said, "I was a witness when Minister Dr. Goebbels wanted to make the attempt to forbid Frau Riefenstahl admission to the stadium"[25]

It should be noted that Jäger's comments on the incident differ from the statements of Mainz, Von Halt, and Riefenstahl, assuming that the two incidents have the same genesis. It does not really sound as if Dr. Goebbels was biding his time at all in the 1958 statements (see Appendix D). However, it does sound as if Riefenstahl's actions were being used as an excuse to get rid of her. It should also be remembered that Jäger tells this story at a time when he is obviously very hostile to Riefenstahl, but his story certainly substantiates the feud existing between her and Dr. Goebbels. In any case, the actions of the Olympic Company on the next day, Friday, suggest that the crew may have thought that Riefenstahl was in danger of being removed or that the whole film unit might be shut down.

FRIDAY, AUGUST 7, 1936

This was the first day Hitler was not in the stands.

The decathlon started on this date, and the first five events took place. At the end, it looked like a clean sweep for the Americans. Robert Clark was first, Glenn Morris was second, and Jack Parker was fourth. Erwin Huber, the German entry, was tenth.

Track and Field

400-meter (Semifinals and Finals)--Won by Archie Williams, United States
5,000-meter (Finals)--Won by Gunnar Hoeckart, Finland
Decathlon--100 meter Sprint (Heats), Broadjump, Shot Put, 400-meter Run, High Jump--Robert Clark, Glenn Morris and Jack Parker, United States

Pistol Shooting

Precision

Basketball

Polo--Argentina wins over Great Britain

Field Hockey

Cycling

1,000-meter Scratch Race

Apparently to counter both the events of the previous day and the increasing dissatisfaction of the authorities, Riefenstahl made several statements to the press. She sounded quite defensive. For Film-Kurier she was "interviewed" by Jäger, who quite obviously set her up by asking whether she was happy with the first week's filming:

> I am only disappointed because of the weather!
> It is scarcely imaginable what an increase in quality the shots would have had by lasting good weather.
> In spite of a lot of unavoidable quarrels, in spite of frightful exhaustion (today I will go to bed at twelve o'clock)--in spite of the weather and a thousand setbacks, I sense that I will see the film through in the next nine days in accordance with my previous program and plans.

> It is already certain that we have material that up to now, and probably never in future, has never been, and never will, be equalled for its uniqueness and extensiveness.
>
> I cannot theoreticise. I cannot explain to you why this nascent film carries a special style, even my style, as I quite distinctly sense.
>
> It is simply so--and therefore I am also pleased.
>
> I believe we are on the right path: if I may say--we will stick to our task and we will accomplish it!
>
> Certainly you know, I do not like doing things by halves, I don't do things by halves, I hate halves....[26]

Riefenstahl's comments to Licht Bild Bühne not only sound defensive, but apologetic. She also sounds as if she had to defend the Olympic film project as a useful enterprise:

> Film rules over the playing field--but it is the servant of sport. It can only serve without friction because the crew of the Olympic film is co-ordinated to the last man--because it knows that the nerves of the athletes can only endure the tension when every distraction--that certainly the film can so easily bring--will be avoided.
>
> So the film is always seen at the arena, but it always withdraws as the servant of the athletic event. Certainly one senses its mastery, where it belongs to create a picture of these festive Olympic days as a material moment....
>
> Part of the tragedy of the Olympic athlete is that he can be seen at his top physical and record shape almost always only once--and if something can take the sting out of this tragedy, then it is alone the film, whose elite-team one now sees using its full amount of experience, strength and readiness, that can do it.[27]

Leaving personalities and politics aside, the filming itself seemed to be going well. Jäger recounted an amusing incident. It may be remembered that the catapult which was to be used to photograph the runners in the sprints was disallowed by the sports authorities. Riefenstahl found a way to use it, however, in the 5,000-meter run. She had it brought in during the midday pause before the decathlon event.

> The starter Miller, from whom Sigi Schultz has gotten such excellent sound recordings, with his classical commands and his classical voice, discussed Leni's idea enthusiastically with a referee. This man with so much expert knowledge of the soul of the athlete, which he has attained in hundreds of nerve-jangling starts, gave the best testimonial for Leni's film crew.[28]

However, the catapult motor and driving mechanism were disallowed. This meant that the camera had to be pushed along its rail by someone chosen from the company. Riefenstahl chose the young Albert Höcht to run ahead of the leaders of the 5,000-meter run, filming the pack from this position.

> --and so Höcht, the Himalaya mountain climber, the young man from the Bavarian mountains, the BMW specialist, Hans Ertl's friend and assistant, started on the inner field on the north side. Dahlmeyer squatted alongside, in order to check the sharpness of the focus. The catapult pulley and motor were disassembled. On the track was attached only a hand camera--and as the 5,000-meter came around the track the fourth time, Höcht flew along the course, four meters before the runners at their murderous, dramatic pace--and filmed them from ahead.[29]

He repeated this feat five times, leaving the other film crew members gasping, and continued through the ninth, tenth, and eleventh laps, without even jiggling the camera as it slid along the rail. Höcht was dubbed the hero of the day, having stayed ahead of the winners Hoeckert, Lehtinen, and Salminen. Someone crowned him with one of the four laurel wreaths that were kept at the Haus Ruhwald for use in retakes of the victory ceremonies.

It was hoped that Höcht's pictures would be a success so that the authorities might reconsider and allow the use of the catapult--motor and all--for some of the remaining events.

In that evening's meeting summing up the first week of the Games, Johannes Häussler reported that 231,000 meters of film had already been shot. He was keeping a reserve of 250,000 meters for the second part of the Games, as well as making sure that he had an adequate stock of all film. It was also reported, as an example of the flexibility of the camera crew, that each Opel driver already had amassed over 3,000 kilometers. Erich Fabowski, the press driver, took the lead with 5,200 kilometers. The darkroom van drivers, Clemens and Richter, had compiled an equally high amount of distance. Erupting from this flaunting of impressive statistics was a real problem. The need for dependable and quick transportation would increase during the second week of the Games as more events began away from Berlin--in Kiel, Grünau or the Wannsee. As the track-and-field events came to an end, the central and easily accessible stadium would no longer be the hub of the Games. This was already signalled by a shift in personnel away from the Reich Sport Field. On this Friday, Albert Kling, Wolfgang Hart, and Wilhelm Siem were sent to Kiel.

SATURDAY, AUGUST 8, 1936

The highlight for this day was provided by the final events of the decathlon, the climax of all track and field events in the Olympics. The United States made a clean sweep, with Glenn Morris first, Robert Clark second, and Jack Parker third. Erwin Huber of Germany, a man who would be important in the Olympic film, came in fourth. The day marked the start of the events in Grünau. Hitler showed up at the soccer stadium to root for the German team, but contrary to the growing German belief that Hitler's presence inspired the German athletes to new heights of performance, Norway beat Germany, the favorite.

Track and Field

3,000-meter Steeplechase (Final)--Won by Iso-Hollo, Finland
Men's 400-meter Relay (Trials)
Women's 400-meter Relay (Trials)
1,600-meter Relay (Trials)
Decathlon--Final 5 events: Discus, Pole Vault, 110-meter Hurdles, Javelin Throw, 1,500-meter run

Swimming

Men's 100-meter Free Style (Trials)

Women's 100-meter Free Style (Trials)
Women's 100-meter Breast Stroke (Trials)
Water Polo

Polo

Soccer

Fencing

Team Epée (Semifinals)
Team Epée (Finals)

Canoeing

Field Hockey

Shooting

Field Handball

Basketball

Cycling

Heinz von Jaworsky, Tietgens, and the others filmed the first day of canoeing at Grünau. Kebelmann photographed the bicycling events. Crews covered polo and fencing. Olympic film people also covered the festivities scheduled for Saturday evening at the Opera House. The regime had commissioned a *KdF-Stadt*--a strength-through-joy town--to be constructed out of wood in the *völkisch* architectural style that was often favored by the National Socialists for Hitler Youth camps or peasant-meeting halls. German and foreign tourists attending the Olympic Games visited the town, and a film crew was dispatched to record the goings-on.

Kurt Neubert had special reason to be pleased, so far, with the photography of the track-and-field events. He had filmed a lot of fine material at the discus and javelin events, and in all the jumping events, too, including the pole vault.

> "These shots," he said, "are at times tinged with a curious comedy, because they show the response of the athletes in their sole concentration with perform-

> ance. A Finn, for example, watches the hammer flying away, spellbound, and accompanies the flight with clumsy movements, that he perhaps is not even aware of. It's exactly the same with the expression of highest concentration in the faces and in the movements shot when they are in the leading group and just before the goal."[30]

Neubert had just received word from Geyer that his discus shots and his broad jump shots were outstanding, up to then the most beautiful work produced by the crew.

Evidently Dr. Goebbels was not alone in being annoyed by Riefenstahl. Bella Fromm, who was not one of Riefenstahl's ardent admirers, reported the director's behavior as follows:

> Leni Riefenstahl, official photographer, wearing gray flannel slacks and a kind of jockey cap, is obtrusively in evidence everywhere, pretending an untiring and exhaustive efficiency and importance. Meanwhile, her assistants quietly, expertly do the work, which Leni signs.
>
> On and off she sits down beside her fuehrer, a magazine-cover grin on her face and a halo of importance fixed firmly above her head. She has priority rights, and cannot bear to have anyone else take a shot that she has overlooked. Page boys dash constantly from photographer to photographer, handing them the dreaded slip: "Leni Riefenstahl warns you to stay at your present position while taking pictures. Do not move around. In case of disobedience, press permission will be confiscated."[31]

Riefenstahl warned off photographers often enough to annoy the regular press--never a wise thing to do. Frederick T. Birchall of the <u>New York Times</u> complained that

> ... her word is law in the matter of all picturetaking anywhere at the games. Any camera man who puts himself anywhere that Miss Riefenstahl thinks he should not be is swiftly approached by an attendant who hands him a pink slip. It says in effect:
>
> "Remove yourself from where you are now--Riefenstahl."

> Receipt of two such slips in one day means permanent removal of the offender, forcibly if necessary.[32]

Ertl reported that Riefenstahl also antagonized the general public and the officials:

> Egocentric, as was her nature, she again and again offended the public as well as, if I am honest, some of her co-workers as well, because she ran--even during the tensest events--from one camera to another, and with large gestures, acted as if she was giving real director's orders. Like a shadow, her personal photographer Rolf Lantin followed, shooting publicity pictures. She only came up to me one time, as my unequivocal "Don't bother me!" even attracted the applause of a referee standing nearby. Other colleagues also had the courage to simply shake her off.[33]

Ertl also pointed out that she would have been just as effective as a director if she had sat in the stands with a notebook. On her behalf, he pointed out that she was trained as an actor and dancer; playing to the crowd was part of her nature. While this may have been so, there is no doubt that her behavior contributed to her problems with Dr. Goebbels and other Party officials.

SUNDAY, AUGUST 9, 1936

There were two major events this day, and both were upsets. In the women's 400-meter relay, the German team was the favorite by far, and in preliminary heats the team had turned in marvelous times. However, in Sunday's final, the team dropped the baton and was disqualified. The United States team seized the victory. The German women were in tears, and Hitler invited them to his box to console them as best he could, telling them that their speed would have made them the fastest women in the world.

In the always dramatic marathon, Juan Carlos Zabala of Argentina was a favorite. He had won the marathon in Los Angeles, and he was in the lead for quite a while on the murderous, 42-kilometer route that extended along the Avus road.

But he could not keep up the very fast pace he had set for himself and collapsed at about the halfway point. The winner was a farmer from Korea named Kitei Son who clinched the gold medal for Japan. Second was Ernest Harper of Great Britain, and third was Shoryu Nan of Japan. Sunday ended the track-and-field events of the 1936 Olympics.

<u>Track and Field</u>

Marathon (Final)--Won by Kitei Son, Japan; second, Ernest Harper, Great Britain; third, Shoryu Nan, Japan
Men's 400-meter Relay (Final)--Won by the United States (Jesse Owens, Ralph Metcalfe, Fay Draper and Frank Wykoff)
1,000-meter Relay (Final)--Won by Great Britain (Frederick Wolff, Godfrey Rampling, William Roberts and G. K. Brown)
Women's 400-meter Relay (Final)--Won by the United States (Harriet Bland, Annette Rogers, Betty Robinson and Helen Stephens)
Women's High Jump (Final)--First, Ibolya Csak, Hungary

<u>Wrestling</u>

Greco-Roman

<u>Swimming</u>

Men's 100-meter Free Style (Final)--Won by Ferenc Csik, Hungary; second, Masanori Yusa, Japan; third, Shigeo Arai, Japan
Women's 100-meter Free Style (Semifinals)
Women's 200-meter Breast Stroke (Semifinals)
Water Polo

<u>Basketball</u>

<u>Field Hockey</u>

<u>Yachting</u>

On this Sunday, there was nothing scheduled for the stadium until quarter past three in the afternoon when the marathon was to begin, so Riefenstahl was able to use the stadium for major retakes and close-ups of the track and field athletes for a large part of the day as well as in the evening. As Jäger put it, she just about staged her own Olympics.

She invaded the Olympic Village at seven in the morning. "Invaded" is the right word in several senses. First, women were officially not allowed in the Olympic Village (the women were quartered elsewhere), and Riefenstahl's visit was a breach of protocol. Second, Riefenstahl went about knocking on doors, waking up athletes from an extremely well-deserved rest. From the men's high jumpers she gathered up the Americans' Albritton (silver) and Thurber (bronze). From the hop, step, and jump, she got Tajima of Japan (gold). And, from the javelin, she got Nikkanen (silver) and Toiwonen (bronze)--both of Finland. She also had the American decathlon winners, Morris, Clark, and Parker.

> A great hour for all participants. The Japanese, the Finns, the Americans--they sensed, and had the feeling for what the cameramen had in mind. A dozen cameras stood in position. Slow motion equipment set at all speeds. Hand cameras in all positions, but all planned out in advance, not improvised. Ertl, Lantschner--they had their great hour. De Laforgue got close-ups--Morris, Parker and Clark threw untiringly. While the others had long since stifled their enthusiasm with lunch, they continued until two o'clock.[34]

Erwin Huber, the German decathlon champion, joined them for retakes and lunch. At lunch on the pleasant terrace of the Haus Ruhwald, Morris drank two glasses of Rhine wine. It was the first alcohol he had consumed in two years.

That afternoon, the marathon race started. The first part of the marathon course was laid out through the Grunewald, along the river Havel. But the course got tougher as it went along a shadowless 16-kilometer stretch of concrete road called the Avus. During the days of the Weimar Republic, this road had been especially constructed for automobile racing. At midpoint, the route simply doubled back, so that after reaching a point called the Avus north loop, the runners turned around and retraced their steps to the stadium. Along the route were observation posts that were numbered or otherwise designated. The people manning those posts reported back to the stadium about the race's progress.

One of the observation posts was control number five. It was located at the entrance to the stretch along the Avus. One could get medical aid there, as well as support from various nations. A table was loaded with various kinds of refreshment--sponges were ready in cold water, all kinds of drinks were available, and lemon and apple slices were on hand. There was also a crowd. Sportsmen, SA men and police were present to keep order, but their duties were probably not too pressing and being at the post allowed them to get a good view.

> Among them appeared two men in silver-grey Olympic film uniform. The camera was set up, distances were measured out, more and more critical glances were directed at the sky, which sometimes was cloudy and sometimes radiant with sun ...
>
> Suddenly a commotion. Loud yells. The cameraman stands ready; his colleague lies in ambush with the camera in order to take a picture of the cameraman at work. Hundreds and dozens of amateur cameras are ready. Then comes Zabala, accompanied by lively applause. Almost three hundred meters behind come the Japanese Son and the Englishman Harper.[35]

There was a pause. Other runners went by. The Olympic cameramen took shots of the group of aides at control number five.

> New call: the first are coming back. Great astonishment: the Japanese leads the Englishman. One hundred and fifty meters behind them Zabala, his head wobbling to and fro, with a despairing expression on his face. And then the others. Dramatic scenes. Two run on the narrow strip of grass. Their wounded feet can no longer endure the hard, red hot Avus. One runner sinks tottering to a chair, is massaged and refreshed with a sponge. The cameramen rush in and shoot.... A camera car from the film company drives on the second Avus course. Film will be shot from it. It is ending.... We start to leave. A small section of the great film of the Olympics has been played out before our eyes at control number five.[36]

Walter Frentz was also quite important in the filming of the marathon. He was stationed in the camera car during the races. As he had done in his shots of Hitler taken in Hitler's car in Triumph des Willens, Frentz demonstrated his knack for keeping a camera quite steady in a moving vehicle.[37] Quite a bit of Frentz's footage shot from this car was used in the final film, and the quality was excellent.

At half-past eight in the evening, Riefenstahl was back at the stadium. It will be remembered that the pole vaulting that took place on August 5 had ended in darkness and could not be photographed. The decision had been made to reenact the event for the cameras.

Glenn Morris had acted as production manager and had brought Meadows, Graber, and Sefton to the stadium. Shuhe Nishida and Sueo Oe were jumping for Japan. Kubisch had ascertained that the normal searchlights were not sufficient to light the stadium. To illuminate the athletes fully, four light trucks from Delschaft were used as well as eight searchlights of five thousand watts each. A few hundred people, who for one reason or another had not yet vacated the stands, began to notice that something interesting was going on; they decided to stay. So did various referees. This group, as well as a crowd of film people, provided an audience, even applauding after each jump. In response, the Americans and the Japanese, seized once more by the competitive spirit, began the pole vault all over again.

> In the film pit, by the run-in, in front of and behind and under the cross bar the cameramen. Neubert, Ertl, von Jaworsky, Hasso, Scheib, Lantschner and more. They are in a fever. Leni laughs. She cheers the jumpers on. Meadows jumps over four meters--with a hurt foot![38]

Finally, late in the evening, the filming ended. The film crew dispersed, heading back to Berlin and the Haus Ruhwald. For some of them, this would be the end of their shooting in Berlin. The next day the major focus of action would shift to Kiel, so Frentz and several other cameramen left for Kiel right away. However, all cameramen had experienced a remarkable recapitulation of the track-and-field events that came to a close on this Sunday.

According to Jäger, Sunday night's filming was to be Riefenstahl's last wholehearted effort in shooting the Olympics.[39]

MONDAY, AUGUST 10, 1936

Yachting was one of the major events this Monday. Adolf Hitler, von Tschammer und Osten, and other Party notables watched the races from the tender Nixe. Also present in Kiel were members of the IOC and Dr. Wilhelm Frick, Reich Minister of the Interior.

The other major event was the beginning of the swimming. Ria Mastenbroeck, the great Dutch swimmer, began her series of Olympic victories by winning the 100-meter free style. The Japanese dominated the Americans in the swimming events, but the Americans Dick Degener, Marshall Wayne, and Al Greene placed first, second, and fourth in springboard diving.

Although the Olympics had almost a week to run, the Olympic exodus had already started. The American track-and-field team would sail on Tuesday to London for the British Empire Games. The Olympic Village was starting to empty, and in Berlin one could already sense an anticlimatic feeling.

Swimming

Men's 400-meter Free Style (Trials)
800-meter Relay (Trials)
Men's Springboard Diving (Compulsory Program)--Won by Degener, United States; second, Wayne, United States; third, Shibahara, Japan; fourth, Greene, United States; fifth, Weiss, Germany
Women's 100-meter Free Style (Final)--Won by Mastenbroeck, Holland
Water Polo (Eliminations)

Cycling

100-kilometer Road Race--Won by Charpentier, France; second, Lapedie, France, third, Nievergelt, Switzerland; team ranking: France, Switzerland, Belgium, Italy, Austria

Yachting

Monotype--Won by Chile
Star Class--Won by Germany
Six-meter Class--Won by Norway
Eight-meter Class--Won by Sweden

Basketball

Field Hockey

Soccer--Italy qualified for the finals, defeating Norway

Monday, for the first time, Riefenstahl was more of an onlooker than an active participant in the filming. Late on Sunday night, while the filming was still going on at the stadium, she, Jäger, and several others left for Kiel. They had not made reservations, however, and arrived on a day when all Berlin was going there as well. When they got to Perleberg, they were advised that there was not a bed to be had in Lübeck, the largest town near Kiel. Finally, Frentz found them lodgings at Lake Schwerin, and they arrived at the hotel at quarter to three, having to be up again by five. Hitler would be in Kiel at nine on the dot, and the fixed balloon the film crew would be using would be at the airport ready to go to work. They were awakened at five and drove sleepily through the festively decorated towns on their way to the harbor at Kiel. They arrived in plenty of time for the events. Hitler appeared on board his private yacht before transferring to the Nixe.

The production manager in Kiel was once again the engineer Bob Fischer. He and Frentz had done an excellent job of organizing the photographing of the yachting event. At their headquarters at 38 Beselerstrasse, with the team of Ernst Laufer, Rogge, and von Holbeck, they had accomplished one of the most difficult jobs of the Olympic filming by arranging for a large fixed balloon to photograph the yachting. The balloon was towed by a minesweeper belonging to the German navy. Fischer and Frentz also had the help of Herr Rosznerski, a renowned balloonist of World War I, Lieutenant Knuth of the German Navy, Dr. Elias, thirty-five members of the German Airship Association, and the crew of sixty of the minesweeper M122, who made these balloon shots possible. The film crew had certainly received the wholesale cooperation of the German navy.[40]

It was also the first time since World War I that the German navy had let a fixed balloon aloft. In order to keep the balloon properly aft of the ship, it was estimated that a four-and-a-half-ton wind must be attained on the stern of the minesweeper by keeping up sufficient seaway.

At first, it had been worked out through paper models how the balloon, after it had been piloted to the minesweeper from the airport, could be tied to the ship without being driven by a strong wind into the stacks or rigging. This was not an easy task in a harbor known for uncertain weather. The plan was not sufficient. It should be remembered that German balloons still used hydrogen instead of helium, as the Hindenburg disaster was to make painfully clear. Lieutenant Bärner had to construct a special sieve stack for the minesweeper so that the hot gasses emanating from the stack would not cause the balloon to explode.

> For a week the balloon ascension was calculated and fussed over. No fixed balloon had risen since the war. The naval leadership that always typically and without prejudice has supported every important national work of others, began, from Rear Admiral Götting to the Olympic leaders in Kiel and to his right hand Lieutenant Rauff, always to say "yes" when it was a question of creating new opportunities for the Leni Riefenstahl film.[41]

The overlapping courses of the competing yachts were extremely complex. Nevertheless, the navy had devised a system so that the minesweeper could be steered to get the most favorable light for the cameraman photographing the races.

Kling, Hart, and Frentz were sent up in the balloon on three different occasions. Working in the balloon was not without its problems. The weather was quite bad when Wolfgang Hart was sent aloft, but Riefenstahl had decided that the photographer's stubborness coupled with his healthy, even temperament would see him through, and Hart managed some wonderful shots in the face of various cold fronts and high winds. The balloon swayed precariously, though, and looked like it was going to throw Hart out. When he landed, he was so pale that it appeared that he had already been sick. Kling had it better. His telephone connections to the ship were good, and those on board carried out his instructions immediately. Frentz had filmed the marathon the day before, when he had been extremely busy. But he was extremely busy on this assignment, too, since he was virtually in charge of the entire operation at Kiel. At the end of this day's filming, immediately after the victory ceremonies, he went to bed totally exhausted.

The group in Kiel had also set up an express service for film delivery through a drugstore on the Hindenburg Embankment in town. By so doing, there would be no delay in getting film from and back to Geyer. At the end of the day, Siem and Schmüggel were still shooting film. Hart came in, wet to the skin because he had been sitting on a buoy in an attempt to get shots of the competition.

The team in Kiel had done extremely well, or so it seems. In fact, in the Olympic film, yachting was one competition for which the fancy technical shots really did pay off. Many of the establishing shots of the yacht races are aerial views, and these probably represent the work of the photographers in the balloons, which was accomplished with the support of the German navy. It should be pointed out however, that the existence of this wholehearted support contradicts Riefenstahl's later claim that the regime had nothing to do with the film.

TUESDAY, AUGUST 11, 1936

In the swimming, Japan won the 800-meter relay in the magnificent time of 8:51:5, breaking the world and Olympic records. Dick Degener, Marshall Wayne, and Al Greene gave the United States a clean sweep in the springboard diving championships. Hideko Machata of Japan won the women's 200-meter breast stroke.

<u>Swimming</u>

800-meter Relay (Final)--Won by Japan (Yusa, Sugiura, Taguchi, Arai)

Men's Springboard Diving--Won by Dick Degener, United States; second, Marshall Wayne, United States; third, Al Greene, United States; fourth, Tsuneo Shibahara, Japan; fifth, Erhard Weiss, Germany

400-meter Free Style (Semifinals)

Women's 200-meter Breast Stroke--Won by Hideko Machata, Japan
Women's 100-meter Back Stroke (Trials)

Fencing

Individual Epée

Rowing

Single Sculls (Trials)
Pairs without Coxswain (Trials)
Pairs with Coxswain (Trials)

Basketball

Third Round

Water Polo

Eliminations

Soccer

Semifinal Round--Austria 2, Poland 1

On Tuesday, Riefenstahl and Jäger returned to Berlin and the Reich Sport Field by car. That evening at about midnight Riefenstahl gathered some of the athletes to see the footage shot of them on Sunday, August 9. This footage was still quite rough and uncut. Glenn Morris, Erwin Huber, Naoto Tajima, and Shuhe Nishida--as well as the car drivers and the film cutters--were all invited to watch the outtakes, which were quite uneven; there were some shots that were good as well as some that were terrible. Toward one in the morning, the athletes said that they would like a screening of Riefenstahl's Das Blaue Licht, so they saw that next. After the viewing, there was a surprise for Anatol Dobriansky, the runner from Greece; the crew had set it up. Dobriansky had accompanied the crew to Kiel and back and was quite tired, but he was also present in the projection room to see the outtakes. Riefenstahl smuggled a hundred meters of his torchbearing into the projection room and had it shown. The footage was excellent and some expectation existed that there would be a reaction from Anatol. When the lights were turned on, however, Anatol was discovered asleep, wrapped in a blue curtain. When he discovered that he had missed his moment on the screen, he complained loudly in a mixture of Greek and French.

There was an outbreak of discontent among the camera crew and the staff of the Olympia Company. This was perhaps unavoidable; they had had little sleep. Their bones ached from lying on the wet grass of playing fields where they waited for a shot. Their quarters at Ruhwald, consisting mainly of cots, were far from luxurious. There were bruised egos, and as the Olympics moved into their second week, a definite general letdown seems to have been felt. The first euphoria of shooting the Olympic Games had passed and the task was becoming merely routine. If Riefenstahl was spending less time on the film, no one would have perceived it as quickly as the cameramen. One cameraman complained because he had not obtained a turn at the only bathtub in the Haus Ruhwald. Another made trouble so that he could get expelled from Haus Ruhwald and sleep at home. Siegert found de Laforgue in his bed and there was almost a brawl between them. Two hundred workers were bound to create dirt, and this bothered some crew members. In the darkroom, one cameraman counted the grains of dust that could cause scratches and abrasions on the film surface. A representative of the 16mm film association complained that the crew was "schmalfilmfeindlich" (hostile to 16mm film). People were calling Jäger and complaining about his writing. Tempers were flaring. In some argument, evidently concerning Professor Hege, one person offered to give another an enema of ground glass and sulphuric acid. At home, the cameramen yelled at their families because

> ... they have come down so badly with Olympianitis that they retreat into their private lives to explode, because it is impossible to do so at work; because Schwarzmann and Michel, the lethal critics, will laughingly give a "five" in their official book to the cameramen who jar their cameras or make a framing error, and that is as bad as a "C" to "D" in the first grade of primary school.[42]

However, Hans Scheib got some excellent film on this day. The major contenders in the springboard diving were

Dick Degener, Marshall Wayne, and Al Greene of the United States; the German, Weiss, and the Japanese, Shibahara (called "Ship ahoy" by the Americans), were also in contention.

With his telephoto lens, Scheib got excellent close-ups of the divers' heads in the moment of concentration before they dove. Later, Scheib stated that he had an advantage in the swimming events as the tempo was not so quick as in the running events, and so the camera could easily follow divers. The disadvantage was that the telephoto lens had a very narrow distance for which the picture could be in focus--less than one foot--and while Scheib could focus on the runners, who at least had a fixed starting line, the same was not true of the divers, who could start their dive on any part of the board they wished. This freedom made it hard to get them in sharp focus. It is evident that Scheib overcame these difficulties in that an excellent series of these telephoto lens shots of Degener, Wayne, Greene, Weiss, and Shibahara were included in the diving sequence of the film.[43] Unfortunately, these shots were edited out of the sequence in 1958--probably because of the extreme visibility of the swastika on Weiss's swimming suit--but they remain in the Museum of Modern Art print of the sequence.

Aside from the stars of the Olympic crew, a huge number of employees were present who were responsible for the hauling of equipment and for the handling of similar tasks. The daily film convoy of Konstantin Boenisch, who provided all necessities for whatever location was in use, moved, each day, fifteen hundred pounds of tracks, camera towers and iron blocks.

Some of his people were getting hurt. The day before, one man broke his foot, another crushed his toes, another cracked his kneecap, while yet another was badly burned by an Olympic torch. These people, too, had their complaints against the film company. Wilhelm Lipke was a stagemaster and overseer of the technical personnel. He filed an official complaint against the company at the behest of the Propaganda Ministry and complained that:

> For instance, we worked eighteen hours a day and were kept in the cellar of the Reich Sport Field, where we got little to eat. If Herr Boenisch had not

> looked out for us, we would have gotten nothing at all. The staff and the remaining personnel were well taken care of in the Schloss Ruhwald, where there was a big new canteen. When we wanted to complain about anything, we were refused or snarled at by Herr Groskopf. We never managed to make headway with Fräulein Riefenstahl in spite of our complaint.[44]

Later, Herr Lipke's whole body (especially one hand) was badly burned by the Olympic flame. He was in the hospital for four weeks, and in spite of earlier promises by the company, he received no medical assistance or other support and had to contract the Reich Labor Service for help. Lipke felt that Herr Groskopf, in particular, was unfriendly to workers and "had learned little of National Socialist thought." Granted that the Propaganda Ministry was collecting these statements to make trouble for Riefenstahl, Herr Lipke's statement implied that much of the behind-the-scenes discontentment was justified.

WEDNESDAY, AUGUST 12, 1936

Jack Medica of the United States won the 400-meter free style title, with the Japanese in hot pursuit. The women made a clean sweep for the United States in the women's springboard diving, with Marjorie Gestring winning the gold medal, and Katherine Rawls and Dorothy Poynton-Hill placing second and third respectively. Germany won the men's team and individual championships in the gymnastics. Germany now had the highest number of points of any nation in the Olympic Games.

Swimming

Men's 400-meter Free Style (Final)--Won by Jack Medica, United States
Men's 100-meter Back Stroke (Trials)
Women's 100-meter Back Stroke (Semifinals)
Women's 400-meter Relay (Trials)
Women's Springboard Diving (Final)--Won by Gestring, United States; second, Rawls, United States; third, Poynton-Hill, United States
Water Polo (Second Rounds)

Men's Gymnastics

All-around Team--Won by Germany; second, Switzerland, third, Finland
Long Horse--Won by Schwarzmann, Germany; second, Mack, Switzerland; third, Volz, Germany
Side Horse--Won by Frey, Germany; second, Mack, Switzerland; third, Bachmann, Switzerland
Flying Rings--Won by Alois Huder, Czechoslovakia; second, Stukel, Yugoslavia; third, Volz, Germany
Parallel Bars--Won by Frey, Germany; second, Reusch, Switzerland; third, Schwarzmann, Germany
Horizontal Bar--Won by Soarvala, Finland; second, Frey, Germany; third, Schwarzmann, Germany
Free Hand--Won by Miez, Switzerland; second, Walter, Switzerland; tie for third between Mack of Switzerland and Frey of Germany

Rowing

Eight-oared Sculls (Trials)
Fours without Coxswain (Trials)
Pairs with Coxswain (Trials)
Double Sculls (Trials)
Single Sculls (Consolation Trials)

Basketball

Quarter-final Round

Yachting

Six-meter class (Final Standing)--First, Great Britain; Second, Norway; Third, Germany

Field Handball

Semifinal Round

During the Olympics, Dr. Goebbels, Goering, and von Ribbentrop all gave huge parties and receptions. Riefenstahl attended the reception at the Goerings' and probably the other receptions as well. Jäger remarked that she was going out nearly every evening to these receptions and was still up at dawn the next day.[45]

The official assignment sheet showed where the cameramen were assigned for this day. Guzzi Lantschner had been asked to cover gymnastics, clearly one of the major assignments. He was assisted by Epkens and von der Heyden. Lambert, Basse, and Hundhausen covered the dressage training for the upcoming riding events. Professor Hege again photographed art, filming the statues at the Dietrich Eckart open-air theater. Frentz was still at Kiel, and von Jaworsky was at Grünau. The supreme event of the day was the swimming, and Riefenstahl assigned a large group of cameramen to the swimming stadium. Hasso was there, taking shots of the spectators--presumably from his crane. Von Friedl was there to take travelling shots. Hans Ertl, of course, also was present at the swimming.[46]

Long before the Games began, the press had given considerable coverage to Hans Ertl's preparations for the swimming events. It is surprising, therefore, that Jäger covered the events so scantily once they had started. This was so probably because most of Ertl's interesting ideas--such as taking pictures of the swimmers from below the surface as he was being towed along in a rubber boat--would have been neither feasible nor allowable in real competition. Most of the really creative material was probably shot before and after the races. One evening, when these rubber boat shots were being projected, in one particular shot a Japanese swimmer got too close to Ertl's camera. Ertl shouted indignantly, "That one kept cleaning my lens with his fingers!" Some of Ertl's best shots were of the diving competition.

> ...[He] built an underwater housing which could take a Sinclair camera, and filmed from inside the pool underneath the 10-meter diving board. To do this, he had to tread water, follow the diver with the camera held out of water, dive with him as he went under, and adjust the distance during the dive, change the exposure setting for the underwater part, and pull the focus and aperture setting again as he came up--all this without a cut and at various camera speeds, sometimes at standard 24 fps, sometimes in slow motion at 48, 72 or even 120 fps.[47]

Some of these shots were used for both the men's and the women's diving sequences, the results indicating that all the pyrotechnics had been worthwhile. In the men's diving sequence--the most famous part of the film-- these slow-motion shots taken by Ertl from below the 10-meter tower do the most to disorient the viewer and to give the sequence the powerful visual impact that occurs quite largely because the viewer cannot establish his position in relation to the diver. This method of shooting was invented by Ertl when he was making promotional films for the 1936 Winter Olympics. Equipped with two up-to-date Bell and Howell hand cameras, he had become fascinated by the various ways in which the ski jumpers on the large jump could be photographed:

> Since my modern American machines could shoot at the normal speed of 24 frames a second as well as slow motion, namely 32 and 48 frames a second, bold ski jumps became peaceful gliding flights, absolutely perfect in form, that later could be analyzed in all their phases of movement on the screen. On my ski voyages and expeditions, I had become well versed in skeet and game bird shooting, which came in handy for my "hunting" with the hand camera for fast-moving subjects. Because of this, I dared to get ever closer to the take-off track of the great ski jump, even when the jumpers shot by me faster and faster. Lastly I crouched--after I had let the jumper know that I would be there--in the middle of the track, somewhere around the fifty meter mark, and let these human projectiles shoot directly over me without losing them from the viewfinder of my lens. In this way I could capture the object in the lower left corner of the frame, then rotate the camera lightning-fast with the jumper who was flying four or five meters over me, in order to show him flying toward the upper right against the sky, until he--pulled down by gravity, tilted downwards, and the camera, now again horizontal, showed him landing by the stadium and masses of spectators.
>
> The so-called Drehschwenk, as I named it, was thus born. In the cinema, it looked as if the ski jumper was an eagle diving on the camera, only at the last moment to sheer off because the intended prey was inedible.
>
> The Drehschwenk was the liberated camera in its highest perfection, and even professionals puzzled later in the theaters about how such shots could be realized.[48]

Ertl simply adapted the Drehschwenk to the situation at the swimming stadium by placing himself at the water line and letting the divers fly by him from the three meter and ten meter boards:

> Since intense activity dominated the swimming stadium day in and day out, I dared bolder and bolder Drehschwenks and varied the frames per second between 24 and 48 frames.
>
> I had the divers, as on the ski jump in Garmisch-Partenkirchen, come out of all corners of the picture, rotated the camera with them, and thus obtained diving figures that appeared nothing short of unreal. Here I could have a thorough fling and transpose this yearning to fly into visual terms and do conjuring tricks on the screen.[49]

Ertl was also quite pleased with his results with the swimmers:

> Somewhat more difficult were the shots in the swimming pool, because I often had to stay underwater up to a minute, although I had no breathing apparatus--not even a nose clip or snorkel. My two helpers built a stool with long legs for the swimming pool, with heavy lumps of lead on its four feet. It had two loops on its so-called seat, into which I could slip my toes and the front part of my feet up to the instep. So I stood up to my breast in the water and I could have them pass my camera, according to my wish, either on top of the water, or when I crouched down, underwater. I succeeded in capturing one of the most beautiful scenes in this way with the world record holder in the backstroke, the American Kiefer. I had him come toward me in the lane next to me at full tempo with the camera above water. As he rushed by me, I went underwater little by little and caught his famous "Kiefer turn" close by me against the wall of the swimming pool, and photographed him again rushing by me underwater, enclosed in a fantastic mantle of bubbles that in the back lighting looked like gold dollar pieces.[50]

Some of Ertl's shots were intercut with the actual swimming competitions. But with the exception of the 200-meter men's breast stroke, the swimming races were shot and shown in the film mostly in long, quite dull, establishing shots that did not show off much of Ertl's camera work. For instance, the shot of Adolf Kiefer, the winner in the 100-meter backstroke, was not used. Riefenstahl appears to have had a lot of good material taken at the swimming stadium that she did not use. Perhaps the enormous amount of time that she took to edit the film did not allow her the opportunity to do more with the swimming events. In contrast to the diving sequences, the editing of most of the swimming races in the finished film was not successfully done.

THURSDAY, AUGUST 13, 1936

Dorothy Poynton-Hill of the United States won the women's platform-diving championship. Dina Senff of the Netherlands won the women's 100-meter back stroke championship.

Swimming

Women's Platform Diving (Final)--Won by Dorothy Poynton-Hill, United States; second, Velma Dunn, United States; third, Käthe Kohler, Germany
Women's 100-meter Back Stroke (Final)--Won by Dina Senff, Netherlands; second, Ria Mastenbroeck, Netherlands; third, Alice Bridges, United States
Women's 400-meter Free Style (Trial)
Men's 100-meter Back Stroke (Semifinals)
1,500-meter Free Style (Trials)
200-meter Breast Stroke (Trials)
Water Polo (Consolation Round)

Soccer

Third-place Play-off

Fencing

Saber Team (Final)--Won by Hungary; second, Italy; third, Germany

Rowing

Fours with Coxswain (Consolation Trials)
Pairs with Coxswain (Consolation Trials)

Pairs without Coxswain (Consolation Trials)
Fours without Coxswain (Consolation Trials)
Single Sculls (Semifinals)
Eight-oared Shells (Consolation Trials)

Equestrian

Dressage

Gymnastics

Women's All-around Team--Won by Germany; second, Czechoslovakia; third, Hungary

Field Hockey

Consolation Round

Basketball

Semifinal Round

At seven o'clock in the morning, Riefenstahl held a conference. Her room was packed with cameramen and her production managers; two journalists were there. She first briefed H. O. Schulze about what he was to do at the swimming events: "... only when there is enough light, otherwise don't shoot," "You shoot from one of the side pedestals in the swimming stadium," and "When the two American favorites are in the lead, get a travelling shot of them with a telephoto lens, I still don't have enough American swimmers. This afternoon I will give you more detailed instructions."[51] Schulze asked several questions and left. Siegert received a similar briefing. Her private secretary, Irma Marie Ernst, noted her instructions. Erna Peters, Riefenstahl's chief cutting assistant, was present to deal with such problems as a print that was too coarse-grained or a film that was streaked with developer. Rolf Lantin gave the report of the previous day's shooting, a document that had the potential of causing the cameramen some grief. Lantin had seen some samples of the previous day's shooting in the new projection room that had been set up at Haus Ruhwald--the room, though primitive, was adequate. Traut asked whether the crew should send cameras to cover the huge forty-two band military concert to be held at the stadium that evening.[52]

Kiekebusch, the chief production manager, was on hand. Riefenstahl's thoughts were quite clearly on the big day coming up at Grünau on the fourteenth. There must have been some trouble with the individual teams or the rowing officials, possibly having to do with permission to use Riefenstahl's fixed balloon, because Jäger talks darkly of the "team arrogance" (Vereinsdünkel) that had been displayed on Tuesday.[53] After being briefed by Sepp Rederer, the film chief at Grünau, Riefenstahl threatened to not cover any of the rowing events except the eights--she had a wealth of material shot of the eights from within the boats during training. The eight-man scull (with a built-in camera that the von Jaworsky brothers had designed) had capsized on Wednesday, dumping von Jaworsky in the water. Riefenstahl wanted to know why the scull had capsized. She also heard from Sigi Schulz, who told her where he planned to place his microphones in Grünau.

The Americans had sent part of their track-and-field team to Bochum for an exhibition meet with the Germans. Jesse Owens had also gone along. Riefenstahl had dispatched de Laforgue to Bochum on Wednesday to photograph the meet. Now de Laforgue was back, and he reported his results to Riefenstahl, who was quite pleased. She called the conference to an end and the working day began.

What Riefenstahl did that day was not reported, but at some point, evidently having received an unfavorable report, she cried out in despair. "It's a pity that we shoot and shoot, and have no idea due to the lack of time, how this or that has turned out, and so we must always go on and shoot more!"[54] Indeed, the problem of keeping abreast of what already had been shot was insurmountable. Over 300,000 meters of film had been shot, and there was no way that any appreciable part of it could be viewed while the Games were still in progress.

Therefore Riefenstahl asked some of the film people whom she most trusted to view a random sample of the film shot. There was another reason for this test. The time would soon be approaching when a large number of cameramen would have to be discharged from the company. Getting rid of people is never an easy task, and part of the reason for the sample was to determine whose work was not up to standard.

That evening at Geyer, the spot check started. Roll

after roll of film was brought from the mountain of film. The Geyer employees had carefully entered the following into their books: 1) the name of the cameraman; 2) the subjects of the corresponding roll of film; 3) a consecutive number; and 4) the day of shooting. A couple of random entries were these: "Hege--4998--fourth shooting day," or "Hart--4937--Kiel." Under these entries fell the exact description of what each roll contained: "Stadium. Public. Polo. Banner," or "Hop, Step and Jump. Slow Motion. Normal." Soon they had what they hoped would be a reasonable cross section. The work of Hege, de Laforgue, von Jaworsky, Kling, Hart, Frentz Schulze, Kebelmann, Schmidt, Hasso and the Lantschner brothers was viewed.[55]

> The projectionists at the two machines are covered with sweat. As soon as a cross section of the material is checked, the bell is rung to change rolls. We see in great haste the slow motion shots of Neubert rush by; there they appear again, Stoeck in the victory ceremony, Bärlund, Wöllke, the women at the high jump, the German women losing the baton. There are Hans Ertl's water fantasies with the most handsome athletes of the Games. There on Block H of the swimming stadium are the Japanese, bowing and nodding to the storms of applause....
>
> Now each gropes his way through a few thousand meters of shots. Is the grain coarse? Where was the camera irreparably jogged in the course of a shot? Where do the daggers of scratches carve lethally through a dark face? Where did light get into a lens? Where did the ghastly weather reduce the slow motion and telescopic lens shots ... into nothing?[56]

The test run was significant. It is noticeable that all of the footage that Jäger cites was taken from events that were included in the final film. This suggests that Riefenstahl had quite a clear idea what events she was going to feature in the finished film and that she wanted to make sure she had covered the events adequately. If she had failed to do that, she would still have had the opportunity for retakes before the athletes dispersed completely. She may have used this test as a basis for retakes.

In the program for the fourteenth, Riefenstahl made some late changes that must have caused her staff headaches. She decided to film the hockey game, a play-off for third place. She also decided to shoot "many races in Grünau, although only the eight-man sculls have been provided for ... since five o'clock early she has re-arranged, re-assigned...." Unless Riefenstahl's refusal to film all of the rowing events was pure bluff, her last minute change of mind must have been extremely disconcerting to the Grünau crew.

FRIDAY, AUGUST 14, 1936

Germany achieved a stunning victory in the rowing finals, sweeping five of the seven final events. This victory was unprecedented, as Germany had never before been a major competitor in rowing. The Germans won gold medals in the single sculls, pairs without coxswain, pairs with coxswain, fours with coxswain, and fours without coxswain. In spite of the bad weather the crowd was ecstatic. Adolf Hitler came to Grünau for the events and was also extremely pleased. The United States won the eights, however, as the University of Washington team edged out the other contenders, and Great Britain won the double sculls. Germany had served notice on the two nations enjoying strong rowing traditions, that Germany was a powerful contender.

Rowing

Single Sculls (Final)--Won by Germany
Double Sculls (Final)--Won by Great Britain
Pairs without Coxswain (Final)--Won by Germany
Pairs with Coxswain (Final)--Won by Germany
Fours with Coxswain (Final)--Won by Germany
Fours without Coxswain (Final)--Won by Germany
Eight-oared Shells (Final)--Won by the United States

Field Hockey

Third-place Play-off

Field Handball (Final)--Germany 10, Austria 8

Basketball (Final)--United States 19, Canada 8

Riefenstahl must have been bitterly disappointed by the film results achieved, considering the spectacular successes of the German teams at Grünau. At Grünau, perhaps more than at many of the other locations, Riefenstahl had tried to devise means to make the shooting a success. After all, a dramatic event would be occurring in which Germany was expected to do well. She had arrived in Grünau with twenty-one cameramen, as well as with permission to use her beloved fixed balloon. Upon her arrival at the regatta she had been greeted by Hitler, and all the people in the stands broke into cries of "Leni, Leni, Leni!" when she first became visible before them.

But the weather, once again, was frightful. Because of the possibility of lightning from storm clouds, the hydrogen-filled balloon was ordered to be brought down.[57] Riefenstahl threw another tantrum, but her hysteria did not change the minds of the authorities. When the balloon was lowered, the gas escaped much too fast and Walter Frentz, although he escaped injury, was plunged into the river Spree.

Others at Grünau also had their share of mishaps. On Wednesday, von Jaworsky had capsized his special eight-man shell and gone in the water. On Thursday, Sepp Rederer had managed to fall in, and now Frentz had gone for a bath. Hans Scheib commented at dinner, "Thank God the whole Grünau film didn't fall into the water."[58] As a result of Friday's shooting, most of the rowing races were shot from a position that looks to have been in the stands. The shots are not particularly interesting, the one exception being the eights for which Riefenstahl intercut footage shot during training. The sequence is also particularly effective because of the extremely interesting use of sound obtained by Sigi Schulz. The exhortations of the coxswains to their crews are very exciting to listen to; these also must have been recorded during training.

At quarter past nine in the evening, the crew was to film a repetition of the festival play that had opened the Games. At the express order of Hitler, the crew did not film this event.[59] Kiekebusch was overjoyed because Grünau had totally exhausted his crew. But it is significant that this story is the first specific example we know about of Hitler directly ordering the film company to shoot a sequence or to not shoot a sequence. This incident contradicts Riefenstahl's claim that she was given a totally free hand in filming the Games.

SATURDAY, AUGUST 15, 1936

The United States again dominated the diving competitions and took first, second, and fifth in the platform diving. But the Japanese dominated the swimming competitions almost completely. The United States narrowly edged the Japanese in the aggregate scores of all swimming events, but this was because the diving events had been included with the swimming events. Norburu Terada easily beat Jack Medica in the 1,500-meter race, and Detsuo Hamuro won the 200-meter breast stroke. Japan was now recognized as a major power, if not the most prominent power, in swimming events.

The Germans were doing quite well in the equestrian events; they were well ahead of all other nations in the total number of medals accumulated. The point was not lost on many observers that the totalitarian nations seemed to be doing quite well in contrast with many of the parliamentary democracies.

Swimming

1,500-meter Free Style (Final)--Won by Norburu Terada, Japan; second, Jack Medica, United States; third, Shumpei Uto, Japan

Men's 200-meter Breast Stroke (Final)--Won by Detsuo Hamuro, Japan; second, Sietas, Germany; third, Reizo Kolke, Japan

Women's 400-meter Free Style (Final)--Won by Ria Mastenbroeck, Holland; second, Regnhild Hveger, Denmark; third, Leonore Wingard, United States

Men's Platform Diving (Final)--Won by Marshall Wayne, United States; second, Elbert Root, United States; third, Hermann Stock, Germany

Water Polo (Final Standings)--First, Hungary; second, Germany; third, Belgium

Equestrian

Combined Dressage--Cross-country (Final)--Won by Captain Ludwig Stubbendorf, Germany; second, Captain Thompson, United States; third, Captain Lippert, Germany

Field Hockey (Final)--India 8, Germany 1

Soccer (Final)--Italy 2, Austria 1 (Overtime)

Fencing

Individual Saber--Won by Endre Kabos, Hungary

Boxing Finals

At eleven at night on Saturday, Walter Frentz filmed the heavyweight fight between Herbert Runge of Germany and Guillermo Lovell of Argentina.[60] Ertl, with his crew, was of course still photographing swimming. Another prominent crew at the swimming meets was Hasso and his assistant, von Hau.[61] The opening shot of the swimming section of the film is a travelling shot taken from behind the stands far off the ground. The footage shows the spectators on the top row from behind; they are gazing raptly at the swimmers below. This shot appears to have been taken from Hasso's crane, and there is a photograph of the crane behind the stands, apparently getting this shot. (The shot appeared in the Deutsche allgemeine Zeitung, August 12, 1936.) Some of the establishing shots of the swimming events also look as if they were taken from a crane position behind the stands.

Neubert and his assistant, von der Heyden, were quite busy at the swimming events. According to Neubert's comments in Film-Kurier, he got some wonderful material, obtaining views never before seen. He used all sorts of positions and varied the speed of the camera from race to race. Just to be on the safe side, the crew shot each race at normal speed so that nothing would escape them. Neubert's comments are significant, because while there is some gorgeous slow-motion work of the diving, very little, if any, slow-motion footage exists for the swimming races.[62] The excellence of Neubert's work in the swimming events can be appraised in the film Olympische Spiele, released by the Olympia-Film Gmbh in 1940. This reinforces the impression that Riefenstahl did not use much of her best footage from the swimming events.

Sadly, whoever was responsible for the marvelous footage of the cross-country riding event is not known. Lantschner had been involved in shooting a lot of the test footage of the riding tryouts at Celle, so he was probably there along with a large amount of the staff. The fencing, field hockey, and soccer events all appeared in the final film, but no one is sure who did the camera work.

SUNDAY, AUGUST 16, 1936

This, the last day of the Olympics, was marked by an almost complete German sweep of all riding competitions.

Equestrian

Three-day Event--Won by Captain Ludwig Stubbendorf, Germany; second, Captain Earl Thompson, United States; third, Captain Hans Lunding, Denmark; final team standings: first, Germany; second, Poland; third, Great Britain

Prix de Nations--Won by Lieutenant Kurt Hasse, Germany; second, Henri Rang, Rumania; third, Captain Joseph von Platty, Hungary; final team standings: first, Germany; second, Netherlands; third, Portugal

The riding events ran well-past their scheduled times, so it was quite late when the closing ceremonies began. They were marked with as much pomp and ceremony as the beginning ceremonies had been. The sun had long since set, so the floodlights were turned on. A squat signal gun went off in the distance, and the giant Olympic bell began to ring. Then the great stadium searchlights began to light up and pierce the sky.

> There were at least a score of these rays of lights at regular intervals. For a moment they beamed straight upward. Gradually they dropped and converged so that they formed a great tent of white above the stadium.[63]

The flag bearers entered. Their order was reversed from the opening ceremony. The host country, Germany, was first; Greece was last. Count Henri de Baillet-Latour made a closing speech. Then fifty-one tall white-clad girls from the Guard of Honor advanced on the flags. Major Feuchtinger gave the command, "Hol nieder Flagge," the tips of the flags dropped and the maidens of honor placed a wreath on each flag. Feuchtinger intoned:

> Kämpfer, siegesfroh, kehrt ins Heimatland, Nehmt zum Scheidegruss die Bruderhand.[64]

The Olympic flag was taken down and presented to Hitler, who was in his box with the guests of honor. It was then presented to William May Garland, the man who had headed the 1932 Los Angeles Organization Committee. Garland handed the flag to Bürgermeister Lippert, who would hold the flag until the 1940 Olympics in Tokyo. The Olympic bell tolled, and the guns boomed. A clear voice called through the loudspeakers, "Ich rufe die Jugend der Welt nach Tokyo." But the 1940 Olympics would not be held in Tokyo or anywhere else.

No doubt, the Olympic Games had been an enormous success for Germany. Observers and journalists from all over the world heaped praise on the awesome efficiency and organization evidenced by the Games. They also applauded the friendship and good will of the German people and the apparent wish for good relations that had been expressed by Hitler and other National Socialist leaders. Janet Flanner of the New Yorker was certainly not a Germanophile, but after attending the Games she felt that the regime had attained a new maturity--an attainment that boded well for the future.

> For Germany, in more than one sense, 1936 has been an Olympian season. Though still stumbling over the downtrodden bodies of the churches (fuller than ever of churchgoers), synagogues, science, and fallen currency, the III Reich has in its third year got into what seems its adult stride. Only a determined deaf-and-blind visitor to any corner of this land could fail to see and hear the sight, the sound, of Germany's forward march.[65]

Frederick T. Birchall of the New York Times was similarly impressed, but he was more cautious than Flanner about Germany's sincerity:

> Foreigners who know Germany only from what they have seen during this pleasant fortnight can carry home only one impression. It is that this is a nation happy and prosperous almost beyond belief, that Hitler is one of the greatest, if not the greatest leader in the world today, and that the Germans themselves are a much maligned, hospitable, wholly peaceful people who deserve the best the world can give them.
>
> On the showing of these two weeks during which

> all black spots have been covered, all political controversy side-tracked, all prejudice and all militarism put aside and forgotten, it is all true. After the flags have been hauled down, the Olympic Village vacated, the streets and hotels brought back to their normal state, one can only hope that it will remain so.[66]

Now we know all too well it was not to remain so. On the pleasant evening of August 16, 1936, however, nobody was aware of what would happen. The Germans were euphoric in their pride over the Olympics, and foreigners had received an impression that would not be dispelled for a long time. Avery Brundage (president of the American Olympic Committee), who met Riefenstahl in Berlin, became an America Firster later in the days before World War II. Charles A. Lindbergh had also been present at the Games, and he was as impressed with this evidence of a "healthy, virile race" as he was with the Luftwaffe's airplanes. The Games had been a huge success.

August 16 was to be the last day for Schmidt, Hundhausen, the Schattmans, von Barsy, Siem, Schulze, and Müller. They had all been busy shooting the jumping events of the afternoon. Riefenstahl ordered von Barsy to take care of shooting the Olympic flame as it was extinguished, and she and Jäger later watched it go out as they stood in the slowly emptying press box. This was Riefenstahl's last order during the Olympic Games.

As the flame died out and the Games ended, that special bittersweet melancholy was felt that is peculiar to the ending of successful Olympic Games. For the film crew, however, there was also tremendous relief that the Games were over. The strain had been enormous. Riefenstahl went to bed at half-past nine in the evening. For some, the Games hardly seemed to be over. At ten at night, Ertl was still shooting swimmers and divers by searchlight. On Monday, too, he would be working--making retakes and shooting extra material.

Assessing the successes and failures of the two weeks proved difficult for the simple reason that the crew itself had no very clear idea of their successes and failures. They had a mass of exposed film that was largely unseen. In the way there is relief when one has finished taking an arduous test (even if one is not sure how one did), the crew was simply glad that the ordeal was over. The problems and recriminations would come later.

On Monday, Ruhwald was again calm. Jäger realized that there were numerous women and children in the immediate vicinity of the villa who were charity cases of the NSV.[67] Nobody had noticed them during the Games. There were two statues of knights, one on each side of the main entrance of Haus Ruhwald that had often been the object of jokes by the comics of the crew. They now carried the inscriptions, "The fallen of Ruhwald," and "The victors of Ruhwald." All was quiet.

No one was aware that the next eighteen months were to hold far different and, in some ways, far more difficult problems for Riefenstahl than the two weeks of filming had held for her.

NOTES

1. This chapter will cover the period between the first of August and the sixteenth of August in which the Olympic Games themselves were held, a period of time that is certainly worthy of its own chapter. What was filmed during these days would have to be the basis for the film, no matter how good the training films and the retakes were. And the epic efforts that the film crew made to record these games are absolutely fascinating. They more than warrant a separate chapter.

The basis for this chapter is largely the series of articles that Ernst Jäger wrote for Film-Kurier entitled "Die Kamera kämpft mit." These reports appeared daily except Sunday while the Games went on. There are obvious dangers in relying heavily on one writer, especially when he is also press chief of the film company. I have therefore avoided wherever possible Jäger's attributions of genius to Riefenstahl's every action as well as other obvious propaganda. And since Jäger, the Olympic film propagandist of 1936, is to a degree counterbalanced by Jäger, the anti-Nazi with a grudge against Riefenstahl of 1939, I have used later quotations from his articles written in America as well. There is so much documentation on the Games themselves that it is relatively simple to check the names of the athletes and the dates of the events cited by Jäger, and of course I have used other sources as much as possible. From all evidence, when Jäger cites dates and gives names of cameramen and locations, he is accurate.

I have also given the highlights and sports results of each day so that the reader can compare the sequence of events in the Games to the altered sequence in the film. I have only given the sports results when they seemed particularly relevant to the film. Because Riefenstahl showed little interest in weight lifting in the film, for instance, I have not given the results. I have also described events to some extent where I felt that a significant event had been omitted by Riefenstahl in the finished film. The reader is therefore advised not to take this chapter as a complete or exhaustive description of the fascinating Berlin Olympics.

2. Leonard Mosley, The Reichmarshall: A Biography of Hermann Goering (New York: Doubleday & Co., 1974), pp. 209-210.

3. Frederick T. Birchall, "100,000 Hail Hitler as the Olympics Open," New York Times, 2 August 1936, sec. 1, p. 33.

4. Idem, "11th Olympics Open Today in Gay and Crowded Berlin," New York Times, 1 August 1936, p. 6.

5. Idem, New York Times, 1 August 1936, p. 33.

6. Ernst Jäger, "Die Kamera kämpft mit," first report, "Die ersten beiden Olympia-Tage," Film-Kurier, 3 August 1936, pp. 1-2.

7. Idem, "Hitler's Girlfriend," part IV, Hollywood Tribune, 19 May 1939, p. 13.

8. Aurelia Friedl later married the cameraman Hans Ertl. Hans Ertl, Meine wilden dreissiger Jahre (Munich: F. A. Herbig Verlagsbuchhandlung), 1982, pp. 191-215.

9. Idem, "Kamera," first report, p. 2. Von Blomberg was the Defense Minister in the original National Socialist cabinet. He was dismissed after he was involved in a scandal in 1938.

10. Ibid., p. 2.

11. Idem, "Kamera," second report, 4 August 1936, p. 3.

12. Ibid.

13. "Hans Scheib, der Mann mit der langen Brennweite," Film-Kurier, 19 August 1936, p. 3.

14. Jäger, "Kamera," third report, 5 August 1936, p. 3.

15. "Hans Scheib," p. 3.

16. Jäger, "Kamera," Fourth report, 6 August 1936, p. 3.

17. Ibid.

18. Ibid.

19. Ibid.
20. Ibid.
21. Idem, "Hitler's Girlfriend," part IV, p. 13.
22. Ibid.
23. Ein Bericht über die Herstellung der Olympia-Films (nach authentischen Dokumenten and Unterlagen). See appendix C, p. 275.
24. Goebbels Tagebuch, 6 August 1936, BA, Nachlass Goebbels, NL 118/63 (1936) p. 169 (102).
25. Letter of Dr. Ritter von Halt, no date, addressed to Filmbewertungsstelle, Deutsches Institut für Filmkunde, Wiesbaden.
26. Jäger, "Kamera," sixth report, "Eine Woche Aufnahmeschlacht," 8 August 1936, p. 3.
27. "Olympia-Halbzeit," Licht Bild Bühne, 8 August 1936, p. 1.
28. Idem, "Kamera," sixth report, 8 August 1936, p. 3.
29. Ibid.
30. "Kurt Neubert-Mit dem Zeitlupen 'Tank'," Film-Kurier, 18 August 1936, p. 3.
31. Bella Fromm, Blood and Banquets, pp. 225-226.
32. Birchall, New York Times, 14 August 1936, p. 20.
33. Ertl, Meine wilden dreissiger Jahre, p. 221.
34. Jäger, "Kamera," seventh report, "Marathon-Sonntag," 10 August 1936, p. 3.
35. "Ein Kapitel Marathonlauf: Film bei Kontrolle 5," Licht Bild Bühne, 10 August 1936, p. 2.
36. Ibid.
37. "Die Arbeit am Olympia-Film," Der deutsche Film, March 1938, pp. 253-254.
38. Jäger, "Kamera," seventh report, 10 August 1936, p. 3.
39. Idem, "Hitler's Girlfriend," part V, p. 12.
40. Idem, "Kamera," eighth report, "Meisterstücke von Marine und Film," 8 August 1936, p. 3.
41. Ibid.
42. Idem, "Kamera," ninth report, "M.a.M.," 12 August 1936, p. 3.
43. "Hans Scheib," p. 3.
44. Affidavit of Wilhelm Lipke, Reichministerium für Volksaufklärung und Propaganda, R55/503, pp. 80-87, BA.
45. Jäger, "Kamera," tenth report, "Ein Hirn ohne Ruhe," 13 August 1936, p. 3.
46. Ibid.
47. Mannheim, "Leni," p. 115.
48. Ertl, Meine wilden dreissiger Jahre, pp. 189-90.

49. Ibid., p. 217.

50. Ibid., pp. 217-18.

51. Jäger, "Kamera," tenth report, 13 August 1936, p. 3.

52. Ibid.

53. Ibid.

54. Idem, "Kamera," eleventh report, "Dritter Tag vor Schluss," 14 August 1936, p. 3.

55. Ibid.

56. Ibid.

57. "In Grünau: 21 Kameras--trotz Regen," Film-Kurier, 15 August 1936, p. 3.

58. Jäger, "Kamera," twelfth report, "Lachendes Olympia II," 15 August 1936, p. 3.

59. Ibid.

60. Idem, "Kamera," thirteenth report, "Letzter Schnappschuss," 17 August 1936, p. 3.

61. Idem, "Kamera," twelfth report, 15 August 1936, p. 3.

62. "Kurt Neubert," p. 3.

63. Birchall, "Games in Berlin close amid pomp," New York Times, 17 August 1936, p. 11.

64. Contestant, happy with victory, return to your homeland, take as token of parting our brotherly hand.

65. Janet Flanner ("Genêt"), "Letter from Berlin," The New Yorker, 22 August 1936, p. 55.

66. Birchall, "Olympics Leave Glow in Reich," New York Times, 16 August 1936, sec. 4, p. 5.

67. Nationalsozialistische Volkswohlfahrt, the National Socialist Welfare Organization.

• CHAPTER IV •

THE EDITING OF THE OLYMPIC FILM

In July of 1937, Riefenstahl showed a *Werkfilm* at the Paris Exposition. The subject of the short film was the making of *Olympia*. To introduce it, Riefenstahl gave a speech. The speech is a good outline of the major events of this chapter, so it will be reproduced here to give some of the major chronological events of the eighteen months following the Games. On July 3, 1937, Riefenstahl said:

> Before I began with the preparations for the Olympic film, I knew that the Olympic film would only be ready after a year and a half. It is therefore no surprise that the film will first appear in the winter of 1937 or the spring of 1938.
>
> I will attempt to explain to you why such a long work period is necessary.
>
> We had until the sixteenth of August at our disposal to photograph the Olympic Games themselves. Until the end of August, footage was shot of the great athletes that were still present.
>
> During all of September, we shot the prologue of our film.
>
> After the ending of this shooting, we had 400,000 meters of picture and 30,000 meters of sound material.
>
> And in order to possess a complete overview of these materials, it was necessary to classify them in an indexed system. Each kind of sport had to be classified into innumerable subdivisions, as for instance, in track and field, the material from each event was organized according to the length, the height, the performance and so on. Even so the time photography had to be specially listed. The material of all the newsreels also had to be classified and

ordered.

For this purely mechanical work, three months were necessary, although twenty experienced people worked day and night.

During this time I could see the material for the first time. I sat for eight to ten hours in the projection room and needed two and a half months there until I had seen the last meter. As I have already explained, we were shooting until the end of September, so I thus lost October, November and half of December--just for the viewing of the shots.

Since one cannot form such a film in accordance with a shooting script, but rather only from the existing raw film, I had to get to know the material. Only then could I begin the creative process.

I required the time from the middle of December 1936 to the middle of January 1937 in order to select the material for the organization and the editing of the film, and to put together the framework of the Olympic film in a form similar to a script. During this work, it became clear that it would be impossible to show the complete Olympiad in one film. In a film that would run in one evening, one would have only the hastiest survey of the Olympics. Even in two films that take up two evenings, it is almost insolubly difficult only to show the most important events and to make them an experience and not merely a transient picture show. The first part will begin with the prologue, torch bearing and opening and will show all the most important track and field events. This section will end with the evening festival play.

The second section begins with the Olympic Village, contains swimming, diving, riding, polo, soccer, hockey, gymnastics, cycling, fencing, sailing, rowing and so on. The conclusion is the closing ceremonies of the Olympic Games.

On January 15, 1937, I could for the first time begin the actual cutting. Since this work is the actual creative part, I have to do it alone. If I were to add another director in order to speed up the work, then a unified work could never be produced. A work in which many directors participated would be a film without feeling, a potpourri of various compositions of many artists which would never produce a harmonic whole.

> Since for each part I must view and check through 200,000 meters of film, I need five months per part for the cutting and a month for the synchronization. For both sections together that makes twelve months --thus until the middle of January 1938.[1]

Riefenstahl's calendar was substantially correct, and it was for other considerations that the Olympic film was not premiered until April 20, 1938. Since this speech provides a good linear basis for the editing of the film, I wish to divide the chapter into the following sections: the post-Olympic filming, the review of the material, the actual editing, and the synchronization.

THE POST-OLYMPIC FILMING

This additional filming went on through August and September, in various locations and at different times. As noted in the last chapter, Hans Ertl was still photographing swimming and diving. Much of the men's and women's diving sequences in the final film was clearly shot in the swimming stadium when it was empty, and from angles and locations that never would have been allowed during actual competition. For instance, close shots of Dorothy Poynton-Hill were obtained that must have been shot after the Games.

Much of the final footage shot by Guzzi Lantschner of the gymnastic events seems to have been made after the competition ended. The whole sequence of Consetta Carrucio, the American gymnast, on the parallel bars was made at a very close distance. Since Carrucio was the top scorer in this event in the Olympics, it is likely that Lantschner shot this event after the Olympics rather than before it. The same is true of the footage shot of the German gymnast Karl Schwarzmann on the high bar.

According to Jäger, Riefenstahl asked Glenn Morris to return to Berlin for retakes.[2] What was shot is not known. In the interesting short film in the DDR, _Olympiade 1936--Kameraleute bei der Arbeit_, there are a few shots of Riefenstahl and Glenn Morris together. In one, Riefenstahl tries her hand at throwing the discus; then she laughs and hands the discus to Morris. A shot exists in which Morris assumes the stance of Myron's discobolus (as in the prologue shot of Erwin Huber), but it is not known whether this material was shot at the session on Sunday, the eighth of August, or later. In any case, none of this footage seems very serious; Jäger intimated that Riefenstahl had been looking for an excuse to call Morris back to Berlin.

Aside from the retakes of the athletes, other footage needed to be shot--animated sections to be made by Svend Noldan that were used in the torch-bearing section of the prologue, some model shots. These were used mainly in the closing ceremonies at the end of the picture when the camera dollied from a great distance through the night to the stadium and then up to the Olympic flame. Riefenstahl evidently despaired of ever setting up this shot in actual space.

Because she had missed footage during the Games, Riefenstahl decided to send Hans Ertl and his assistant to Nuremberg in September. There was a sport festival taking place there in conjunction with the 1936 Nuremberg rally. Since many of the same German athletes would be competing, it was hoped that some extra footage of the athletes might be useful. As we will see, this venture was to have unforeseen consequences.

During this period, Riefenstahl met a man who would be a good friend to her for the next few years. The man--Hubert Stowitts--is also significant because Riefenstahl's admiration for his work is an indication of the aesthetics they both shared.

Stowitts was an American from Nebraska.[3] Like Isadora Duncan whom, in some ways, he resembles, Stowitts became a modern dancer who emphasized personal style over classical training. He had been a good athlete in his youth, and in later years was interested in the combination of athletic motives with dance forms.

Stowitts was extremely interested in the nude male figure. He had been a famous partner of Pavlova, but he had retired and then taken up painting seriously. He painted many subjects, but was especially interested in the male physique. In 1936, in conjunction with the Olympics, he had painted a series of UCLA and USC male athletes; he called the series "The American Champions." Stowitts had hopes that the exhibition would be approved by the U.S. Olympic Committee for inclusion in the American art exhibit in Berlin, but the portraits, lovingly painted of nude models, shocked the committee. Stowitts sent the paintings to Berlin for exhibition at his own expense. National Socialism has always had a penchant for explicitly painted nudes, and his work was quite well received by the critics. However, because Stowitts' show included Black and Jewish athletes, it was closed by Alfred Rosenberg. Significantly, however, and perhaps inevitably, one of the major admirers of his work was Leni Riefenstahl. Stowitts wrote his mother on September 19, 1936:

> The exhibition closed on Tuesday. Another triumph! The press was wonderful; the papers were full of it and the critics were ecstatic in their praise, even the conservative propaganda papers of whom everyone was afraid. There were articles in seven different papers that I know of. The day after the closing Leni Riefenstahl telephoned and asked if it were possible to see them. So we transported them back to the dirty laundry rooms at the Blucher Palais. I lunched with her yesterday at her home and spent the afternoon at her studio.
>
> She has a marvelous idea of putting some of the paintings in the prologue of her 'Olympia' film if they can be stylized in some way; so on Monday they will experiment with smoke colored filters and out-of-focus effects to see what can be done. If it works out successfully it would mean a great deal of publicity, since the film will have a world wide release. Riefenstahl is really a genius; she made the clouds and the mountains speak in 'The Blue Light'.[4]

Riefenstahl did not put any of Stowitts' paintings in the prologues. However, as will be discussed below, one section of the prologue, shot at the Kurischer Nehrung, was a series of figure studies of some of the more prominent German athletes. Inspiration for this section may have been due in part to Stowitts' paintings.

With Riefenstahl's help, Stowitts got jobs in Germany during the winter of 1936-1937. He was asked by Ufa to choreograph <u>Fanny Elssler</u>, a big-budget film starring Lillian Harvey, and he danced the male lead in one major dance production. Stowitts appears to have remained extremely dedicated to Riefenstahl; he was quite close to her for the remainder of his stay in Germany. They went to dance concerts and movie premieres together, and Stowitts said that he was the only person in Germany besides members of her staff who was permitted to see her Olympic footage.[5] Stowitts was to be helpful to Riefenstahl later when she came to America.

Another extremely important part of the post-Olympic shooting got under way at the end of the actual Games. This was the shooting of the remainder of the prologue, the section dealing with the female temple dancers invoking the Olympic flame. Willy Zielke was assigned to this task by Riefenstahl, but before he could begin actual photography, he first had the interesting assignment of finding the best female bodies in Germany to photograph. With the government's official blessing, he went to the three best schools of dance and gymnastics in Germany; the Bode, Laban, and Wigman schools.[6]

> ... and I was able to get permission to enter these three schools after I had a long talk with the head mistresses, that the matter was aboveboard and proper, and nothing would happen to the girls, it was an assignment from Adolf Hitler, from the *Führer* and guaranteed by Dr. Goebbels. And when they were named, these women immediately stood up very straight and said, 'Jawohl! Jawohl!' It was all very Prussian, disciplined.[7]

And so, shortly after, all the students at one of the schools were gathered together, and Zielke found himself in a cold and uncomfortable room, generally used for dance exercises:

> I just sat there, and then I pressed a button. It rang a buzzer, and then the girl came in, dressed as Eve. And she would go to the podium, make a few movements, dance, piroutte, *pas de deux* and so on, then she also turned around backwards with her back to me, then around again, again from the front, and then she would withdraw. I sat very still, said no word. It lasted at most five minutes, no more. And I already had the names of these young ladies written down. And then, I wrote either a red cross or a blue cross. Red meant 'first choice' blue 'second choice', or a zero--nothing.[8]

Zielke repeated this process at all three schools, and then returned to his hotel, no doubt slightly dazed. But he remembered that a few of the girls had made a very strong impression. Out of three hundred, he had no great difficulty in choosing twelve. He took photographs of these, and Riefenstahl approved of his choices.

Zielke and his production assistant Rudolf Fichtner had been instructed by Riefenstahl to film this section of the prologue on the Kurischer Nehrung; it was to substitute for the Adriatic in Greece. The Kurischer Nehrung is a narrow spit of land that leaves the Baltic coast east of Danzig, extends across the sea in a northeasterly direction and nearly reaches the Latvian province of Courland, from which it gets its name. Topographically, the Nehrung rather resembles the Outer Banks of North Carolina, being mainly comprised of sand dunes. The whole Nehrung is now firmly within the borders of Poland. But, in 1936, the southwestern part of the spit was in Germany. The white dunes were quite picturesque, and they had served as a film location before. The area was once used for a low-budget desert film, the local fishermen hired to act as Arab camel drivers. The local Luftwaffe flight school had also made some short training films in the Nehrung, and in 1934, Frank Wysbar had used both the sand dunes and the flight school in his feature film Rivalen der Luft (which featured, among others, Guzzi Lantschner).

In August, Zielke's group arrived and established themselves near the end of the Nehrung, only a kilometer and a half from the border with Latvia; the area was called the Grabscher Haken. It was surrounded by barbed wire, and the group needed special permission from the army to film there. The barbed wire was there not only to mark a border. The area was part of a designated wilderness area designed to protect the last herd of elk in Europe. Occasionally, Field Marshal Goering would come to shoot the elk, but aside from him, the area was quiet and very private. Nearby was a settlement called Pillkoppen, which boasted a good hotel and could supply the group to some extent. This area of the Grabscher Haken had very beautiful sand dunes and these were perfect to photograph. Since tourists were not allowed in the area, Zielke's nude photography would not become a major attraction; the dunes would not be marred by footprints.

The group lived in tents and suffered all the usual discomforts. The women's tents bore the names of the planets and several satellites--Mercury, Mars, Venus, the moon, and so on. The army built a large tent for Zielke and Fichtner. It had beds, a wooden floor, and an artificially cooled laboratory so the film would remain cold. Because of the relentless wind and drifting sand, the cameras had to remain covered and be cleaned constantly. Zielke got hold of a motor boat, which he named the Pik Dame. In it, he scouted locations; he also used the boat to get food and water.

The operation was far from small. Zielke had a mass of lighting equipment that he had gotten from Ufa. The equipment required a generator, cables, power lines and other gear. A field kitchen had to be built to care for all the personnel. The lighting equipment was very heavy. Walking through sand with it was extremely tiring, so special paths were created to carry the equipment through the dunes.

There were other problems--technical and otherwise. The team was plagued by such a severe shortage of fresh water that it hired a water dowser to look for a spring. Often the winds were too high to film, and there were other weather problems.

But the major difficulty for Zielke was the dunes and how to keep them intact. Many rules were laid down to protect them from footsteps or other damage. Zielke became enraged when they were at all disturbed. He explained their importance as follows:

> Dunes give simultaneously the background, the yellow background, and the blue sky. They are two contrasting tones. The dunes give a light background; the blue sky with a filter gives a middle grey background, even a dark grey background; and this was very important. The background must be smooth, so that the body is well profiled against it and stands out in relief against it like a statue. This is the secret of every film shot--the background is a very important thing: a calm background, then is the picture a picture.[9]

In spite of all the problems, Zielke finished shooting the temple-dancer footage in two weeks.

He had one more major task. This was to accomplish the very complex dissolve from the statue of Myron's Discobolus to the living decathlon athlete, Erwin Huber. Zielke first had to get a plaster cast of the statue. The copy chosen stood in Rome, so it had to be taken down from its pedestal and a new cast poured, an act that called for the permission of Mussolini. Zielke believes that the most expert museum in Germany (the Glyptothek in Munich) cast it. So that it would photograph better, Zielke had asked that a grey color be added to the plaster; brilliant white is extremely hard to shoot well.

When the Discobolus arrived, it caused another problem that angered Zielke greatly:

> ... the Discobolus of Myron was sent to us in a big box--it was life size: and then it was lifted up. And then the idiots of workers simply pulled off the top of the box and let the wind blow the straw that was inside the box all over the dunes. It was a catastrophe. I thought I would go crazy, that I would hit the people. I was never so angry in my life as at that moment. All the beautiful dunes full of straw.[10]

The incident was indeed serious. The dunes were deemed so important that members of the company had standing orders not even to throw a cigarette butt into them. If the backgrounds to the shots were gone, the whole production would come to a standstill. Very fortunately, a wind came up that night. It blew the straw away as well as repaired all the damage. When Zielke emerged from his tent the next morning, the dunes were perfect. This was very lucky. If there had been rain, the straw would have stuck to the dunes. With this problem out of the way, Zielke could continue planning the shot.

> ... then we built a turntable out of wood so that this Discobolus would turn on its own axis. And that was my idea. I did not want to have it standing there, so stupid, so rigid. Rather I said to myself, when he throws the discus, he turns around like so and then he throws the discus. And from this movement from within of the turning naked body with the discus, I had the opportunity of mixing. Because the real discus thrower turns this way, as I

> have said; then I could mix these turning motions at the cutting table, so that these two figures cover each other and simultaneously turn. And later I did this with the cutting of the film. And there was a very long dissolve from one shot to the other, two and a half meters long ... a band of film that slowly goes into the other and dissolves.[11]

While Zielke was filming this shot, Riefenstahl arrived at the Kurischer Nehrung with some of her principal cinematographers. The papers seem to have been advised of her presence because a reporter from the Preussiche Zeitung quickly turned up. She gave him an interview and gave the following explanation of the Discobolus shot:

> "What we're shooting here? Well, the film will consist of several sections. Along with the purely sporting events, the shots that were taken during the Games, will also be shown pictures that show the beauty of movement coming into its own: in visual form, the Olympic idea of the ancients will be expounded. What we are doing here is supposed to become the prologue.... Next we will take the shots that show the visual forms of ancient times as well as stylized movement. The figure of the Discobolus, for example that is standing there, by means of Huber, who is superimposed over it will slowly begin moving. So we make the transition from the classical Games to modern sport...."[12]

Then, according to Zielke, she coolly thanked him and told him that he could return to Berlin. The whole scene had the flavor of a dismissal, and Zielke still does not know why he was sent home. Riefenstahl and her crew stayed at the Kurischer Nehrung and were responsible for the prologue footage that dealt with the male athletes running, jumping, and working out with weights and javelins. The athletes included Erwin Huber, Luz Long, and Anatol Dobriansky. The short film in the Institut für wissenschaftlichen Film in Potsdam called Olympiade 1936--Kameraleute bei der Arbeit shows one superb shot of a cameraman lying supine in a wheelbarrow while he is pulled along, aiming his camera almost straight up at Erwin Huber and shooting as Huber runs alongside the wheelbarrow holding a javelin over his head. This shot of Huber was in the final film.

These final incidents at the Kurischer Nehrung suggest some sort of a rift between Riefenstahl and Zielke. But there is no question that this location produced some of the finest cinematography in the film, and that Zielke's work there was brilliant.

THE REVIEW OF THE MATERIAL

By mid-September, Riefenstahl could look at all the material and begin to think about how to use it. According to Jäger, Dr. Goebbels struck some time during this period. Goebbels believed he had sufficient ammunition to oust Riefenstahl as director. The picture had been shot, and there was no reason to wait any longer. He raised five points against Riefenstahl: 1) the virtual kidnapping of Anatol Dobriansky from Greece; 2) the insult to the referee; 3) the annoyance of the Reich Sports leader von Tschammer und Osten regarding Riefenstahl's preference for filming the Americans; 4) her attentions to the Black athletes Ralph Metcalfe and Jesse Owens; and 5) the fact that Anatol Dobriansky and several skiers had gotten into a brawl at Haus Ruhwald over Glenn Morris. Goebbels held that these facts proved Riefenstahl incapable of cutting 400,000 meters of film, and he wanted to replace her with Hans Weidemann, the vice-president of the Reich Film Chamber, who had made the Winter Olympic film.[13]

This story is largely substantiated by Friederich A. Mainz, although slightly different reasons are given for Dr. Goebbel's dislike of Riefenstahl:

> The press chief of Tobis and the functionary of the Propaganda ministry Senior Civil Servant Räther told me that Frau Riefenstahl was supposed to be unendurable, and was rejected by the controlling functionaries of the regime and the Party. In spite of this, Frau Riefenstahl worked with demoniac energy and threw herself into her task. The witch hunt against Frau Riefenstahl which emanated principally from the Propaganda Ministry, grew wider and wider. Another person told me that Frau Riefenstahl was supposed to be half Jewish, had earlier had traffic with Jews, was supposed to have, the same as before, Jewish relationships and to be politically undependable. It was prophesized to me that Frau Riefenstahl would

> never finish her Olympic film.... [ellipsis points in the original document].[14]

According to Jäger, Dr. Goebbels went to Hitler with his complaints. Hitler was quite upset and directed Weidemann to film the Nuremberg rally to be held in mid-September, adding that he did not wish to see Riefenstahl for a while. Jäger said that Riefenstahl ignored all this, even when Dr. Goebbels closed her publicity office and started checking her accounts to see what had happened to the funds. Riefenstahl took a long vacation with Frau von Opel, the daughter-in-law of the international auto magnate. Frau von Opel suggested that Riefenstahl might get further with Hitler if she got rid of her slacks and cap and did something about her appearance. Riefenstahl took this advice and showed up at the party congress looking extremely fashionable. Hitler saw her, and according to Jäger, although they were too far away from each other to speak, he greeted her with a friendly smile. In this intense atmosphere of court politics, such a gesture was extremely meaningful. Not a word was passed, but somehow Weidemann's 1936 Party Congress film never reached the screen.[15]

This is an interesting account of the events following the Games, and it may in part be true, although all evidence suggests that it took more than Hitler's smile at the rally to get Riefenstahl out of her difficulties. Moreover, Weidemann's troubles may have stemmed from the fact that Dr. Goebbels did not particularly like Party rally films. The part of Jäger's story that is verifiable is that Dr. Goebbels did think that Riefenstahl was incompetent, and that he certainly did want to replace her. Riefenstahl is also absolutely correct when she says that she was attacked by Dr. Goebbels partly because he thought that the job was simply too large for a woman. The following incident--and Goebbel's subsequent reaction to it--are indicative of his thinking:

> In order to get at least these shots of the German Olympic victors, L. R. assigned the cameraman Hans Ertl with his assistant Bertl Höcht to get the lacking shots at a sports festival in Nuremberg. They were prevented by force from making these shots by the then chief of the Reich Film Chamber [sic], Herr Hans Weidemann. As Hans Ertl in his declaration under oath stated on 8.29.48, he was simply pulled out

> of bed by the SS and ordered together with his assistant Höcht to make the very same shots under Weidemann's authority. On Ertl's protest that he was supposed to be engaged to shoot film for Riefenstahl's Olympic film, Weidemann answered that that was all the same to him, and bestowed on Frau Riefenstahl the quotation from Götz.[16] Further Ertl declared in his statement under oath: "Thus and similar appeared the 'protection' that Frau Riefenstahl and her staff of workers could enjoy from the highest party circles."[17]

Riefenstahl evidently was upset enough by this incident to go to the Ministry and directly to Dr. Goebbels. He entered in his diary a response that would be typical of all his responses to Riefenstahl for the next six months:

> September 18, 1936 (Friday)
> Ministry: Riefenstahl has complaints about Weidemann. But she is badly hysterical. A further proof that women cannot master such assignments.[18]

According to Riefenstahl, the Propaganda Ministry found other ways to apply pressure. She claims that there was a press ban on reporting on the film. On her birthday, August 22, 1936, Ernst Jäger had had a headline inserted in the popular Berlin daily <u>BZ am Mittag</u> congratulating Riefenstahl. Dr. Goebbels got angry over the excessive coverage of Riefenstahl in the press and ordered the ban. Riefenstahl relates:

> In September 1936, after the ending of the Olympics, Herr minister-councillor Berndt by order of Dr. Goebbels officially told the German Press in the assembly room of the Propaganda Ministry that it was officially forbidden in word or in picture to report about Leni Riefenstahl and her Olympic film. This press ban against L. R. remained in effect for 1 1/2 years and was only lifted two months before the world premiere of the films, since they were already finished and a further boycott was pointless.[19]

I find this claim of Riefenstahl one of the most difficult to verify. In the Bundesarchiv, there are numerous collections kept by different newspapers of the directives (given both orally and in writing) to the German press by Propaganda

Ministry personnel, Herr Berndt and Herr Stephan, for example. I went through three of these collections personally; the Sammlung Brammer, the Sammlung Traub, and the Sammlung Sänger. In none of these collections was I able to find a direct allusion to a ban on press coverage of the film during the time span that Riefenstahl described. The only ban I could find went into effect about the time that Riefenstahl said that it was lifted, approximately two months before the premiere. The Propaganda Ministry imposed a press ban until two weeks before the release of the film. Because the release of the film was delayed numerous times, the press ban was consequently extended numerous times. But there is no direct allusion in any of these collections to a press ban in either 1936 or 1937.

And though the ban may have existed, it was far from complete. Articles appear from time to time in 1937 about Riefenstahl and the Olympic film (in the glossy magazine _Der deutsche Film_, which was published under the auspices of the Reich Film Chamber itself). The ban appeared to be lifted in June and July of 1937, when Riefenstahl was to attend the International Exposition in Paris. She had nowhere near the publicity that she had had during the Games, but a possible explanation is this: While shooting the games was dramatic, it was very hard to make a good story about cutting a film.

There is at least some negative evidence of a press ban. When such a ban was mentioned in print on January 4, 1938, the directive stated that the ban was to be _extended_ until January 31; it did not state that the ban was newly imposed.[20] This suggests that an ongoing ban had been in effect. But it would be interesting to know whether Riefenstahl has affadavits in her possession substantiating her claim.

Other Propaganda Ministry pressures on Riefenstahl included the dismissal of Ernst Jäger, an event already alluded to:

> In October of 1936 L. R. was told by State Secretary Hanke of the Propaganda ministry that she was immediately to fire her press chief Ernst Jäger, who was married to a Jewess and expelled from the _Reichschrifttumskammer_. Aside from this, it was also imparted to her that Dr. Goebbels did not want her to show too many victorious black athletes in the

> Olympic film.
>
> In spite of the risk involved, L. R. refused to fill these demands. This had the result that Dr. Goebbels gave the order to the Film Kredit Bank, which was maintained by his ministry, to stop all further credit to the Olympia film G.m.b.H. With this the war between Dr. Goebbels and L. R. reached its highest point.[21]

This writer has been unable to find any independent evidence that Dr. Goebbels told Riefenstahl to cut footage of Black athletes. But Jäger substantiates her story even in his later anti-Riefenstahl articles. However, it certainly is true that Dr. Goebbels refused to extend any more credit to the Company. He was not without good reason for doing so.

As Ernst Jäger has stated, Dr. Goebbels had Riefenstahl's accounts audited. From October 3 to 8, 1936, a team descended upon the Olympia-Film Company to do a surprise audit. It produced a report demonstrating that the business end of the company was in a horrible mess.[22] The report gave numerous examples of sheer incompetence that had been made worse by a remarkable amount of white-collar crime. The company had no safe or strong box, and Groskopf, the financial head, had been walking around with between 14,000 and 15,000 RM in his pocket and giving money to people when he was asked to do so. Although, according to her contract, Riefenstahl was to have received an initial payment of 700,000 RM with an additional payment of 200,000 on November 1, she had in fact already gone through 1,200,000 RM of her 1,500,000 by September 16. It should be noted that a smart shopper could buy a dress in Berlin for less than ten RM in 1936, so one can see how much money she actually had at her disposal. Some parts of the report, which goes on for fourteen pages, approach high comedy:

> 6) To voucher 217 and 218: In the months of February and March 1936, tests with 16 millimeter film were carried out and for this purpose Herr Otto Lantschner and Herr Kraisch were sent to Davos. The costs for allowances, expense money, and travelling expenses and other special costs amounted to 5,185.40 RM. On these vouchers, it is still to be established why these tests had to be made in Switzerland, and why they could not be made in a shorter

> time....
> 13) In the bill for expenses submitted by Noellke, the expense of 5.75 RM for one bottle of Asbach appears, with the remark, "by order of Traut." The amount is to be collected....
> 29) On June 9, 1936, a motorboat was bought for the price of 1400 RM. Why this boat was not used during the events in Grünau, but rather considerable sums for the rental of motorboats had to be paid is still to be established....
> 32) The Olympia-film company bought a used car from the Daimler-Benz Company for 2571RM. On 4/27/36, the car was delivered to the employee Gustav Lantschner for the price of 1,000 RM (payable in installments within a year). What grounds were relevant for this transaction? Why did the firm keep the car in its own possession when it was bought solely for business reasons and as a rule only should be used for business purposes?....[23]

Further investigation revealed that Riefenstahl had either given or sold at a huge discount to her special favorites among the cameramen, the company's property. In addition, furniture that the company had ordered for Ruhwald or the Geyer Works had then been taken home by various officials of the company.

The accountants also said that the accounts were in such a shambles that it was virtually impossible to say what had happened to the Olympia property and funds before October of 1936. Dr. Goebbels said that some of the bookkeeper's complaints were not so important--he wrote, "Let's not be petty" at one point on the pages of the audit[24]--but there is no doubt that the way in which the affairs of the company had been handled put him in a rage. On October 25, 1936, he wrote:

> Investigation of the Olympic film; Riefenstahl has made a pig mess (Sauwirtschaft) of it. Intervene![25]

And intervene he did. He ordered that the books of the company be subject to a monthly audit. Riefenstahl fought this with all her might. In a memorandum, Dr. Ott, the financial expert of the Propaganda Ministry, suggested the books be audited by the Film Kredit Bank, but this idea was objected to by Riefenstahl:

> Fräulein Riefenstahl resisted this with all the means at her disposal and always emphasized that she must have independent control, and that she would not let herself be talked out of this by anyone. Moreover, she cited the Führer as her authority.[26]

As we have seen in chapter one, the Film Kredit Bank had not been established to deal with Reich-sponsored films. Therefore, Dr. Goebbels rejected this idea initially and instead ordered Judge Bruno Pfennig to become a financial advisor to the company. The Film Kredit Bank, however, did in fact assume auditing responsibilities for the company and reported to Pfennig. Thereafter the receipts and expenditures of the company were subject to a strict review by the Propaganda Ministry.

Clearly, by this time, bad blood existed between Dr. Goebbels and Riefenstahl. It must be said that, on the basis of the business records up to this point, Dr. Goebbel's doubts about Riefenstahl's competence were not without foundation. Regarding Reich funds, her company had certainly been guilty of negligence. And, evidently, the first reports that the Propaganda Ministry received implied that the footage shot by the company had been mediocre. On the basis of these reports, Goebbels ordered investigations of the complaints against the company, all this with an eye to building a strong case against Riefenstahl and to finding the taxpayers' money.

At least with regard to the charges of financial mismanagement, which are the only ones that are verified by the Propaganda Ministry records, the writer finds himself in the unusual position of being in some sympathy with the Propaganda Minister. It may be excusable to overlook submitting a voucher in triplicate while buying film or a new filter to shoot an Olympic event that is about to start, and indeed Walter Groskopf made this defense. But the expense-account padding and the hanky-panky found in the auditor's report went far beyond that. The defense may be made that the amount of stealing that went on was no worse than what occurs in any present-day large-budget production where bookkeeping becomes an act of artistic creativity. To the extent that this is a defense at all, it should be pointed out that the Olympia-Film GmbH was the recipient of government funds, doled out by an arm of the government that, according to Riefenstahl's own testimony, had little love for her. To this extent, the Propaganda Ministry complaints were not unreasonable.

The Ministry's anger did not long deter Riefenstahl. By November, she had looked at a sizable amount of the footage. At this time, apparently, she decided that she would have to make two films to cover the games adequately. This meant that she would need funds over what she had already been allotted; she had already depleted the funds she had been given initially. She filed a request with Dr. Ott in the Propaganda Ministry for an additional 500,000 RM. Dr. Goebbels was certainly not going to grant such a request at this time; the ink was hardly dry on the financial audit of Riefenstahl's company. He wrote on top of Dr. Ott's request "500,000 RM are out of the question."[27] Riefenstahl then came to ask Dr. Goebbels personally for the funds. Dr. Goebbels wrote in his diary:

> November 6, 1936
> Fräulein Riefenstahl demonstrates her hysteria to me. It is impossible to work with this wild woman. Now she wants 1/2 million more for her film and to make two out of it. Yet it stinks to high heaven in her shop. I am cool right down to my heart. She cries. That is the last weapon of women. But, that does not work on me any more. She should work and keep order.[28]

Faced with this hostility, justified or not, Riefenstahl felt that she had no recourse except to appeal to the <u>Führer</u>:

> 23) There was no longer any possibility for L. R. except to clarify the situation through a personal consultation with Hitler, to whom L. R. had not spoken alone for a period of 1 1/2 years. However, Dr. Goebbels succeeded in preventing every discussion with Hitler for another two months, so long that L. R. experienced a total collapse of her health. Only in December 1936, with the support of Hitler's adjutant Fritz Wiedemann did L. R. succeed in speaking to Hitler.
>
> This occasion established that Hitler had absolutely no idea of what was going on, and at first did not want to believe her. Only when she laid the supporting evidence before him which made everything obvious, for instance, the press ban against L. R., the blocking of credits, the abduction of cameramen under duress by the SS, etc., Hitler became very

> stirred up and considerate. As then L. R. explained that she could not continue to work in Germany under such conditions, Hitler said that she would receive a decision in a few days.
>
> It has never become known what Hitler arranged with Goebbels in this matter. But 5 days after this conference, L. R. was told by the adjutant of the Reich Chancellery that a new arrangement had been struck with Dr. Goebbels, by which she would have no more difficulties with the Propaganda Ministry. This certainly had the result that she could work undisturbed from then until the beginning of the war; however at the same time, because of this decision, a new wave of envy and mistrust by her colleagues came about. A whispering campaign maintained that such a privileged position meant that L. R. was Hitler's mistress. This was all too happily believed, and these libels spread further and further. So these wicked rumors have penetrated deeper and deeper, so that by this means the fate of L. R. took a tragic turn even until today and has most strongly limited her creative power.[29]

It is very hard to dredge up much sympathy for Riefenstahl's "tragedy" allegedly due to all those people who misunderstood her special relationship with Adolf Hitler. The events in Germany between 1933 and 1945 gave all of us millions of real tragedies to ponder. What happened to Riefenstahl has not been without a rough justice--a fact that she still refuses to admit--and this inability to accept the consequences of her actions is reprehensible. Whether she slept with Hitler is beside the point. What is important is that she cannot very well admit to having been able to go to him whenever she needed to and, at the same time think that this course of action would be overlooked by a lot of people--some of them Hitler's victims--who did not enjoy the same privilege.

But, with the exception that the Propaganda Ministry continued to check her accounts, her description of the events seems accurate. In January of 1937, all harassment of the Olympia-Film GmbH abruptly ceased, and the Propaganda Ministry became extremely cooperative.

Although in November Dr. Goebbels had disapproved a further advance to the company of 500,000 RM, by January his ministry endorsed the extension of another 300,000 RM. On January 25, 1937, the Propaganda Ministry wrote to the Finance Ministry asking for the special allocation of these funds to the company and said in part:

> With respect to Chapter 8, Title 6:
>
> The available material on the Olympic Games, contrary to expectations, has turned out to be extensive and first rate. It would be unjustifiable not to exploit this material that can above all be used for propaganda purposes. On this ground an increase of 300,000 RM to the amount provided for was necessary.[30]

It also turned out that the reports that Herr Groskopf and other administrative types had been guilty of malfeasance were highly exaggerated. The Propaganda Ministry may not have been totally happy with the situation, but it clearly was not going to go against Hitler's clearly expressed wishes. Dr. Goebbels was still not pleased with Riefenstahl, however. On February 21, 1937, he wrote in his diary:

> Frau Stahl [Riefenstahl?] demands an exorbitant contract. She is completely hysterical.[31]

And Dr. Goebbels was still vindictive towards those who had helped Riefenstahl. In the spring of 1937, Frederick A. Mainz, the director of Tobis, was dismissed by Dr. Goebbels because of the distribution contract that he had made with Olympia-Film GmbH. He later stated under oath:

> I was the former production head of Tobis and the sole director of Tobis-cinema A. G. The discussions over the contract were carried out and concluded between the legal advisor and myself. In this matter, Herr Dr. Scheuermann told me that all parts of the Olympic film GmbH were supposed to belong to Frau Leni Riefenstahl.
>
> During the production of the films, that were only finished around 1 1/2 years after the end of the Olympiad, I was eliminated, namely on May 3, 1937. The former Propaganda Ministry, and the Reich Film Chamber acting through its agents, President Dr. Lehnich and the Bürgermeister Dr. Max Winkler, made representations to me to the effect that I had damaged

> Tobis because of the inadvisable guarantee of 750,000RM--and that this deal would conclude with a great loss for Tobis. At that time, I offered to bear the loss myself if the profits from the Olympic film were assigned to me. This offer was refused. Later I discovered from *Herr Bürgermeister* Winkler, from Frau Riefenstahl and my former co-workers of Tobis, that both Olympic films had done a huge business, and many millions had been made on the films. I satisfied myself that both in Germany and abroad, the film met with a resounding commercial success. *Herr Bürgermeister* Winkler perceived belatedly that the contract concluded by me had obtained exceptionally satisfactory results. Tobis got back the guarantee of 750,000RM paid out by it soon after the premiers of the film.[32]

By 1937, Riefenstahl's position was again secure, and she did not have to concern herself with what Dr. Goebbels thought. Also, Dr. Goebbels' comments about Riefenstahl's hysteria seem to have been exaggerated. By January 15, she had seen all the material, had appraised it, and had worked out the basic plan for the Olympic film. Riefenstahl has said several times that once she had worked out the architecture of the film, the rest would fall into place. In the next section, we will see in more detail what she meant by this.

THE EDITING

Finally, the Propaganda Ministry was leaving Riefenstahl alone. And having seen most of the material, she could now start the task of editing. The task was going to be extremely difficult and time consuming. According to Riefenstahl, however, she had already visualized--right from the beginning--two films and the prologue:

> [The idea of two films] was clear to me from the beginning. When I had no Manuscript ... I had only the idea of the prologue, but not yet written down.... I had it right away. In the first second, when I thought about it, whether I should make the film, I had the idea, almost as it is. In order to cross over to the time of today.[33]

Riefenstahl is probably not exaggerating about the prologue here, otherwise she would not have picked Professor Hege's brain so thoroughly and sent Zielke to Greece so soon. But one cannot make a film out of a prologue, and the rest of the film still had to be constructed.

> The problem was how the overall film was to be made. Many said to me that you cannot do that; you can either make newsreels or a lot of sport films, or you make a film in which everything is mixed up, a fantasy where everything is cut on movement, but has no value from the point of view of sport. And it was clear to me that it would work by far the best if I could make it in two parts. And if there were two parts, what should be included comes automatically. I couldn't put track and field and swimming and ev-verything together, and then later in the second part do the same thing. It certainly must have a style. I tried to put the most important sports in track and field into one film, and since track and field is the heart of the Olympics, it followed automatically that the decathlon, that along with the marathon and the 100 meter dash is the most important area, that I could not use the decathlon in part one anymore--it would certainly be repeating itself--, and must be in the second part. This automatically produces the result that it must not be in the beginning or the end, but somewhere in the middle. Since I had no prologue for the second part, I had to look for an introduction, and the Olympic Village offered itself. And since swimming and diving also even uncut are already a high point, the automatic result was--the closing ceremony coming somewhere around the end--so that the diving from the tower could come before the closing ceremonies. The elementary, more lyrical sections if possible at the beginning, otherwise I would have had no intensification. Now I saw on viewing the three day riding that the audience would laugh when the riders fell with their horses in the water. And then I thought that this would have the most effect if this was preceded by something that was somewhat gripping. And of all the events what was the most gripping? The rowing, because of the strain of the rowers. It was very dramatic. Only the riding could come after that,

> because it was a relaxation, and this was supported through the music, a convalescence for the ears since the drama of rowing was built through a background of noise intensity.[34]

This is an extremely interesting quote, for several reasons. First of all, it shows the importance of sound to Riefenstahl, to the point where it assumed a priority in choosing where to put events within the film. It also shows how much she planned the cutting in terms of highs and lows and alternations between tension and relaxation. It further suggests that paramount for Riefenstahl was finding an overall form or architecture for the film.

> ...Before I start cutting, I first of all reflected, here [Triumph des Willens] and also in Olympia, on the architecture: where the sequences are coming, what comes at the beginning, what is suitable for the end, thus the order. And therefore I must see where the best material is, where intensifications are possible. And that was of primary importance. And then came the cutting, and there I concentrated on one complex and tried only to intercut the pictures and movement.[35]

Looking at the material caused surprises, some pleasant and some unpleasant. The most unpleasant was to find that 70 percent of the film was unusable because of technical problems or because of errors caused by the cameramen, which meant that 300,000 out of the 400,000 meters was worthless. This discovery must have appalled Riefenstahl, and it probably convinced the Propaganda Ministry that she was incompetent. But there were good discoveries as well:

> I was very enthusiastic about the shots of the pole vaulting which were extremely good. Then the shots of the Olympic Village, Frentz had done a lot of those. I was very enthusiastic about Ertl, who had done the relay races, the 100 meter, 400 meter relays, men and women. Ertl did all of these, from the tower in the middle. And the marathon, naturally, the marathon shots.[36]

She was also happy with the beautiful cloud shots used at the end of the diving sequence:

> There are clouds that one sees while shooting that they are good; when there are clouds that are not washed out, that have a contour, yes? And then there is often a half fog, half cloudy-grey sky. And these.... Luckily I had many shots taken, because I had reckoned from the beginning with a lot of rejects; and we didn't use the bad ones, when there were bad clouds, and used the ones with good clouds ... because we shot so much material in training. We couldn't during the actual events, we would have disturbed the athletes.[37]

Because of the awful weather, the footage at Grünau was as bad as she had expected, and she decided to use less footage from there than she had originally hoped.

Riefenstahl has a very strong reputation as an editor. But editing never takes place without a context, and Riefenstahl also knew when not to cut. In addition, many of her best effects came from planning well before the Games began. A good example of editing strategies dependent on previous planning is the 1500-meter run. From the beginning, she had hoped to get this race in one take; and she got her cameraman Hans Ertl to photograph the entire race in one shot. On the other hand, the 10,000-meter race lasted for half an hour, so she used a series of cutaways to the various spectators to abridge the time of the race.[38]

Many of the most interestingly edited sequences feature the mixed use of actual footage from the Games and more stylized and subjective shots made during training or after the Games were over. A good example of this sort of edited sequence was the marathon. The first part of the sequence was largely shown in terms of footage shot during the Games, and this section of the sequence was given a straightforward narration. However, in the last part of the sequence, close-up shots of Kitei Son, Nan, and the American Indian, "Tarzan" Brown, are featured. These shots were obtained during training. There are also subjective shots of what the runners are seeing. Riefenstahl explains how she got these shots of the legs running:

> I had an idea that we could convey the exhaustion of the runners by showing the effort of rhythmically pulling their feet off the ground with every step.

> We tried to think up various ways of doing it and made innumerable trials. The bits now in the film were the only usable lengths of nearly 1000 feet of shooting. What we did was to suspend the small 16 1/2 ft. camera, the kinamo, in a wire basket with a remote release and had the marathon runners carry this during training, so they could release the camera themselves in their chest, pointing down at their legs. The result of the first trials was unusable; everything was blurred with camera shake. We tried again different framing speeds and then took a bigger camera with 100 feet of film because the Kinamo's film lengths were too short. Eventually we ended up with a few short bits of footage which we cut into the sequence of the marathon run.[39]

The editing here sets up an odd tension between the reportorial footage and the more stylized shots. The extremely subjective result is uncommon in documentary film. The same polarity is found in the diving sequence, the rowing eights, gymnastics and the swimming events.

Riefenstahl's editing of the film inspired a controversy that still is very much alive. According to Willy Zielke's recollection, his assignment was not only to shoot the film for the prologue but also to edit it. He therefore edited a version of the prologue in a very special way. Instead of cutting, he used extremely long, slow dissolves, some lasting as long as eight or ten seconds. The method of obtaining these dissolves was so unique that Zielke published an article in *Der deutsche Film* entitled "Die Überblende."[40] The effect Zielke obtained was a mystical, dreamy one, the images of ancient Greece melting into one another. Zielke remembers sadly:

> [Riefenstahl] took my film, that I had cut, finished, and she cut it completely differently on her table.... First, she made it smaller, shorter, and second, she changed the whole mythology ... I made it more unreal and dreamy, and she made it more concrete. This is why she never came out of the stadium ... there she had the spirit of the competition, one after the other, continued, tempo--that she had there.... The prologue is something imaginary, it has no tempo, it is hundreds of years long, Greece, soul, mythology, and I cut it thus, so dreamlike. And she treated

> it crudely, thus one could say the fine, the soulful was kaputt, it did not emerge.... When I looked at what she had made of it, I got a toothache. But I said to myself, it is not my film, right?[41]

Riefenstahl disagrees. After giving Zielke full credit for his wonderful photography, she states:

> But he was not able to do one thing, and that made him very sad. He made a rough cut of the prologue that I still possess and must be someplace in my archive. It was completely unusable. I had to cut everything myself.... I worked two months on it, only on the cutting. What he had was all mixed up, you know? So it had no architecture. Now everything is in accordance with a defined dramatic form....[42]

Certainly Riefenstahl seems to have retained Zielke's slow, dreamlike dissolves at the beginning of the sequence, where the temples and statues are portrayed. The break in style to something more objective comes after the Discobolus "becomes" Erwin Huber. For me, at least, the change in style works, since the change in subject matter from the inanimate to the living makes the stylistic change seem in keeping. Zielke's original cut, however, would be extremely interesting to see.

The length of time it took to edit the film was due in part to the fact that Riefenstahl continually tried new versions of different sequences:

> I could have edited the film in half the time ... if I hadn't been so thorough, but I had to try everything, every kind of cross-cutting experiment. Once I had edited a section or a sequence, for instance the marathon, it ought to have been finished and OK. But then I started wondering whether it couldn't be done still better, so I made perhaps 100, 200 or more trial editings. It was my time and it didn't earn me any money, but it was a challenge. I tried for the best possible result I felt I could get out of it, irrespective of time, health or anything else, least of all money.[43]

On May 18, 1937, Judge Bruno Pfennig of the Reich Film Chamber, who was advisor to the Olympia Film Company and in close contact with Riefenstahl as well as with Minister-Counsellor Ott, the financial expert of the Propaganda Ministry, reported to Dr. Goebbels:

> Because of the difficulty of the subject matter and the exceptional volume of recorded materials, the cutting of the film proceeds quite slowly. Instead of the originally planned film to take place in one evening, Fräulein Riefenstahl will produce two such films to take up two evenings. The purchaser, Tobis, is also in agreement. While it was next considered to bring out part one in the Fall of 1937 and the other one in the spring of 1938, Fräulein Riefenstahl now wants to bring out both films together (or one directly after another). She hopes to speed up her work so that the world premiere can take place in February 1938. Considering the great difficulties of the work, a guarantee for the maintenance of this completion date cannot be assumed. The first scenes that have been put together into rough cuts by their nature do not permit any judgment whether the film will be finished by the date that is hoped for.
>
> In addition, one must especially bear in mind that the synchronization afterward will entail considerable work, especially while foreign language versions with partially different footage--because of the special considerations of the performances of the pertinent nations--still have to be prepared.[44]

The report went on to say that Dr. Ott and Judge Pfennig regarded it as imperative that the film be released before the quiet summer months when film attendance was very low.

In the spring of 1937, probably to keep interest in the Olympic film from totally dying, it was decided to present a Werkfilm (at the Paris International Exposition that was to take place that summer) about the making of the Olympic film. It is not clear who was responsible for this decision, but it is interesting to note that the project was not financed by the Olympia-Film GmbH. The expenses of making the film were shared by Tobis and the Reich Film Chamber directly.[45] Otto Lantschner had been shooting footage of the cameramen since the outset; his commission had been to film the filming, and his footage was extensively used. However, the director of the film was Rudolf Schaad, who was credited as a technical assistant to the Olympia company. Otto Lantschner and Walter Traut were listed as his assistants in the credits, and Walter Gronostay wrote the music. The format of the film is as follows: Two persons, an Englishwoman and a Frenchman, are walking across the Reich Sport Field. They begin to talk about the marvelous accomplishments of Leni Riefenstahl in photographing the Olympic Games. (According to a newspaper article, the "American" woman is Karin Evans and the Frenchman is listed as St. Germain.)[46] The film is narrated in English and French and flashes back to scenes of the filming of the Games--for example, Walter Frentz at the catapult, and the photographing of the hammer throw with the aid of a step ladder, or Riefenstahl, Frentz, and Guzzi Lantschner in one of the pits. A section follows that covers some of the work involved in cutting the film, and then a section appears that shows some of the heats of the 100-yard dash. This is the only section of the film that deals with actual footage from the Games. The film ends with a section of the festival play accompanied by Handel's "Hallelujah Chorus." The shots of the cameramen at work are extremely interesting.

The film can be seen at the Library of Congress under the title Behind the Scenes of the Filming of the Olympic Games. Evidently, other material was seen in Paris, including a section of the prologue, but this is not included in the Library of Congress material.

Armed with this piece of footage, Riefenstahl would go to Paris and impress the world with the accomplishments of German film. It was the first of her semiofficial jaunts since the torch bearing in Greece, and it also suggested that the Propaganda Ministry had made peace with her.

The Paris International Exposition was a depressingly apt metaphor for Europe in the summer of 1937. Designed to be a showpiece of the Front Populaire, it was supposed to have opened on May 1, 1937, but there were numerous setbacks, caused in part because the planners kept enlarging their ideas long after the original plans had been approved; also, labor disputes caused delays. Union members, who were angry at Léon Blum, the Premier of France, refused to allow additional labor to be hired to complete the building. They wanted jobs guaranteed for all laborers even after work on the fair was completed. There were constant work stoppages. Other unions in Paris threatened to strike, and finally Blum said he would resign if there was further union pressure.

The opening had to be postponed until May 24. The Germans, who had just opened an equally large exposition in Düsseldorf (Schaffendes Volk), enjoyed the French discomfiture. Der Angriff made fun of the French exposition, and Hermann Goering said that "no strikes and no social problems" had delayed the opening of the Düsseldorf Fair.[47]

When the fair finally opened, virtually nothing was completed, not even the gates. The British Pavilion was a month from completion. The American Pavilion was still only scaffolding. The government had considered a further delay but decided that opening even in this shambles was less embarrassing than further postponements would be. Only the Belgian, German, Russian, and Italian pavilions had been completed; they had used labor from their own countries. Jacques Doriot, the ex-communist, who was now a fascist and later was to become infamous during the German occupation, crowed in the pages of his newspaper, Liberté:

> They mocked the President and public by piling them into a motorboat on the Seine as the only practicable way of making a tour of the exposition and avoiding the holes in the ground and the mess of construction.[48]

It was a long way from the efficiency of the 1936 Olympic Games, and again it seemed to many as if only the totalitarian nations could accomplish anything. However, if the French performance was tragically symbolic, so was the German one. It was announced that only Germans who had obtained a police license certifying their 100 percent political reliability would be allowed to travel in France, as they might be "contaminated" by contact with German émigrés. Léon Blum said that the exposition would be a fair to show the future. This was only too true.

Certainly not unrelated to Riefenstahl's proposed visit to Paris, a nasty little scandal involving Riefenstahl and Dr. Goebbels cropped up in the French press. On June 14, 1937, Paris-Soir ran an article entitled "The Disgrace of Leni Riefenstahl."[49] The article went on to claim that at a reception given by Reich Minister Dr. Frick, Dr. Goebbels had called Riefenstahl a Jewess and ordered her to leave the reception. The story leaked into Germany via Strassbourg radio. Dr. Goebbels was furious when he heard it. In his diary, he wrote:

> June 16, 1937
> Foreign press prints a mean vilification against Leni Riefenstahl and me. I issue a very sharp denial.[50]

At the Propaganda Ministry press conference, the newspapers were ordered to issue extremely sharp denials as well, and not to avoid such expressions as "filth peddler."[51] Complete instructions were issued regarding how to handle the denials:

> This report is supposed to have been picked up by a great number of French and other foreign papers. It is a complete fabrication. To the report denying the story from DNB (German Information Agency) should be added some commentary in which something like this is said: Paris-Soir is a boulevard sheet, living on sensationalism. This foreign rag, evidently no longer stopping with women of society, attacks the honor of a well-known artist and does not stop at reporting public nonsense which claims that a Minister at a dinner party would publicly cause scandal in such a place.
>
> Leni Riefenstahl has a meaningful assignment from the state, to create the Olympic film, and because of this stands in a particularly close relationship with Dr. Goebbels' Ministry. The commentary should be sharp and can also be sarcastic.[52]

Film-Kurier ran the story as follows:

> It was officially communicated: Paris-Soir has printed a report that Frau Leni Riefenstahl was insulted by Dr. Goebbels at a dinner party at the home of Reichsminister Dr. Frick and was sent away. The report was picked up by a large number of papers, above all in Paris and Vienna. It is a complete fabrication.[53]

Jäger reported the background as follows:

> The truth is that a German Foreign Ministry man, to excite publicity for the long-awaited-and-already forgotten Olympia film, concocted the story in Paris in order to force Paris later to print a denial, which would be added publicity for the picture and Leni Riefenstahl.[54]

Perhaps. But it is not very likely that Jäger's version is correct. The Foreign Ministry still had reasonably high professional standards and was staffed with professional diplomats. Their duties did not include promoting motion pictures by creating scandals and using the names of high government officials. According to the entry in his diary, Dr. Goebbels was obviously as shocked as anyone; it is hard to believe that such a scheme would have been hatched without his knowledge. This was terrible publicity for the regime. Furthermore, why would a member of the Foreign Ministry care about the Olympic film?

The incident does seem like a typical example of press agentry; perhaps Ernst Jäger himself was behind it. Riefenstahl had claimed that a press ban was in force, preventing reporting about her or the film. This story would have been sure to break the ban--it certainly worked.

When Hitler heard about the incident, he, too, was furious and was determined to show that relations between Dr. Goebbels and Riefenstahl were at least cordial. Soon after, Goebbels accompanied Hitler to Riefenstahl's villa for lunch. Hitler took along his photographer, Heinrich Hoffmann. The entire Riefenstahl family was gathered, and for hours Hoffman took photographs of Goebbels, Hitler, and Riefenstahl. Goebbels wrote:

> With the Führer to Leni Riefenstahl for lunch. She has had a very nice house built for herself. We chat a long time. She is so high-strung.[55]

At least "high-strung" is an improvement over the usual "hysterical."

As a device to awaken French interest in the Olympic film and in Riefenstahl, the scandal worked admirably. When

Riefenstahl arrived in Paris on July 2, the Paris-Soir (perhaps as an atonement) ran a sensational presentation under the title, "Leni Riefenstahl Is in Paris." The article ran for three pages. It contained numerous pictures, including one of the pictures that Dr. Hoffmann had taken of Hitler, Goebbels, and Riefenstahl. In addition, Riefenstahl got extensive coverage in the Daily Express, a paper which tended to be pro-German during this period.[56]

That evening, a large press reception was held at the international theater "Ciné-Photo-Phono." The reception was given under the auspices of the Reich Film Chamber, and although the official line was that Riefenstahl was in Paris as a guest of Tobis only, Dr. Lehnich, the President of the Chamber, took the opportunity to mention the Olympic film:

> ... in the Olympic film that was especially made for this evening's showing you will see Germany within the framework of the Olympic Games of 1936, as with the help of film, it works for the Olympic idea. To our great joy, the creator of the Olympic film, Leni Riefenstahl is with us today.
>
> ...Without exaggeration, one can certainly say up to now no film has so powerfully championed the idea of peaceful co-operation of nations as the case will be with the great Olympic film, which will be in two parts running two hours each. Today only a small sample and a report about the development of the great Olympic film, but proof enough of what view the new Germany assumes in the friendly competition of nations.[57]

The film was received enthusiastically. Riefenstahl then gave the speech that was cited at the beginning of this chapter. She also apologized for not having been able to show an excerpt of the finished film itself. Sadly, because she had not started dubbing the film, that turned out to be impossible.

On July 3, Riefenstahl was among the guests at a breakfast that the German Ambassador gave for the various notables present at the exposition. On that evening, Triumph des Willens was shown outside of Germany for the first time.[58] According to the German press, the audience was enthusiastic. This obviously was not mere press propaganda; later, Triumph des Willens was awarded the Diplôme de Grand Prix by the exposition, and the prize was personally bestowed by President Daladier.[59] Riefenstahl later argued that the award was proof that Triumph des Willens was an innocent documentary film and not propaganda.[60] But French politics were extremely polarized in the latter days of the Third Republic; the jury, by making this award, may well have been making a pro-fascist or, at least, an anti-Front Populaire statement.

For several reasons, the trip to Paris was a personal triumph for Riefenstahl. One of her films had won a major prize in a foreign land, indicating that Riefenstahl films were not purely a domestic German commodity. If, before, she had been in trouble with the regime, the Paris trip implied that these times were past, and, if Dr. Goebbels still had any serious ideas of sacking her, he never would have allowed her to be so public. She had again assumed her semiofficial status as ambassador, a role she would often fill during the next two years. And to the extent that the press ban of which she complained was at all effective, she had certainly broken it wide open.

Although Riefenstahl was not going to start adding the sound to the film until January of 1938, by July of 1937 Dr. Paul Laven, the main narrator, was being filmed and was consulting with Riefenstahl. Laven would be a man of considerable importance to the finished film. He was a sports announcer on German radio, perhaps the most famous sports announcer in Germany, as well known to Germans of the period as Jim McKay or Chris Schenkel are to Americans. Riefenstahl used him in the finished film in a rather interesting way. Instead of merely having an anonymous narrator, the standard practice on most documentary film, she had Paul Laven and his colleagues Rolf Wernicke, Henri Nannen, and Johannes Pagels reenact their reportage of the events for German radio. So, within the film, at times we see the narrators, who of course are narrating to us, as actors within the Games narrating with microphones to an unseen radio audience. This is an effective device, and no doubt, was partly done as a tribute to German radio service, which had given brilliant coverage of the Games to Germans, and which had also provided all the nations of the world with excellent technical facilities so they could cover the Games for their own countries. For foreign viewers, the idea may, in some sense at least, have backfired. One of the more chilling shots of the film is one in which Dr. Laven--a stocky, humorless-looking man in severe spectacles--puts his hands on his hips and addresses the microphone in clipped, strident tones as if he were the Gauleiter of the Reich Sport Field. As a screen presence, he was not altogether ideal.

But Riefenstahl's concept necessitated Laven's presence because numerous shots of him and the other announcers had to be made against back projection of the crowds in the stands. Shots were also made of him announcing the events in the decathlon and at kilometer eight of the marathon. In addition, it was important to have him present as the events took shape in the cutting room, as he would have to work out his dialogue for the events well in advance. It was of course quite important for Riefenstahl to have more or less of the final recording of the narration to use before she started the difficult job of mixing voice, sound effects, and music. And whatever Dr. Laven's faults as a screen presence, he had a fine voice and was an excellent announcer. He was also quite articulate about the importance of the narration to the Olympic film, and on the eve of the film's premiere, wrote how this narration was in itself quite original:

> We had no idea how completely novel it would be to fulfill the assignment of being the speaker for Leni Riefenstahl's Olympic films. The documentary work was supposed to preserve the memory of the Games and the progress of the competition in an artistic-dramatic form and to make it a thrilling experience. But just as this powerful document of the greatest sports event up to then obtained its actual effectiveness through its artistic form, so the utilization of the speaker was more than a question of reportage. First, the speakers had to discover a not yet known Sprechkunst.
>
> A commentary such as those used in the newsreels was impossible in this artwork. A mere emulation of the reporting of events, such as the radio speaker is accustomed to giving, would in any case have been out of place. It was already quite apparent that the speaker in the Olympic film would not only play the role of an announcer, but also that he had to take on, in a certain sense, a dramatic role.
>
> At the inception of this new Sprechkunst stood improvisation. With all her other urgent work, Leni Riefenstahl took the time to follow up on the develop-

ment of the ad lib text, to help create it, to help to put it into words, and to develop it into its most effective form. Let us compare this work with the assignment of the television announcers.

It was astonishing how the English speaker Marshall knew how to use his television experience here, and immediately found his own style, that was, of course, utterly different from the French and German conception. With him, one could indeed study the difference between the assignment of the speaker in television and pure radio. The description of events receded completely in importance, because what one sees does not have to be repeated. Only occasionally, when it appears necessary for orientation and clarification, can the speaker 'underline' and amplify the event portrayed.

What was original and difficult for the speaker in the Olympic film, but also what was revolutionary, lies in that which the Englishman signifies by the English word "inside," that word formed from within, from personal experience and understanding, out of practical knowledge and intuition, whose effect lies in the frugality of the expression and in the refinement of tone and tempo. While in mere radio, the speaker can "let go," and the individual words play no special role in the pouring out of this barrage of sentences, with the "picture talk" (Bild-besprechung) of this Olympic film, it was exactly the opposite.

This "inside" speaking is, however, the fruit of long practical experience that has to be combined with sensitive and real competence born of experience. Fresh simplicity and a great amount of industriousness are the preconditions. Leni Riefenstahl asked still more from us. The thrilling Games demanded not only this "inspired" speech, but also a passionate dramatic art of expression, so that also in the "temperament" of the speaker, the powerful tension and passion would bring the spectator as well as the contestant at the Olympic Games to grasp the artistic statement. So the speaker had then a star role, so that word; picture and music could become equally strong aspects of this unique artistic work.

Up to now, the speaker stood only at the edge of the film. One thinks of the role of narration in

> the "spirit voice" in a Kulturfilm or a newsreel. From the Olympic film (Tobis), both can learn much about how to obtain a stronger artistic effect from speech in the future, and television as well will get real stimulation from this newly developed Sprechkunst.[61]

A few additional words are in order regarding the narration. Riefenstahl has tried to refute the charge that the narration in the long German version has National Socialist overtones. In her refutation, she states that the English and the German narration are similar. (see Appendix D, p. 286.) However as Dr. Laven himself said, the information given may be similar, but the tone could not be more different. For example, in the marathon sequence three marathon runners from Finland were filmed running together in a group. The English announcer Marshall referred to a previous run by them in the 10,000-meter race:

> The three men from Finland, as usual, are running in close formation, confident and menacing. They still have 13 miles to go.

The English narration is dry, clipped, and matter of fact. It contains the additional overtone of finding the Finnish habit of running clumped together rather humorous and quaint. Compare this with the pomposity of the German narration with its use of the alliterative and rhetorical repetition of the word ein and its emphasis on the heroism of the athlete:

> Drei Läufer! Ein Land! Ein Wille!
> Einundschwanzig Kilometer liegen noch vor ihnen!

At times, the English narration is so English, at least to American ears, that it becomes comical. After Dorothy Odam dropped out of the woman's high jump at 1.62 meters, the announcer said with a sigh, "Bad luck, Dorothy, but well done." When Oe of Japan missed a jump, having competed continually for something like five hours, the announcer said, "Oh well, he must be tired." The English narration, then, had an informality and humor that could not have been more in contrast with the humorlessness of the German narration, whose sole emphasis was on the athletes' competitive struggle.

Top: Kurt Neubert and Eberhard von der Heyden with the slow motion camera.
Bottom: Henry Javorsky with his Debrie Parvo L camera. (Courtesy Henry Javorsky)

Mittwoch, d. 12. 8. 36.

No.	Name	Assignment
1.	Dietze	O [illegible]
2.	Neubert	[illegible]
3.	[illegible]	[illegible]
4.	[illegible]	
5.	v. Jaworsky	GRÜNAU
6.	[illegible]	[illegible]
7.	Hafft	Kiel
8.	Kebelmann	V. Marathon N. Grünau
9.	Frentz	Kiel
10.	Lantschner G.	TURNEN V. N. 6[00] Start
11.	Schattmann	
12.	[illegible]	[illegible]
13.	v. Friedl	[illegible]
14.	Lamberti	7 [illegible]
15.	[illegible]	
16.	Gottschalk	
17.	Hundhausen	Dressur V. N.
18.	Siehr	Kiel
19.	Siegert	
20.	Lantschner O.	[illegible]
21.	Groschopp	O [illegible]
22.	v. Barsy	O [illegible]
23.	[illegible]	[illegible]
24.	Basse	7 DRESSUR 24. Z. [illegible]
25.	Scheib	
26.	de Laforgue	[illegible]
27.	[illegible]	[illegible] Olympisches Dorf.
28.	[illegible] O	
29.	[illegible]	V. Plastike. [illegible] Eckart
30.	[illegible]	TURNEN V. N.
31.	[illegible]	V. Dressur – N. TURNEN
32.	[illegible]	[illegible]
33.	[illegible]	[illegible]
34.	[illegible]	[illegible]
35.	[illegible]	[illegible]
36.	Lemki O	
37.	[illegible]	
38.	[illegible]	Turnen V. N.
39.		
40.		

Top: The camera assignments for Wednesday, August 12, 1936.
Bottom: Hans Ertl photographing divers with his underwater camera.

Hans Scheib with the 500x telephoto lens.

Willy Zielke. (Courtesy Willy Zielke)

Top: Adolf Hitler and Riefenstahl meet members of the German Olympic team. Hans von Tschammer und Osten is behind and to the right of Hitler. (Courtesy National Archives)

Bottom: Riefenstahl's press reception on the eve of the Games. From the right: Sylvia Weaver and Harrison Chandler of the Los Angeles Times, Hans Wolfram of the California Staats-Zeitung, and Riefenstahl. The speaker is Joachim K. Rutenberg, an employee of Film-Kurier as well as the Berlin representative of the American film trade journal The Motion Picture Herald. (Courtesy the Billy Rose Theatre Collection, The New York Public Library at Lincoln Center, Astor, Lenox and Tilden Foundations)

Top: Riefenstahl with athletes from the decathlon. From left: Erwin Huber, Robert Clark (top), Jack Parker (below), and Glen Morris. (Courtesy National Archives)

Bottom: Riefenstahl and cameramen with Archie Williams after he had won the 400-meter run. (Courtesy National Archives)

Herbert Windt

Doctor Paul Laven and Leni Riefenstahl. (Courtesy Leni Riefenstahl)

THE SYNCHRONIZATION

In late 1937, Riefenstahl began to synchronize the film. This is not to say that she had not already been thinking about the music and the sound. As already stated, as soon as she had roughly blocked out the montage, she began to make notes about the sound treatment of the various sequences. Indeed, according to their sound treatment, she had already placed certain sequences within the film.

Adding the sound track proved to be a horrendous task. First of all, although extensive sound recordings had been made during the Games, most of them were unusable. In the stadium, Riefenstahl explains, the sound never stopped, it was always a roar. After hearing ten minutes of it on a sound track, the ears could no longer stand the noise. She had to re-record the sound track. None of it is original. Later, Riefenstahl stated that dubbing the film almost drove her mad.

For the New Year's issue of Film-Kurier (proof that the ban on reporting about Olympia had been suspended), Riefenstahl produced a statement on the progress of the film. In it were indications of the difficulty she was having with the dubbing.

> At this New Year of 1938, two years have gone by since I began the work on the film of the Olympic Games. This is because my studies and preparations had already begun by the Winter Olympics of 1936.
>
> By the end of its first six weeks, the new year should see the completion of the two full features and should bring forth their immediate premiere in Germany and the world. In the meantime, I am still deep at work.
>
> Because as enormous as the preparations were, as unique the proportions of the footage shot, and therefore as doubly difficult as the inspection and cutting were, equally so complex and many faceted is what is called "dubbing," which, in an ordinary feature film or a documentary, would be accomplished in a few days. "Adding the sound track" ("Vertonung") here means the re-creation of the whole atmosphere, independent of the pictorial effect.
>
> The sound-, word-, and background noise film of the Olympics exists. The foundation is formed by

> the original sounds and reportage that the radio recorded during the Games. To this, a carefully harmonized score of Herbert Windt is fitted. I had to experiment a lot with this novel sport music. Also, the re-recording of reports and languages demands extreme dramatic forcefulness and exactness, in order to achieve the full harmony of the sound picture with all its affective elements.
>
> My wish for the new Year and the end of the last phase of work on the Olympic film: may the strength and beauty of the youth of the world find the film form that is worthy of the highest spirit of the Olympic Games. May the film make visible for millions of men all over the world the ideals and energy to which the Olympic city of the New Germany gave such an unforgettable setting.[62]

This following excerpt from Mannheim's interview with Riefenstahl may give further indication of some of the troubles she was having with the dubbing of the film:

> The only sound recordings of those days were on optical film. Sound editors could, in theory, handle up to seven sound films and, in practice, about four before noise levels became intolerable. Leni arrived in the Tobis mixing studios in Berlin with up to 16 soundtracks per shot--speakers, music, four or five different crowd noises, near and far shouting groups, and so on. And she refused to give up a single one.
>
> Once everybody had halfway calmed down, sound engineers spent a week inventing new noise-filtering techniques. It wasn't the end of her problems: "In the mixing studio, I might find that a commentator was speaking just when the image-matched music reached a climax, or that the yelling crowd was drowning out the speaker who was explaining something important. So, when it couldn't be done with mixing, I had to recut the sound as well as the picture, to lengthen one shot to take in a sound effect completely, or shorten another one to cut out clashes. And to modify the sound or the image, every one of the eight to sixteen sound tracks needed altering. With optical sound, you couldn't erase and, if I cut out 10 frames of the picture, I had to cut 10 frames

> from every single sound track--an absolutely inhuman task."[63]

Riefenstahl explained why so many sound tracks were necessary:

> The normal ones are only speech: music, two tracks, because the victory hymns were extra, right?... But I needed many tracks in order to get the background noises for the scenes. And certainly we could not use the normal tone, for instance, at the stadium or the soccer field. It was impossible because of the [imitates stadium noise]. You understand. When you look at the Olympic film, the background noise there is a composition, but you must have a good copy for that, not just a dupe. That is the only way possible that the atmosphere was produced. And that was out of only five or six background noises that I had previously mixed together. So, [at the beginning of the event] you hear the tension, the sound track is not dead, but very quiet. Then tracks that are moderately wide, and then very wide and loud. And that was all mixed on one, like notes, like an orchestra. And that's why I needed so many sound tracks.[64]

With the sound mixers only capable of handling eight tracks, she had a problem that was extremely difficult to solve.

> So I had to take these tracks and mix them in advance, on one band. And it was fiendishly difficult. One of the main successes of the Olympic film is the sound and the background of sound. And the mixing. I worked almost three months.[65]

The _Sprechchöre_ were another problem. She had her heart set on using them, but since the actual recordings from the stadium and elsewhere were unusable, she also re-recorded all of them, going so far as to get Americans studying in Berlin to do the American cheers and getting Japanese in Germany to do the Japanese cheers. She recorded them on a separate sound track, and the cheers then were mixed with the other background noises that had been previously mixed together. One can see why the sound track was so important to the success of the film and also why it was such a major headache--

by far, for Riefenstahl, the most difficult part in making the film.

At times, she put the sound track first in importance in choosing where to put sporting events:

> You know, I tried to alternate music and sounds. I did this when there had been noise too long; then I would intercut a sport that music accompanied. I cannot underscore a run with music, that's impossible, but the hop, skip and jump has something so dancelike about it, it demands music. Or another example: the pole vault was cut in two parts, the first in daylight, the second in the night. Now it never would have worked, in my opinion, to show all five hours of this competition as a competition. As a result, I came to the conclusion that it would be enough for the competition aspects to show the last jumps that took place at night. The first part by day, in which the athletes jump in such a dancelike, light way, I cut completely on movement and could underscore this part with the appropriate music. It is very restful and pleasant, when you can relax after so much running and yelling.[66]

Riefenstahl used the sound track to produce tension and relaxation, highs and lows, just as she used her visual editing to create the same effects. She also used the sound track in another way:

> I have always a representation inside of me and I always take every precaution so that the sound and the image never total more than a hundred percent. Is the image strong? The sound must stay in the background. Is it the sound that is strong? Then the image must be secondary. This is one of the fundamental rules I have always observed.[67]

To give an example, she returns to the 1500-meter run, which was shot all in one take:

> In the 1500 meter run the camera never leaves the runner, the camera accompanies the runners through all four laps. And because of this, the drama lies with the announcer. So the announcer

> must produce the drama and the tone ... the tone, the background sound, must be like an orchestra, and rise and fall for the intensification--you can't always intensify, it has to decrease once more, because a person cannot stand a constant intensification....[68]

Most of the running events and the rowing at Grünau are events for which Riefenstahl needed the sound to be particularly strong.

The music made an enormous contribution to Olympia, and its composer, Herbert Windt, was one of the best film composers in Germany. Windt was born on September 15, 1894 in Senftenberg in Saxony and attended the Gymnasium in Kottbus. He then studied music with Klatte at the Stern'schen conservatory. After 1910 he studied at the Musikhochschule in Berlin with Franz Schreker. When World War I broke out, Windt volunteered for the twelfth regiment of Hussars and fought for three years on the Eastern and the Western fronts. He was severely wounded fighting for the forts at Verdun. After the war, he returned to Professor Schreker's master classes. In 1921, he received the Mendelssohn Prize for a chamber piece; in Berlin, in 1923, he received a composition prize. Some of his major works included Andante Religioso and the opera Andromache, written in 1932. He wrote a radio cantata, Flug zum Niederwald, in 1935. Windt was a member of the NSDAP.

By 1936, he was quite well known as a film composer and was closely associated with heroic and nationalistic films. His strong point was the composition of "heroic" music, and his first major success in this area was his score for Morgenrot (1933). Walter Gronostay, another major composer of the period, wrote:

> Windt's music was a great success. Amazingly, it had been established that music with real substance could substantially help a film. These sounds were not the fruits of a salon music grown ripe at the turn of the century. Here, there were no diminished seventh chords, with which the mediocrities up to then musically underlined every emotion and feeling.
>
> A great heroic tension goes through the music of Herbert Windt--. Certainly one feels here and

> there the spirits of Wagner and Strauss, but a personal spark always shines through and finds its form in highly individual rhythms and tart harmonies.[69]

Gronostay had one major criticism of Windt's work:

> Nevertheless, the music often does not lie in the center of the film, but along side it.[70]

Gronostay's criticism assumes a place for music in film which is fairly conventional; that is, the music should be at the service of the narrative. Gronostay's criticism is not without merit. Sometimes, Windt's music overwhelms the image, but he had other dreams for film music. It was to do more than merely accompany images, and he was to write an unconventional score for Olympia. "The time will come," he said, "in which music will reign sovereign and will not be the last whose advice is asked for and whose achievements will be requested."[71]

Some of Windt's film scores previous to Olympia were Du sollst nicht begehren (Ufa, 1933), Rivalen der Luft (Ufa, 1934), Flüchtlinge (Ufa, 1933), Wilhelm Tell (Terra-Film, 1934), Hermine und die sieben Aufrechten (Terra-Film, 1934), Die Reiter von Deutsch-Ostafrika (Terra-Film, 1934), Mein Leben für Maria Isabell (Lloyd-Film, 1935), and Fährmann Maria (Pallas-Film, 1936), a score which David Stewart Hull found "luminous." Windt was also an old colleague of Riefenstahl. They had collaborated on Sieg des Glaubens and Triumph des Willens.

Riefenstahl describes her relationship with Windt as follows:

> Herbert Windt was very much involved with the success of the film. His music is very good.... I cut first, and when it was ready, I explained to him what I had in mind, for instance in the prologue. Let's take the prologue, which is completely supported by music, yes? I had conceived the music, and said, 'It would be beautiful, Herbert, if you could do it so that when new themes appear in the picture, the heads or the temples or so on, that you change the theme exactly synchronous with the picture.' A melody with the picture together. And he did it per-

> fectly.... I had the pieces played before we recorded them with an orchestra. We brought a piano into the cutting room, by the cutting table, and then played them. If it pleased me, good and OK. If not, I said, 'The music is too independent, it's stronger than the picture. I conceive it this way.' Then he would compose the music again, and he always got it the second time.... For instance, he had composed wonderful music for the pole vault and javelin. But it didn't fit the image, it was wonderful music. I was very unhappy, because I could not compose. I said, 'Herbert, I don't know, it must have more tension, and be quieter,' and so on. And then he did it. But the melodies are all from him.[72]

Of special significance to the Olympic film was the fact that Windt had composed the marathon music to accompany the German radio broadcast of the marathon. This music was composed as an experiment, and importantly, it indicates the direction of Windt's musical thinking:

> The Marathon, the greatest athletic event of the Olympic Games, was to obtain for broadcasting an unusual frame to meet the importance of the sporting event. It was originally intended to add dramatic scenes from former Marathons to the large number of commentaries as the intervals between each in the two hours of the race could be gauged in advance. But then the eye-witness accounts would have been in direct competition with the prepared word and this would only have delayed the action. It was therefore decided to arrange for music, an orchestral suite, to frame the commentaries instead of word pictures. Herbert Windt was chosen as composer. After the revolution he proved himself one of the most important musicians for film and broadcasting and only recently achieved extraordinary success with his musical composition "The Flight to the Niederwald."
>
> Herbert Windt had several months in which to complete his work. The task would have been easy if he had illustrated in an orchestral suite the events to be expected: The rapid start, the fight, the tiring, collapse and victory. Instead of wasting an abundance of harmonies and chords the composer contented himself with a few themes which he wound to-

> gether in counterpoint and always repeated. He arranged his composition in three movements, a short scherzo for the beginning, and an unending, occasionally slow, occasionally rapid phase portraying the rhythm of running, then a short victorious, imposing finale. It was decisive that one single rhythm impressed the whole, the rhythm of running, that never stopped and that kept together the themes which were often harmonically unrecognisable.
>
> After the start of the marathon the programme organisers only had the task to change, in the right moment, from the first movement of the music into the great suite of uninterrupted running and to start the progressive and nearly breathless finale of the music at the proper moment. It was also necessary to see that the commentaries were set in at the correct place, for in each case, the music had to lift the last word of the speaker and carry it on.
>
> This succeeded astonishingly well. The listeners assisted at [sic] the Marathon in its greatness and unendingness, in its battle and its decision, as at one great and uninterrupted dramatic happening. It was certainly a chance happening that the collapse of the former marathon victor Zabala found exciting and even terrible expression in the music immediately after. But this is only proof that the audacious attempt of a combination of reality and art was completely successful.[73]

Windt adapted the original radio music to the marathon sequence in the film. In the music for the marathon event, Windt's desire was not to accompany a sporting event with dramatic music but to merge the sporting event, with its own narrative structure, to a definite tripartite musical form that imposed its own logic and order on the event.

The marathon music is particularly striking during the last section of the running as the athletes become exhausted. The music was supposed to provide a counterpoint to the growing fatigue of the runners. Windt described it as follows:

> Leni Riefenstahl had also produced shots that were shot from the heads of runners [the famous basket shots], so that the spectator, as it were, sees with the eyes of the runners. His view goes out over the

> ground, his legs fly unceasingly forward--under them the earth rushes behind. In these pictures, Leni Riefenstahl was able to create dramatically that condition that sets in after so many kilometers in every long distance run: exhaustion! His legs become heavier, his rhythm slower, his gait more sluggish, his image more oppressive. But the music does not accompany the sequence of events happening to his body. On the contrary, it, the music of the runner, his mood, his flight of ideas, his spirit, his will, his driving idea, elevates itself over the body which begins to tire, flies before him, and pulls the body further on. Here was a magnificent success in forming a dramatic counterpoint of body and spirit as a thrilling experience.[74]

This is one example of the ambitions that Windt had for the score to the film. His success is arguable, but there is no doubt that Windt's music is vital to the impression which _Olympia_ left on the viewer.

Windt was not the only composer heard in the film. The Olympic fanfare of Paul Winter was heard in part one, Richard Strauss' "Olympic Hymn" was used twice, and the music Walter Gronostay composed for the _Werkfilm_ also turned up accompanying the polo sequence in part two. Gronostay wrote the music for the pentathlon riding event after Windt became exhausted. Werner Egk had written an Olympic festival piece. According to Riefenstahl, some of this music was also used; still, the major musical contributor to the film was Herbert Windt. He started work on the score late in 1937.

On Sunday, January 9, 1938, a large part of Windt's score was recorded, including the torchbearing sequence and the opening and closing music for parts one and two. A large mass chorus of 340 persons, the Kittelsche Choir, recorded a long and short version of Strauss' "Olympic Hymn," as well as the choral music that Windt had written for the dying out of the Olympic flame at the closing ceremonies. The orchestra was the Berlin Philharmonic, and the recording was done at Philharmonic Hall.

The session began at four in the afternoon. Tobis had set up three recording machines and seven microphones. Professor Kittel was to direct his choir, but the overall authority was vested in Sigi Schultz, the head sound man for the film. In the entrance vestibule of Philharmonic Hall, a portable viewing area had been set up, with projection by Ufa. This allowed Riefenstahl, her composers and the sound men to view the film simultaneously with the recording of the music. In that way, they could immediately check juxtaposition of the film sequence and score. Numerous repetitions were necessary. It was established that the microphones were particularly sensitive to some of the high notes of the women singers and that their parts had to be diminished in volume. As always in a recording situation, the balance between the choir and the orchestra had to be carefully regulated.[75]

The singers took a short break for refreshments. When they returned, everything sounded hard and shrill. The hall had become colder, causing a change in acoustics. There were other problems. In one sequence, the music appeared to be a few beats too short. After some show of temperament, the problem was quickly solved. Windt seemed pleased with the session, and he stressed the importance of its success:

> This is one of my most important days for recording music. If it doesn't come off, the results would be particularly serious, because the Philharmonic is going on a tour. We are recording very important parts of the music today.[76]

He did not want to be too specific about his music yet:

> I still have thirty minutes to record, then we'll hear.... It is a quite novel 'sport/music' that we will be introduced to, music-drama when it must be, frivolous-courageous when the situation permits (as in the Olympic Village), or sometimes scarcely noticeable, like an unconscious thought, only just 'there' among the sounds, speaking chorus, and the 'music' of the pictures themselves.[77]

By the end of the year, Dr. Goebbels appeared to be reconciled with Riefenstahl. He wrote in his diary:

> November 26, 1937
> In the evening, dinner with the Führer for the Hungarians. I explain to the Führer about the Olympic film of Leni Riefenstahl. He is very happy that

> it is such a success. We want to do something in order to prepare a small token of esteem. She has earned it. She has renounced fame and recognition for so long.[78]

One wonders if Goebbels was being sarcastic. In any case, the entry indicates that Dr. Goebbels knew what the film looked like and that he was keeping tabs on the cutting of the film. And while Goebbels often went away from talks with Hitler with his ideas turned completely around, this entry indicates that Goebbels was telling Hitler that the film was first-rate.

On December 22, 1937, Dr. Goebbels had another meeting with Hitler, and they discussed the film. Dr. Goebbels' diary reads as follows:

> Both Olympic films to be premiered at the same time at the beginning of February. Plan in grand style.[79]

It can be verified that, about this time, the Propaganda Ministry imposed a ban on reporting on the film. This may have been prompted by delays in finishing the film, or by internal problems that might have made Dr. Goebbels fearful of having the press build the film up too soon, or perhaps by Goebbel's wish to censor the film's content. The ban was extended many times. At the press conference on January 4, 1938, it was announced:

> <u>Directive no. 12</u>
> The ban on reporting the Olympic film is extended until January 31. The world premiere will take place around February 15. The propaganda for this film should begin 14 days before the world premiere.[80]

Then on January 24, 1938:

> <u>Directive no. 133</u>
> The premiere of the Olympic film is again postponed, and certainly until the first and second of March. The ban is extended for the press until February 15.[81]

On February 12, 1938, the ban was further extended, although several illustrated magazines, including the <u>Stuttgarter Il-</u>

lustrierte and the Kölnische Illustrierte Zeitung, had already produced articles that could not be withdrawn.[82]

The date for the premiere was postponed until mid-March, but on March 18, 1938, at the press briefing, the Propaganda Ministry announced:

> Directive No. 385.
> No word should be written about the Olympic film. The world premiere has been postponed until more politically calm times.[83]

This directive was amplified verbally:

> No word should be uttered about the Olympic film; in addition the premiere is again postponed. The film is supposed to have been shown to a small circle already and has provoked a lively enthusiasm, but at this time other things are in the foreground. There is nothing more to be done on the film, but it is said to be too beautiful for its premiere to take place among the events happening at this time.[84]

What the directive referred to were the events taking place in Austria. For quite some time, the German government had been increasing pressure on Austria. For all intents and purposes, the Austrian government had been asked to give itself over to German control. In desperation, Dr. Kurt von Schuschnigg, the Austrian Chancellor, called for a plebiscite. The Austrian people would choose whether it wished Austrian unification with Germany and cessation of independence.

When Hitler heard of the proposed plebiscite, he decided to act immediately. On March 10, 1938, the border between Germany and Austria was closed; German troops massed on the border. On March 11, Goering presented ultimatums to the Austrian government, which, under duress, were finally accepted. The new law proclaiming Hitler the president of Austria was presented to the Austrians on Sunday, the thirteenth of March. It was the end of an independent Austria, and on March 14, Hitler made his triumphal entry into Vienna.

He spent the next four weeks whipping up public support for another plebiscite. The question was whether the German and Austrian people approved of the Anschluss, the annexation of Austria into the Reich. With the propaganda facilities of both countries at his disposal, and with German and Austrian National Socialists manning the polling stations, he certainly did not need to worry about the results. An enormous campaign was launched by the Propaganda Ministry, and the German film industry was also asked to do its bit. The Film-Kurier ran a long article by Riefenstahl in favor of saying Ja on April 10, the day of the referendum:

> Years ago the Führer said once, if the artists knew what great tasks were reserved to them in a more beautiful Germany, they would come to the movement with greater enthusiasm. Today every artist knows just as it has become clear to every fellow German: reality yields more than even artistic fantasy can imagine. Greater Germany has become a reality; we have seen it grow from year to year with increasing certainty and emotion. The creator of Greater Germany is at the same time its most artistic man.
>
> With warm hearts, we greet our Austrian brothers into the Reich. Valuable new energies flow from them as well as to the artistic will and struggle in Germany.
>
> The greatest of German days of destiny, on which the Führer freed his homeland, worked a miracle on all of us. Time after time the voice of the Führer has called to us, 'Begin!' during these years, and time after time the artists obeyed the call to fall into the troops of millions in order to declare their allegience to the Führer and his deeds for Germany's freedom, honor and greatness. The vote on the tenth of April will be a unanimous affirmation of our Führer Adolf Hitler.[85]

But to the rest of the world, the decision to seize Austria by force signalled precisely how aggressive Germany had become. In 1936, there were a large number of foreigners who were active supporters of Germany. In 1937, as German rearmament became more and more a threat, these people were still vocal in their support, but they were becoming more defensive. With the annexation of Austria, Germany inspired increasing fear and dislike. The feeling continued to grow during 1938. Some politicians still may have wished to appease Germany, but there were fewer and fewer real pro-Germans internationally. This trend was to have a profound effect on the future of the Olympic film.

While the Propaganda Ministry was postponing the premiere of Olympia and making plans for the future of the film, Riefenstahl was shipping a copy of the film out of Germany to Hubert Stowitts in southern California. A month before the official German premiere of the film, Olympia was being run--for the benefit of athletic teams--in the back rooms of sports clubs in America. On March 5, 1938, Stowitts wrote:

> On April 1st I am showing Leni Riefenstahl's Epic of the Olympia Games as a Charity Benefit at the Ebell Club Theatre. On March 13th I am showing it at the Jonathan Club, a dinner at which twenty Olympic Champions will be guests at my table. The film is breathtaking in its beauty, and I have the only copy being shown anywhere. It has not yet been released even abroad.[86]

He wrote Joseph Paget-Fredericks on April 17, 1938 that he was trying to arrange showings at the Town House and at the Bohemian Club in San Francisco and that the showing at the Wilshire Ebell Club had been a great success.[87] Evidently, Stowitts had a 35mm print, without sound or at least without narration, because he was giving his own commentary at the showings. Stowitts also arranged a showing of the film at the Ross Auditorium in San Diego under the auspices of the Junior Chamber of Commerce for the benefit of the new San Diego track team. On Saturday, May 21, 1938, he showed the film at a matinee and evening performance at the San Diego Athletic Club for the benefit of the track team.[88] Clearly, even before Adolf Hitler had seen the film, it had received a wide showing in front of sports groups in the California area.

Riefenstahl may have had several reasons for sending Stowitts a print of the film. First, she may have been afraid of a Hollywood boycott against distribution of the film and was trying to develop early interest in the project. Second, if she was afraid of Propaganda Ministry censorship of the film, sending Stowitts a copy was a sure way of saving at least one complete print. Third, she had developed very close ties to many of the American athletes, and she may have wanted to give them the first chance to see the film. In any case, it speaks much about the close relationship between Stowitts and Riefenstahl that she had entrusted him with a copy of the film for his own road show even before the film was shown to Adolf Hitler and the German Party elite.

In Germany the ban on reporting ended, and a major press campaign ensued. A series of articles appeared in which Riefenstahl described the process of cutting the film in extremely general terms. Because the film had not been released sooner, she sounded defensive in many of these articles. In this writer's estimation, the articles did not provide very effective propaganda. They all harped on similar issues and almost forced the reader to wonder why it took two years to cut a film. But at least Riefenstahl was again being written about.

If, as Ernst Jäger had stated, von Tschammer und Osten had wanted to have Riefenstahl removed as director of the Olympic film, it appears that by April, 1938, he had seen the error of his ways. To make publicity more effective, he issued a statement that appeared in the Tobis press book and was widely printed:

> Just in the year when we stand before the N.S. competitive games in Nuremberg and above all before the accomplishment of the German Gymnastic and Sports Festival of Breslau in 1938, the most meaningful national festival of track and field in the world in terms of extensiveness and performance, I salute the Olympic film, which re-awakens the memory of August 1936 and its events.
>
> I expect from the Olympic film a new wave of enthusiasm for the deeds and the success of German sports people. I expect from it a deepening of the understanding of my work by all who experienced those days in Berlin, and a dissemination to all those who will now see what up to now could only be imparted to them by other means. I especially expect that the German youth, renewed and strengthened, will answer the call of the Olympic bell and help us carry the call from generation to generation.
>
> I expect all this with certainty, because I know that the film, through the singular performance of its creatress, is a unique document, not only because of the up-to-then greatest achievements in international sports, but also far beyond this, a song of songs of human spirit and affirmation of life.[89]

On the eve of the premiere, the press section of the Propaganda Ministry issued an odd directive to the press. It read as follows:

> Herr Bade on the Olympic Film: The film will be released (tomorrow) in a particularly festive fashion, and certainly both parts. In three weeks, the first part and later the second part will be released publicly. On the grounds of saving time, tomorrow, the second part will be missing the decathlon, since track and field is already extensively covered in the first part. In the regular showing, the decathlon will of course be seen. One should therefore come to no false conclusions. Tomorrow, it would also be best that, above all, the overall impression of the premiere be reported and to report at length only about the first part; one should treat the second part in a detailed fashion only when it appears regularly in theaters. The review of the film should be disseminated from the sports-and filmic point of view and, as said, in the first reports, be limited to general impressions.[90]

It is difficult to understand this directive in any way other than the Propaganda Ministry was not happy with part two and was planning cuts. The instructions were significant. If any section of the film shows blatant tampering for propaganda purposes, it is the cutting of the decathlon.

Riefenstahl explained the numerous delays in the release of the film:

> After the finishing of the Olympic Film in February, 1938, there were again difficulties with Dr. Goebbels. First the world premiere was again and again postponed, so that the finished film had to remain sitting for two months. Then the last obstacle came, the censorship. L. R. knew that there was a dangerous hurdle here, since censorship was under the authority of Dr. Goebbels, and the censor's cuts would radically change the form of the Olympic film. To escape this, since L. R., with reason, was afraid for her 'black athletes', she let her copy be cut to bits again and again, and made up excuses until the premiere so that she succeeded in the seemingly impossible task of showing both Olympic films uncensored at the premiere. In addition, neither Hitler nor Dr. Goebbels had seen a meter of this film before this premiere. After the great success of this premiere,

> at which the foreign press was in attendance, it was no longer possible for Dr. Goebbels to demand a cut version.[91]

However, Germans generally did not have access to foreign papers and so would not have read about the premiere. Furthermore, newspapers do not generally go into a great deal of detail about film premieres. So Dr. Goebbels still could have made cuts if he wished to do so; the films were not to have been released publicly for another three weeks.

Some evidence does exist of last minute cuts. Many stills from the film, as well as press books and some posters, show an exhibition of mass gymnastics and part of the dance festival that were to have been included in Fest der Schönheit. One picture of dancers forming Olympic rings is particularly prominent. Yet, as far as I know, this particular sequence has been cut from every film version, including the long German one.

I can think of no reason, however, why these particular sequences would have bothered the Propaganda Ministry. One possible explanation for cutting the dance festival was that it was a special brainstorm of Dr. Diem and made a rather strong antiwar statement. But it is difficult to see why the mass gymnastics exhibition would have been cut. Ironically, a still of the men's gymnastics exhibition is often used as an example of the fascist regimentation in Riefenstahl's film--even though the sequence was not included. Why these cuts were made remains a mystery. Perhaps the film was seen as being too long.

Another reason for last minute cuts or minor amendments could have been the increasing German pressure on Czechoslovakia. As a result of the annexation of Austria, Czechoslovakia now stood partially enveloped by a pair of jaws: On the south lay what had been Austria; on the north was Germany. Almost as soon as Austria had fallen, Hitler had increased the pressure on Czechoslovakia for the return of the Sudetenland. Propaganda stories of the ill-treatment of the German minority in Czechoslovakia increased, and the German press started an anti-Czech campaign. The military was already preparing plans for the invasion of that unfortunate country. Although the Czechs had done rather well in gymnastics and canoeing, they were virtually ignored in the film. However, whether mention of Czechoslovakia was deleted as a result of last-minute editing is not known.

On April 20, 1938, Adolf Hitler's forty-ninth birthday, the Olympic film was premiered in his presence. The showing must have been one of the major triumphs in Riefenstahl's life. Dr. Goebbels had prepared the premiere and had written that preparations for the premiere were to be carried out on a grand scale. They were indeed. The Ufa-Palast am Zoo in Berlin, the theater often used for major premieres, was specially decorated by the architect Franz Pöcher. The blood-red swastika banners alternated with the white Olympic flags and their golden rings. Searchlights played over the whole facade. Pöcher had also had constructed two large towers decorated with laurel wreaths, and on the connecting wall between them could be seen, in huge letters, the names of the two films, Fest der Völker and Fest der Schönheit. The event was to start at seven at night.[92]

Hitler had already spent a busy day. At ten o'clock that morning, he had attended the march past of the SA regiment "Feldernhalle," one of the few military units in the SA. (The SA would soon be incorporated into the Luftwaffe and would go into action fully armed during the entry into the Sudetenland.) At eleven, he was at a huge army parade before the University. The parade was led by the Austrian (now German) First Infantry regiment from Linz (Hitler's birthplace). The new militancy was certainly in the air.

Shortly before seven in the evening, the festivities began. An honor company of the SS-Leibstandarte Adolf Hitler stationed themselves in front of the theater. Car after car stopped there. Riefenstahl arrived and was greeted by the general director of Tobis, Herr Lehman, who escorted her to her loge. Hitler arrived just before seven. He inspected the honor guard, and escorted by Dr. Goebbels, entered the theater. As he entered, the entire audience--whether arrayed in uniform or in full evening dress--rose and applauded. Almost every prominent person in pre-war National Socialist Berlin was in attendance, and it was perhaps the last time that such a group could have been assembled.

The entire diplomatic corps had sent delegations. The Ambassadors from Italy, France, Turkey, Chile, Brazil, Argentina, Great Britain, Spain, Japan, and the United States of America were there. The envoys of Lithuania, Czechoslovakia, Switzerland, Greece, Ireland, Finland, Portugal, Uruguay, the Union of South Africa, Iraq, Afghanistan, Yugoslavia, Hungary, Belgium, Estonia, Panama, Sweden, the Netherlands, Guatemala, Venezuela, Iran, Siam, and the *chargés d' affaires* of the Dominican Republic, Colombia, Cuba, Peru, Rumania, Egypt, Denmark, Bulgaria, and Luxemburg were also present.

In Hitler's box could be found Reich Sport Leader and State Secretary von Tschammer und Osten, who had the seat of honor, Dr. Goebbels, Dr. Frick, von Ribbentrop, Funk, Reich Press Chief Dr. Dietrich, State Secretaries Hanke and Pfundtner, SA-Obergruppenführer Brückner, and SS-Gruppenführer Schaub.

Countless other high-ranking Party members sat in the surrounding boxes. They included the president of the Secret Cabinet Council, Freiherr von Neurath; the Reich Ministers, Dr. Gürtner, Count Schwerin von Krosigk, Dr. Frank, Darré, Rust, Kerrl, Dr. Dorpmüller, Dr. Ohnesorge; the head of the Reich Chancellery, Reich Minister Lammers; the head of the Presidial Chancellery, State Minister Meissner; the *Reichsleiters*; the Hitler youth leader, Baldur von Schirach; the Staff Chief of the SA, Lutze; the Reichsführer SS Heinrich Himmler; the National Socialist Motorcycle Corps leader Hühnlein; the inspector-general for German Roads, Dr. Todt; General Architectural Inspector, Albert Speer; the president of the Reich Tourist Office, State Minister Esser; the president of the Reich Film Chamber, Dr. Lehnich; the Reich representatives in the States; the Gauleiters Streicher, Lohse, Forster, Bohle, Stürtz, Joseph Wagner; the Reich Women's leader, Frau Scholtz-Klink; the Mayor of Berlin, Dr. Lippert; SS-Gruppenführer, Sepp Dietrich; SS-Gruppenführer, Heydrich; and the chief of police, General Daluege.

The military was also represented. Among these were *Generaladmiral* Raeder, the head of the high command of the Wehrmacht; General of Artillery, Keitel; Luftwaffe generals, Milch and Kesselring; Infantry General, von Witzleben; Panzer General, Guderian; Infantry Generals, Liebmann and Adam; and Artillery General, Dr. Becker.

The newly annexed Austria was also represented by Dr. Arthur Seyss-Inquart and the other officials of the new government, as well as by chief of the Political Section, Dr. Rainer.

With the advantage of hindsight, it is difficult to read this list without shuddering. In a few years, this group of people would mostly be dead or in the dock at Nuremberg and charged with the perpetration of war crimes. More than a few of the guests attending the premiere knew of Hitler's plans for Czechoslovakia; it must have been strange for them to watch a film ostensibly dedicated to the youth of the world. On the other hand, one wonders how many of them were capable of grasping the irony.

The various Olympic committees were also well represented. The IOC members present were Artillery General von Reichenau, Duke Adolf Friedrich von Mecklenburg, Ritter von Halt, and von Rosen of Sweden. Also present were the ten directors of the Organization Committee, as well as all members of the German Olympic Commission. All the German winners of gold, silver, or bronze medals, some 239 of them, were in the theater.

A number of prominent film persons were also in attendance, including Reich Film Advisor von Demandowsky, the vice president of the Reich Film Chamber Weidemann, the producer Karl Melzer, as well as many other prominent leaders in the industry. Many stars of the industry also showed up: Lilian Harvey, Lida Baarova, Luise Ullrich, Jenny Jugo, Marianne Hoppe, Maria Paudler, Hilde Weissner, Hilde Körber, Generalintendant Gründgens, Willy Fritsch, Harald Paulsen, Mathias Wiemann, and Anny Ondra, accompanied by her husband, boxer Max Schmeling, who was a celebrity because of his bouts with Joe Louis.

Before the film commenced, the music corps of the Leibstandarte Adolf Hitler played the Olympic fanfares while a fire blazed within a pedestal on the theater stage. Then, under the baton of Herbert Windt, the Berlin Philharmonic played Marathonlauf 1936, which was dedicated to Kitei Son.

When the film was shown, the audience reacted favorably. Hitler himself led the applause at the end of part one; he pressed Riefenstahl's hand and thanked her. At the end of part two, he presented Riefenstahl with a bouquet of white lilacs and red roses. By order of the Crown Prince of Greece and the president of the Greek Olympic Committee, the Greek envoy presented Riefenstahl with a twig from an olive tree; the twig had been taken from the sacred grove at Mount Olympus.[93]

It was a premiere that would make any producer in Hollywood twitch with envy. (The great David Selznick got only the mayor of Atlanta for his Gone with the Wind.) With this kind of publicity behind the film, and the complete endorsement of the regime, the film was bound to do well in Germany. Dr. Goebbels ordered every paper to give the opening extensive page-one coverage, and this was done.[94] The entire state mechanism was thrown behind the film.

It must have seemed to Riefenstahl that her problems were over. The film still had to return a profit, but it had an excellent chance of doing so. She had more than delivered the goods in spite of the preceding eighteen months of frustration and very hard work. She was the most prominent film maker in Germany and enjoyed the personal favor of Adolf Hitler. Nothing could go wrong now.

On the next day, however, Hitler did not have the peaceful competition of nations on his mind. He was making plans that would affect Riefenstahl's future as well as the future of all Germans, and ultimately, the future of the whole world. On April 21, 1938, he conferred with General Keitel at the Reich Chancellery to prepare concrete directives for Case Green--the invasion of Czechoslovakia.[95]

NOTES

1. "Leni Riefenstahls Rede in Paris," Film-Kurier, 5 July 1937, p. 2.
2. Jäger, "Hitler's Girlfriend," Part V, p. 13.
3. Lynn Garafola, "The Odyssey of Hubert Stowitts," an unpublished manuscript, a copy of which is in the possession of the author. Ms. Garafola graciously shared copies of the letters that Stowitts wrote to his mother and to Joseph Paget-Fredericks in reference to Riefenstahl.
4. Hubert Stowitts to Blanche Stowitts, 19 September 1936, Stowitts Family Collection.
5. Hubert Stowitts to Joseph Paget-Fredericks, 12 November 1936, Joseph Paget-Fredericks collection, Bancroft

Library, University of California, Berkeley.

6. Willy Otto Zielke, interview with author held at Bad Pyrmont, Germany, 18 May 1983, p. 5.

7. Ibid., pp. 5-6

8. Ibid., pp. 6-7. Incidentally, Zielke reports that Riefenstahl was not one of the nudes he photographed at the Kurischer Nehrung.

9. Ibid., p. 10.

10. Ibid., p. 10.

11. Ibid., p. 11.

12. "Filmburg auf der Nehrung hinter Stacheldraht," Preussische Zeitung, 17 September 1936.

13. Jäger, "Hitler's Girlfriend," part V, p. 13.

14. Riefenstahl, "Ein Bericht über die Herstellung der Olympia-Filme," p. 6.

15. Jäger, "Hitler's Girlfriend," part V, p. 13.

16. An allusion to Goethe's Götz von Berlichingen, in which the challenge "Leck mich am Arsch! (Lick my ass!)" was used.

17. Riefenstahl, "Ein Bericht über die Herstellung der Olympia-Filme," p. 7.

18. Goebbels Tagebuch, 18 September 1936, BA, Nachlass Goebbels, NL 118/63 (1936), Fol. 1, p. 214.

19. Riefenstahl, "Ein Bericht über die Herstellung der Olympia-Filme," p. 7.

20. Sammlung Brammer, 4 January 1938, vol. 11, p. 3.

21. Riefenstahl, "Ein Bericht über die Herstellung der Olympia-Filme," p. 7.

22. "Bericht über die in der Zeit vom 3. bis 8. Oktober 1936 stattgefunden Kassen- und Rechnungsprüfung bei der Olympia-Film G.m.b.H." RMVP, BA R55/503, pp. 1-30.

23. Ibid., pp. 8-14.

24. Hans Barkhausen, "Footnote to the History of Riefenstahl's Olympia," citing BA R55/503, p. 48.

25. Goebbels Tagebuch, 25 October 1936, p. 251.

26. RMVP, BA, R55/503, p. 30.

27. Ibid., p. 48.

28. Goebbels Tagebuch, 6 November 1936, pp. 268-269.

29. Riefenstahl, "Ein Bericht über die Herstellung der Olympia-Filme," pp. 7-8.

30. Report of the RMVP to the Finance Ministry dated 25 January 1937, Reichsfinanzministerium, BA, R2/4754, p. 211.

31. Goebbels Tagebuch, 21 February 1937, NL 118/64 fol. 1, p. 75.

32. Riefenstahl, "Ein Bericht über die Herstellung der Olympia-Filme," p. 7.

33. Weigel, "Interview mit Leni Riefenstahl," p. 403.

34. Ibid., pp. 403-404.

35. Ibid., p. 401.

36. Riefenstahl, Interview with author, p. 18-19.

37. Ibid., p. 20.

38. Mannheim, "Leni", p. 114.

39. Ibid., p. 116.

40. Der deutsche Film, vol. 1, 1937, pp. 74-77.

41. Willy Otto Zielke, interview, p. 13.

42. Leni Riefenstahl, interview with author.

43. Mannheim, "Leni," p. 114.

44. RMVP, BA R55/503, p. 52.

45. Ibid., p. 156.

46. "Der Olympia-Vorfilm: Immer wieder Interesse in Paris," Film-Kurier, 7 September 1937, pp. 3-4.

47. Otto D. Tolischus, "Reich Shows Uses of Its Materials," New York Times, 9 May 1937, p. 33.

48. P. J. Philip, "Paris Exposition Is Inaugurated; Most of Buildings Uncompleted," New York Times, 25 May 1937, p. 29.

49. "La Disgrâce de Leni Riefenstahl," Paris-Soir, 14 June 1937, p. 1.

50. Goebbels Tagebuch, 16 June 1937, p. 240.

51. Sammlung Brammer, Bundesarchiv, Zsg 101/9/15 June 1937.

52. Sammlung Sänger, Bundesarchiv, Zsg. 102/5/15 June 1937, p. 385.

53. "Lügen über Leni Riefenstahl," Film-Kurier, 16 June 1937, p. 1.

54. Jäger, "Hitler's Girlfriend," part V. p. 13.

55. Goebbels Tagebuch, 1937, p. 400. This entry is dated August 13, 1937, in the version typed from Dr. Goebbel's original handwritten entries, but this entry is followed by the words "in d. Reihenfolge der Fotokopien." It would appear that the compiler interpolated the date incorrectly since Heinrich Hoffman's photographs were published by 2 July 1937.

56. "Ovationen unter dem Eiffelturm," Film-Kurier, 3 July 1937, p. 1.

57. "Die Ansprache Dr. Lehnichs," Film-Kurier, 3 July 1937, p. 1.

58. "Parteitag-Film in Paris," Film-Kurier, 5 July 1937, p. 1.

59. Riefenstahl, "Ein Bericht über die Herstellung der

Olympia-Filme," p. 3.

60. Ibid.

61. Paul Laven, "Neue Sprechkunst beim Olympia-film: Der Sprecher als 'Star'," Olympia: Fest der Völker, erstes Presseheft, p. 61.

62. Leni Riefenstahl, "Kraft und Schönheit der Jugend mögen filmische Form gefunden haben," Film-Kurier, 31 December 1937.

63. Mannheim, "Leni," p. 117.

64. Riefenstahl, interview with author, p. 11.

65. Ibid., p. 34.

66. Weigel, "Interview mit Leni Riefenstahl," p. 404.

67. Michel Delahaye, "Leni and the Wolf," Cahiers du Cinéma in English, no. 5, p. 54.

68. Riefenstahl, interview with author, p. 11-12.

69. Walter Gronostay, "Deutsche Filmmusiker: III. Herbert Windt," Der deutsche Film, 1937, vol. 1, p. 316.

70. Ibid.

71. Hans Alex Thomas, Die deutsche Tonfilmmusik von den Anfangen bis 1956 (Gutersloh: C. Bertelsmann Verlag, 1962), p. 139.

72. Riefenstahl, interview with author, p. 16.

73. "The Marathon-Race as a Musical-Dramatic Event," Olympia-Weltsender (Berlin: Deutscher Verlag für Politik und Wirtschaft, [193-]), p. 90.

74. "Musikalische Pionierleistungen im Olympia-Film," Olympia : Fest der Völker, the first pressbook published by Tobis, p. 59.

75. "Philharmoniker spielen Filmmusik," Film-Kurier, 10 January 1938, p. 3.

76. Ibid.

77. Ibid.

78. Goebbels Tagebuch, 26 November 1937.

79. Mannheim, "Leni," p. 117.

80. Sammlung Brammer, vol. 11, p. 3.

81. Ibid., p. 49.

82. Sammlung Sänger, 12 February 1938, vol. 8., p. 106; "Illustrierte Presse über den Olympia-Film," Licht Bild Bühne, 22 February 1938, p. 1.

83. Sammlung Brammer, 18 March 1938, vol. 11, p. 217.

84. Sammlung Sänger, 18 March 1938, vol. 9, p. 68.

85. "Leni Riefenstahl zum 10. April," Film-Kurier, 9 April 1938, p. 3.

86. Hubert Stowitts to Joseph Paget-Fredericks, 5 March 1938, Joseph Paget-Fredericks Collection.

87. Ibid.

88. Ibid.

89. Licht Bild Bühne, 14 April 1938, p. 1, citing press book for Fest der Völker, p. 11.

90. Sammlung Sänger, Vol. 11, 19 April 1938, p. 49.

91. Riefenstahl, "Ein Bericht über die Herstellung der Olympia-Filme," p. 9.

92. "Begeisterte Aufnahme des Olympia-films", Film-Kurier, 21 April 1938, p. 1.

93. Ibid.

94. "Rundrufe vom 21.4.38," Sammlung Brammer, vol. 11, p. 301.

95. Domarus, Hitler, Reden und Proklamationen, vol. 1, p. 633.

• CHAPTER V •

THE HISTORY OF THE FILM AFTER ITS RELEASE

Writing the history of a film is usually comparatively easy. The film is made, it is released, it either makes or loses money, it is retired from circulation, and--if the film makers are lucky--one or two copies of it go into archives so that the film is not forgotten. But this was not the fate of Olympia, which was not only a film but a major propaganda event of the Reich. All over Europe for almost a year after its world premiere, it was presented with much pomp. Then history caught up with it. As relations with Germany worsened in 1939, the film was no longer warmly welcomed. While the war was going on and Germany was fighting most of the nations portrayed in the film, its circulation was limited.

Peace did not make the film less controversial. Riefenstahl was accused of being sympathetic to the National Socialist regime; Olympia shared this onus then as it does even now.

One of the reasons Olympia remains an issue to film historians in a way that many other films of the National Socialist period do not is that it is too good to be ignored. Karl Ritter's films can be dismissed as pure propaganda, and Heinz Ruhmann's films can usually be classified as pure entertainment, even if they were made in 1938, but Olympia cannot be categorized so easily. Because it cannot be categorized, and because of its status as an art film, Olympia is a ghost that will not rest. Through the years, viewers' reactions to the film have changed in accordance with the times.

In addition, the film has changed. Five national versions existed before the war; even then Riefenstahl had made a de-Hitlerized version. Since those years, censors of various nations have cut the film, military authorities have censored it, motion picture companies, (by merely seizing it as enemy property) have made their own versions when the film was unprotected. Riefenstahl herself severely cut the film when it was re-edited in 1958 and had to be approved for showing by the German authorities. When somebody says he has seen Olympia, he should always be asked which print he has seen. A complete Olympia may not be in existence. The film's numerous editings reflect the political changes that have taken place in the world during the last fifty years, and many people who categorically state that the film is not political have not seen the long German version. Of those people who saw the version shown on Hitler's birthday in 1938 today probably less than forty are alive.

So the film's history after its release is not without interest. It tells us much about the illusions that sustained Europe as the war drew closer, and it also tells us much about Europe and the world after the war, when Olympia had already assumed the status of a relic from a previous barbaric age, like the Iron Maiden of Nuremburg or the Tower of London. This chapter will deal with the history of the film from its grand premiere to the present.

From April 1938 until the Munich crisis in October 1938, the film had an almost uninterrupted series of successes. The film and Riefenstahl were both acclaimed in virtually every country of Europe. Riefenstahl hobnobbed with royalty, dictators, and the celebrities of the continent, rather like the fabled opera singers and courtesans of the nineteenth century whose carriages were drawn through the streets by students and whose champagne was drunk from their slippers. The Europe she saw and toured on the film's behalf now seems to us as ancient and legendary as a fairy tale. Adolf Hitler would soon destroy it. But at the time, the European tour must have been exhilarating to Riefenstahl. She was the toast of Europe.

After Berlin, the next major premiere was in Munich, shortly after Hitler's birthday. Munich was the second most important city in Germany at the time; it was the official headquarters of the NSDAP, the largest city in southern Germany, and the capital of Bavaria, which was a stronghold for Hitler's followers. On Tuesday, April 26, the premiere took place under the auspices of Gauleiter Adolf Wagner. The showing began with the performance of three dances by the Gunther Dance Group under the leadership of Maja Lex. Then the film was screened. Present were Minister President Siebert, representative to Gauleiter Nippold; Reichleiter Oberbürgermeister, Fiehler; Bürgermeister, Dr. Tempel; SS-Obergruppenführer police president, Freiherr von Eberstein; SS-Gruppenführer, Schaub, Hitler's adjutant; General Schobert; Obergebietsführer, Klein; Generalarbeitsführer, Baumann; Reichshauptamtsleiter, Dr. Dressler; City Commander, Lieutenant Colonel von Mann; Gaupresseamtsleiter, Dr. Werner and many others. Numerous members of Riefenstahl's staff were there, including Herbert Windt, and Lieutenant-Colonel Paul Winter, whose Olympic fanfare was included in part one. In the place of honor sat the Olympic victors from the Gau of Munich and upper Bavaria, who were accompanied by the representative of the Reich, Party Leader Schneider.[1]

On the next day, April 27, Riefenstahl flew to Vienna. That evening, she gave a lecture at the Concert Hall entitled, "Film Making in the Service of an Idea." Part one of the film was premiered on Thursday, April 28.[2]

On May 1, 1938, Olympia was awarded the National Film Prize for 1937-1938, an indication of the film's importance to the regime.[3] No doubt the film was excellent, but it had had its premiere only ten days before and had not even been released to the general public. The more normal course of events would have been, in 1939, for it to have received the best film prize for 1938-1939. The reason for this rush can only be attributed to the wish to keep film propaganda rolling prior to the film's release in Germany and in Europe. These National Prizes were distributed on May Day, which the National Socialists had appropriated as the Day of German Labor. On May 1, 1938, Dr. Goebbels gave a speech on the importance of the arts. He made special mention of the Olympia film, and of Riefenstahl, who sat in the audience.[4] This was all recorded by the newsreel cameras, presumably to drum up additional publicity. In addition, Dr. Goebbels sent Riefenstahl a telegram on the occasion of the receipt of the National Prize:

> It is a special joy to me that the highest recognition for the outstanding achievement of the Olympic films Fest der Völker and Fest der Schönheit was awarded to you in the area of film for the year 1938. On this occasion, I wish to express my warmest and sincerest congratulations
>
> Heil Hitler
> Reich Minister Dr. Goebbels[5]

On the tenth of May, Olympia moved on to Zürich, where the premiere took place under the auspices of the Association of the Sport Reporters of Zürich. Riefenstahl was present and officially greeted by engineer R. Schlegel, the vice-president of the Swiss football and Athletic Association. Members of the diplomatic corp were present, representatives of the cantons and the city of Zürich, the heads of the sports leagues and 120 gentlemen of the press. There were over 1100 people in the Scala Theater. The press and public were enthusiastic.[6]

However, while Olympia went from capital to capital gathering critical acclaim and impressing the European public with the art and culture of new Germany, the international situation was worsening. In May of 1938, the second of the series of crises that were to happen with such awesome regularity in this year took place. This was the May Crisis over Czechoslovakia. On May 20, the skilled Czech Secret Service obtained indications of troop movements in Silesia and Saxony in eastern Germany. Czechoslovakia assumed that mobilization or even invasion was imminent. Germany denied that it had any such intent, but the Czechs were not mollified; the Germans had said precisely the same thing when they had mobilized against Austria only three months before. There was a crisis, and for once all of Czechoslovakia's allies stood firm against Germany. In addition, Russia was not expected to let Czechoslovakia be invaded. The Czechs mobilized. Hitler was furious, but he had no choice except to order the foreign office to advise the Czechs that Germany had no aggressive intentions against their country. This action was widely seen as a humbling of Germany, and Hitler never forgave Czechoslovakia. He was now bent on taking the country by force.

It is significant that Olympia was not released in Czechoslovakia in 1938. As far as this writer knows, it was the only country in Europe that did not receive the film. German films were still received regularly in Prague, and it is not known whether the Germans withheld the film, or whether the Czechs did not allow the film to run.

It was not until June 3, 1938 that part two of the film was finally released in Berlin to the general public. Film-Kurier explained the long delay of six weeks by saying, "The overwhelming success of the two films, that have meantime been awarded the National Prize, made a lengthening of the running time increasingly necessary." But the length of time needed to bring forth part two could also indicate that cuts had been made.

Fest der Völker was premiered in Athens on the occasion of the Greek Sports Week during the second week in June in Athens. The Greek Governor-Minister Kotzias sent the following telegram to Riefenstahl:

> After a truly triumphal showing, at which His Majesty the King, Their Majesties the crown Prince and Crown Princess Frederike and a thousand young Greek athletes were present, I wish to express to you my sincere thanks for the wonderful gift that you have sent to our athletes. I wish to convey to you also the effect of the really deep admiration that the whole public felt for the masterly filmic rendering of the classic Olympic idea. I most heartily congratulate you on the award of the Aristeon of Greek sports, which has the honor to express its appreciation for your marvellously beautiful achievement.[7]

On Monday, June 20, 1938, the second French-German Congress began in Baden-Baden. This congress was held under the auspices of the Comité France-Allemagne, a committee with an extremely shady past and an infamous future. It had been started in 1933 by Fernand de Brinon and Otto Abetz. De Brinon was a pro-German French journalist, and Otto Abetz was the chief German agent in Paris. De Brinon was shot after the war for collaboration, and Abetz was to become German ambassador to the Vichy government. The committee had been established to better French-German relations, but it was often used to launch National Socialist propaganda in France. The congress was held for the purpose of discussing the development of French and German cultural life, and, on June 22, Riefenstahl and Sacha Guitry discussed French and German film.[8]

On June 23, the French version of the film premiered in the presence of King Leopold of Belgium at the Palais des Beaux-Arts, the largest theater in Brussels. The other guests of honor included Minister President Spaak, Minister of the Interior Dierckx, Minister Marck, and Minister of Justice Tholien. In addition the King's Minister, Major Van den Heuvel, the Belgian Olympic Committee, and the diplomatic corps including the German envoy, Baron von Richtofen, were in attendance. Riefenstahl of course was present.

The film was shown under the auspices of the Front Sportif Belge, an organization whose purpose was to promote sport in Belgium. The chairman of the committee was State Minister Count Lippens, who was also president of the Belgium Olympic Committee. The proceeds of this showing went to the Front Sportif Belge. The film was well received, and the press was quite friendly.[9] Jäger reported later that King Leopold flirted outrageously with Riefenstahl.[10]

On the same day, on the evening before the celebration of the third anniversary of the Pro-German Stojadinovic Regime in Yugoslovakia, Fest der Völker premiered in the Urania-Theater in Belgrade. Numerous representatives from the regime and the court were present. The diplomatic corps was there, as well as many officers of the Yugoslavian army and air force. The Yugoslavian Olympic team attended, and Tobis was represented by Dr. Simon and the men of Tobis's subsidiary in Belgrad, Tesla-film. Germany was officially represented by its envoy to the court, Victor von Heeren, as well as by all other members of the legation, the Landesgruppenleiter of the NSDAP and the Yugoslav General Consul Frank Neuhausen. Again, the film was well received, but it was not the major event that it had been in Brussels, where both the king and Riefenstahl had been present.[11]

On July 1, part one of the film under its French title Les Dieux du Stade premiered at the Normandie in Paris. Riefenstahl was present, and a large gala was planned, although it was not reported in any detail by the French or German press. Riefenstahl gave a short speech to the French press, saying that the film was dedicated to Baron Pierre de Coubertin, the French founder of the modern Olympic Games, and that she hoped the film would please the French public.[12] Evidently it did. Licht Bild Bühne reported that the film had gotten extremely favorable reviews in both the left-wing and right-wing press.[13] Riefenstahl later compiled a list of the papers that had given the film good reviews. The list included Paris-Midi, Intransigeant, Le Jour, Liberté, L'Ordre, Le Figaro, Marianne, Action Française l'Effort, and Dupont Magazine.[14] The presence of certain names is no surprise. Intransigeant and Le Jour were extremely right-wing. Liberté was a fascist newspaper, run by Jacques Doriot and financed in Berlin. Action Française was a royalist paper edited by Charles Maurras, highly anti-Semitic and, by 1938, pro-National Socialist. A number of respectable papers with a large circulation, such as Le Figaro and Le Matin, which attracted a bourgeois readership, also gave the film very good reviews, but I am unable to find evidence that the left criticized the film favorably. This tends to verify the belief that propaganda is only effective if its audience is predisposed to believe it or at least has no strong feelings against it. It is not effective against crystalized opinion.

The same article in Licht Bild Bühne made some interesting comments on the propaganda victory that the film had achieved. It also gives an insight into the anxiety that the National Socialists were feeling about the Germans who had left Germany for Paris because of their opposition to the regime. In retrospect, it is hard to imagine how the émigrés could possibly have been regarded as a real threat to Hitler. They were a nuisance, at the most. However, Dr. Goebbels spent an excessive amount of time in the press denouncing the émigrés, and by doing so, calling attention to them. The regime treated them as if they were a personal insult:

> The result of the film's success dumbfounded the local émigrés and their yellow press, which in the face of the great triumph up to now, has found no better solution then to hush up the event. That the whole Parisian press from left to right, overpowered by the greatness of the showing and the unheard of achievement of its German creatress, would so glorify this film, which is National Socialist in the best sense of the word, had not been expected in these circles, and in the disappointment of these local atrocity-fairy tale manufacturers is a mixed strong frenzy over the uselessness of the now almost five-year long hate campaign. In the face of this penetrating document of our time from the new Germany, many a tissue of lies will in fact burst apart, and many foreigners will alter their fundamental ideas about the Third Reich.[15]

By July, it was clear that Olympia was a very big hit. The Propaganda Ministry noted that even the extremely hot weather of the summer did not deter people from seeing the film. It is difficult to establish how much the Olympic film had cost since every time new copies were run or a new version was made, these costs were added to the expenses of the company, but by this summer, it was generally established that the film had cost 2,350,000 RM, of which 1,800,000 RM had come from the Propaganda Ministry and 550,000 had come from the Film-Kredit Bank. Olympia was a very expensive film, but there was no doubt that the film was going to make a lot of money. By the end of September, part one had already run for twelve weeks in Paris and Riga and for eight weeks in Stockholm; it was playing to packed houses in nine countries.[16] Part two was only beginning to be exploited. Riefenstahl later estimated that the total receipts of the film were between seven and eight million RM.[17] The records of the Propaganda Ministry show gross receipts of over 6,000,000 RM a month during the first-run months of 1938, so this figure is probably correct. This meant that Riefenstahl's position would be strengthened when dealing with the Propaganda Ministry; henceforth, her requests were rarely turned down. Olympia was not only getting good reviews--it was good box office.

The Propaganda Ministry, however, did not get reimbursed quickly. The Olympia-Film GmbH was responsible for many of the costs of distributing the film, such as making trailers, making different language versions, and striking new copies--and it was already starting the production of short films. The result was that its overhead was extremely high and that it needed available cash. In addition, there were complaints that Tobis was withholding funds from the Olympia Company, a common dispute between a producing company and its distributor.[18] Olympia did not fully reimburse its creditors for quite some time.

On about July 20, a group arrived in Rome to start making the Italian version of the film. This group included Walter Traut, dialogue director Bartsch, sound man Hermann Storr, Johannes Lüdke, and Frau Steffen. All together, nine persons were involved in the making of the Italian version. They were working out of the synchronization section at Cinecittà. Two men who were active in Italian radio and had reported the Games to Italy from Berlin did most of the narration of the film. These were the reporters Carioso and Notari. As in the other versions, they would also be seen in the film because they had actually been in Berlin. Professor Nicolai, the chief of propaganda of the Italian Olympic Committee, was supervising the Italian text that would go with the film. In order to get a perfect dubbing, the group had brought along the 30,000 meters of sound recordings that Schulz and the others had gotten in Berlin. The Italian version was to be finished by the sixth of August so as to be ready for the Venice Film Festival.[19]

In late July and August, Riefenstahl went on a massive Scandinavian tour on behalf of the film. On July 31, in Copenhagen, a garden party and press reception were given in her honor. The first part of the Olympic film was to have its first run at the Grand Theater on the evening of Tuesday the second of August.[20]

The premiere in Copenhagen was another success, even though the film was shown not in the Grand Theater but in a hall with the unlikely name of the Odd Fellows Palais. The showing was presented under the auspices of his majesty Prince Axel, the Danish representative of the IOC. The committee in charge of the festivities included Mayor Dr. Ernst Kaper, member of the German Olympic committee in Berlin; Rear Admiral C. Carstensten; General Consul Svend Langkjär; Director Urban Gad; Chief editor of the _Berlingske Tidende_, Svend Aage Lund; and editor Jörgen Bast. After the premiere, the _Berlingske Tidende_, gave a huge banquet at the Royal Yacht Club, and Riefenstahl was toasted. On the next day, most of the Copenhagen newspapers gave _Fest der Völker_ extremely favorable reviews.[21]

Riefenstahl went on to Stockholm and Helsinki. On August 4, her plane landed at Bromma Airport at Stockholm, and an hour later, she was taken to a press reception at the Grand Hotel. She stated, possibly with some relief, that after the premiere at Helsinki, she was going to start work on _Penthesilea_. _Fest der Völker_ had been already running for six weeks in Stockholm; she was there to be awarded the Polar Order for her work on the film. The order had never before been awarded to a foreigner.[22]

In Helsinki, she attended yet another premiere. Among those invited were Field Marshal Mannerheim; Chief of Staff General Oesch; General Valve; Social Minister Fagriholm; Economic Minister Heikkinnen; and the president of the Olympic Committee, Krogius. Diplomatic representatives from Denmark,

England, Japan, Poland, Hungary, Brazil, Latvia, Rumania, and Italy were present. At the beginning of the performance, two Finnish athletes, Gunnar Hoeckert, the Olympic winner of the 5000-meter run, and Volmari Iso-Hollo, the bronze medalist in the 10,000-meter run, greeted Riefenstahl, who gave a short speech thanking everyone. The German envoy gave a tea in her honor following the performance.[23]

The next major premiere was at the Venice Film Festival. Part one was shown on August 26, 1938, with so much pomp and circumstance that it is hard to see how the jury would not have granted it some sort of prize. The press had already seen it at an advanced showing and described it in glowing terms, so the actual showing had long since been sold out. It appears that Dr. Lehnich, president of the Reich Film Chamber, had been doing some politicking on behalf of the film. The day before the premiere, Lehnich invited the major figures in the Italian film industry to a dinner at the Hotel Excelsior. Included were Count Volpi di Misurata, His Excellency Paulucci di Calboli Barone, and Dr. Benedetto Croce. Representing the Germans were the German consul in Venice, Hübner; Reich Section Leader Carl Neumann; Minister-Councillor Ernst Leichternstern; the business representative for the Reich Film Chamber, Karl Melzer; Curt Belling; engineer, Albert Göring; and representatives of Tobis and Olympia-Film GmbH. Tobis also had its press reception. Riefenstahl was present, giving numerous interviews. The groundwork had been carefully laid for the showing.

The evening of the presentation was a great success. The showing took place at the Palazzo del Cinema, and as in Berlin, the whole audience was in evening dress. As Riefenstahl appeared, everyone rose to greet her with loud applause. She was escorted to her place of honor by the Italian Minister for National Culture Alfieri, under whose auspices the gala had been given, and by Dr. Lehnich.

Among the guests were the German Ambassador in Rome, von Mackensen; the Duke of Genoa, His Excellence Paulucci de Calboli Barone; Count Volpi di Misurata; Head of Italian Film Production Freddi; the Secretary-General of the Italian Olympic Committee, General Vaccaro; Countess Ciano-Mussolini. Representing the Germans were Minister-Councillor Dr. Leichternstern; the German Consul in Venice Hübner, the business representative of the Reich Film Chamber; as well as representatives of the Fascist party leadership and the group leader of the NSDAP in Venice.[24]

After the performance, Dr. Lehnich gave a reception at the Hotel Excelsior for state VIP's as well as for the prominent film people who were in Venice for the festival. Telegrams were sent to Hitler, Mussolini, and Goebbels. The one to Hitler read:

> Impressed by the splendid progress of the premiere of the Olympic film at the film festival, that was a great success for Germany, we greet you and congratulate you.
>
> Alfierei, Volpi, Lehnich

The telegram to Mussolini read:

> The festival premiere of the Olympic film is a great success for Germany and also at the same time, for the film festival.
>
> Alfierei, Volpi, Lehnich

And to Dr. Goebbels:

> On the great success, which Germany has achieved with today's premiere of the Olympic film, we most heartily congratulate you. May Germany continue to make further extraordinary contributions to the progress of film culture.
>
> Alfieri, Volpi, Lehnich[25]

On August 30, again with Riefenstahl present, part two of the film was shown. The hall was again packed, and the audience responded well. For some reason, _Urlaub auf Ehrenwort_ was shown, too, on the same evening. Both films were well received.

On September 1, _Olympia_ was awarded the festival's first prize, the _Coppa Mussolini_. Dr. Goebbels sent Riefenstahl a telegram of congratulation:

> To Frau Leni Riefenstahl, presently in Venice; On the most honorable award that your Olympic film achieved in Venice, my deepest and most sincere congratulations.
>
> Reich Minister Dr. Goebbels[26]

The film had achieved another great victory. An interesting sidelight: The British and American representatives at Venice, who were hoping for an award for Disney's Snow White and the Seven Dwarfs, went home in protest over the award to Olympia.[27] Although Snow White was an excellent film, its loss to Olympia could hardly be seen as a blatant political decision. It should be remembered that though it was a fascist nation, Italy could make some surprising awards. At Venice in 1937, it had given a prize to Renoir's Grande Illusion.

Less than a year before the Germans invaded Poland, Olympia appeared there. On September 15, 1938, part one started simultaneous runs in Warsaw, Kattowitz, Krakow, Bydgoszcz, Biala, Lemberg, and Sosnowice. A gala premiere was set for September 23 under the auspices of the Polish foreign Minister Colonel Józef Beck. Colonel Beck had good reason to be pro-German at this time. All during the summer of 1938, Ambassador Hans-Adolf von Moltke in Warsaw had been in contact with Beck. Beck had promised that Poland would take no action against Germany (if and when Germany attacked Czechoslovakia) if Poland could be ceded the section of Czechoslovakia called Teschen. Poland had been promised this section and was content, little realizing that after Czechoslovakia, it would be next to fall.[28]

Along with Beck and Ambassador von Moltke, the Honor Committee for this gala event consisted of the Polish Minister of Culture, Swietoslawski; the minister of Transport and chairman of the Polish sporting leagues; the mayor of Warsaw, Starzyndki; a member of the IOC, Minister Matuzewski; General Rouppert; and the chairman of the Polish Olympic Committee, Colonel Glabisz. Glabisz had done much for the film in Poland and especially recommended that the film be shown in Polish schools.[29]

At about the time Olympia opened in Poland, the events in Czechoslovakia were about to come to their tragic conclusion. What happened is well known. After six months of German sword rattling and unrelenting pressure, Czechoslovakia's allies, England and France, refused to come to Czechoslovakia's aid and to honor their treaties. Hitler had screamed for the Sudetenland and at Munich he was disappointed because it was given to him. He had wished to conquer Czechoslovakia by force. On the thirtieth of September, Hitler had gained not only the Sudetenland, but also control over most of the natural barriers in Czechoslovakia. The rest of the country was his to take whenever he wished.

But friendship for Germany had been dealt a major blow. The Germans had been so aggressive at Munich that virtually no one could still make a case on behalf of Germany. There were still appeasers of Germany, to be sure. But it was increasingly difficult for Europeans to take a pro-German position out of friendship or sympathy with National Socialism. Esteem for Germany had plummeted with the Anschluss of Austria. After Czechoslovakia, it all but disappeared. The situation in England in 1938 followed this increasingly anti-German trend:

> Sympathy for Germany was less, however, than at any time for the last few years. People were governed more by a sense of fear than by a real desire for friendship. The gap between "appeasers" and "enthusiasts" became very clear. They were both working for the same end, the avoidance of war, but the approval of Germany which had been so common in previous years was now more and more confined to the "enthusiasts," many of whom themselves began to moderate their views. Throughout 1938 and 1939 we see a continuous move whereby pro-Nazi or pro-German activities, in their public expression, became more and more confined to extremist movements, and to the statements of a few prominent enthusiasts.[30]

There was a brief euphoria in England and France, at least temporarily, but there was soon a public reaction against Neville Chamberlain, against Daladier, and especially against Germany. Hitler, increasingly arrogant after Munich, made a speech within ten days telling Britain to "drop certain airs inherited from the Versailles epoch." Relations between the nations worsened. The peace offensive of 1936 seemed very far away.

During the Czech crisis, Olympia premiered in Rome. Mussolini was too busy to attend, but there was another lavish ceremony. That afternoon, the Italian Institute for Cultural Exchange gave a reception. Present were the German ambassador and his wife, General Director Roncaglia as the representative of his excellence Paulucci, representatives of the mayor, the Fascist Party and the Students League. A gold medal was awarded to Riefenstahl, and she gave numerous statements to the press.

That evening, Olympia was shown at the Supercinema in the presence of the following: the prefects of Rome; the mayor; Under State Secretary Ricci; General Vaccaro; high officials of the Italian government; representatives from the army, navy, air force; and the fascist militia. The German ambassador and his wife, as well as the Greek envoy and members of the diplomatic corps were also in attendance.

After the showing, which was a large success, Riefenstahl gave an interview on Italian radio that was translated for the listeners.[31]

She then left Italy and swung north once again to Scandinavia. This time, Olympia was being premiered in Oslo. On October 13, Riefenstahl had a private audience with the King of Norway, Haakon VII, after which a dinner was given in her honor by the crown prince. That evening, Olympia was premiered in the Colosseum, the largest film theater in Oslo. The king, crown prince, and numerous representatives of the government attended. After the showing, Riefenstahl was invited to another dinner, this one given by the League for the Promotion of Cultural Relations with Germany. The chairman of the league, Professor Selmor, made a speech calling Riefenstahl the torchbearer of the Olympic idea. Two copies of the film were given as presents to Norwegian sports groups. The showings of the Olympic films had, for many days, already been sold out in Oslo.[32]

On the fifteenth of October, at the University of Lund in Sweden, Riefenstahl gave a lecture about the production of the Olympic film. On the sixteenth of October she was once again in Copenhagen. On the next day, Christian X, the king of Denmark, received Riefenstahl privately. On the eighteenth of October, Riefenstahl was once again at the Odd Fellows Palais for the premiere of Fest der Schönheit. On the nineteenth, she flew back to Germany.[33]

Her October Scandinavian tour marked the end of her successful rounds on behalf of Olympia. From then on, the film was to have very tough going.

Tobis and the Propaganda Ministry were extremely interested in getting the film distributed in England, but no distributor was much interested in picking it up. At last, on October 25, Tobis sent its director, Kurt Hubert, to England to try to find a distributor for the film. Hubert had a difficult time. His mission was criticized by "Tatler" in the Daily Film Renter on the basis that the Olympic film was propaganda:

> The film of the Olympic Games is over here! You know--the precious picture which won the Mussolini Cup at the Venice Festival and resulted in Britain and America deciding it was just a racket and that they would stand for no more of it. I needn't tell you the film is a bit old, because it was made in Berlin some two years back. It's presented by Tobis, whose foreign manager, Herr Hubert, I understand, is in town. Frankly, I see no reason why we should encourage the gentleman to remain on this mission, and certainly don't see why anybody should be interested in the picture, seeing that it's blatant and undisguised German propaganda. They can ship the thing back as soon as they like.
>
> If anybody will tell me, even at the risk of precipitating another international crisis, *why* we should show German propaganda on our screens, I'll be very glad to hear it. Personally, I'm very strongly opposed to it, and that goes for a lot of other people. The trade would be well advised to have nothing to do with this precious film, to which for my part I wouldn't even give house room! As for its chances of success in this country, I would say they were about one in ten million--and I'm very well content for it to be so! [34]

Herr Hubert was far from hopeful about finding a slot for the film. Aside from the article in the Daily Film Renter, which he described as vindictive, Hubert found the prevailing mood in Britain extremely anti-German. The seizing of Austria and the Sudetenland were having their effect. The most he could produce was the possibility of a limited run in one theater:

> As a consequence of the ever tenser situation and the exceptionally strong anti-German feeling in England, it has become impossible for the film to get a national distribution, which only would have been possible

> through the Associated British Picture Corp. Ltd. However, the Associated British Picture Corp., with whose General Director Maxwell I used to be very friendly, told me after numerous discussions that he was ready to put one of his theaters, namely the Rialto Theater at my disposal.[35]

Hubert had hopes that if the film got even a limited release in Britain, it would become such a hit that a large chain would almost have to distribute the film. In his final report, he recommended this course of action to Tobis, Max Winkler, and the Propaganda Ministry. His recommendation was not acted upon, however, and Hubert left England on November 1. Variety noted his leaving and felt that his mission had been a failure.[36] On the day that Hubert left, "Tatler" took one more crack at Olympia:

> I see no reason why we should have this film on our screens--it is likely to provoke disorder, no matter where it is shown--and I'm hanged if I can see why we should lend our halls for German propaganda. I'll raise my voice against it every time--and continue to do so. Not that I imagine there's any likelihood of this opus of marathon length being taken up by the industry. Again I say with even greater emphasis than I did--we don't want the blooming thing, and, as far as I'm concerned, it can be chucked into the ashcan....[37]

And this seemed to be the end of any hope of general distribution in England. Ambassador von Ribbentrop did however have a complete English print of the film at the German Embassy in London, and he showed it to favored guests.[38] Olympia did not get a general showing in England until after the war.

THE AMERICAN JOURNEY

In discussing Riefenstahl's trip to the United States, one must discuss Ernst Jäger's series of articles, "How Leni Riefenstahl became Hitler's Girlfriend." Jäger fills the pages of these articles with every lurid story about Riefenstahl that he can think of. He intimates that she was Hitler's mistress, that she was stupid, petty, coarse and opportunistic. Anyone who is looking for material to use against Riefenstahl will find a mine of material in Jäger's articles. However, Jäger is so angry and vituperative that he almost sabotages his aim.

Riefenstahl is already on record as saying that Jäger's stories are a pack of lies. The objection could also be made that Jäger certainly was not averse to writing prose adoring Riefenstahl and also Adolf Hitler when it paid him to do so. Suddenly, when it seemed safe and profitable, he became an anti-Nazi. The objection can and should be raised: Was Jäger, or was he not, a hack journalist who would write anything for money?

I will be using Jäger's articles extensively in describing Riefenstahl's trip to America, and I refer to them for the following reasons. First, he was there, so his reports are first hand. Second, wherever I have been able to check, Riefenstahl did what Jäger said she was doing. Third, by all verification Jäger was a competent journalist. Riefenstahl later complained that "J. watched over her wherever she went, and took notes on everything she said or did."[39] He may not have been a paragon of virtue. As a matter of fact, defecting to America, he left a Jewish wife in Germany with no means of support. Jäger defected after Kristallnacht, when the future of German Jews already appeared hopeless. The only way Frau Jäger could survive was to ask for funds from the Olympia Company, which she did.[40] The image of Frau Jäger asking for Propaganda Ministry funds in order to live is chilling.

Nevertheless, since Jäger accompanied Riefenstahl almost everywhere she went in America, I have used his information, limiting myself to hard facts: names, dates, and places. I have omitted lurid details when they could not be corroborated. Interestingly, just as he substantiated the Goebbels-Riefenstahl feud, Jäger still corroborates much of what Riefenstahl has been saying since 1945.

Why did she make the trip to America? Olympia was already a smash hit in Europe, and she did not need American receipts to break even. Since her contract did not then provide her with a percent of the gross, it was of no advantage to her financially to get the film released in America. So why did she come?

Ernst Jäger accused Riefenstahl of wanting to circulate National Socialist propaganda:

> Leni's intentions in New York were first of a business nature: she wanted to sell the Olympic film. She was not so much interested in the purchase price of $325,000, as in winning converts. It seemed logical to her that her propaganda-through-sports film would attract sports-loving America to the man behind the picture--Hitler.[41]

If there is one statement of Jäger that Riefenstahl would now strongly contest, it is probably this one. It is difficult to find any substantiation for Jäger's statement, which of course does not necessarily make it untrue. But assuming it was true, it probably was not the only reason that Riefenstahl came to America. Riefenstahl was gregarious, and taking a trip to America that was paid for by government funds must have seemed like a good bargain. She was proud of her film and wanted to show it to as wide an audience as possible, certainly an understandable impulse to anyone who has created something to be proud of. And Riefenstahl may have enjoyed the challenge. She had managed to sell herself to a group of very tough men in Germany and may have wanted to do the same in America.

Riefenstahl sailed for America on board the _Europa_. She had two travelling companions, Ernst Jäger and Werner Klingeberg. Jäger had been chosen by her in part because he was an old friend of Riefenstahl and needed the work. In addition, however, he knew the film world and Hollywood. He had been dealing with the agents of the big Hollywood firms in Berlin for years, and he had taken a trip to Hollywood in November of 1935. Klingeberg, the leader, had been active in preparations for the Olympic Games of 1936, and he held the position of international secretary for the Olympic Games of 1940. He also knew America quite well. He had been at Los Angeles in 1932 where he had studied the Games. Then he went to the University of California at Berkeley for a year before returning to Berlin. He spoke English with an American accent.[42] What perhaps neither Riefenstahl nor Jäger knew was that Klingeberg had been a National Socialist since 1931 and was possibly a member of the _Abwehr_.[43] It was on the boat train that the two men met each other for the first time. Jäger snarled, "Klingeberg had seen few films in his life and never one of Riefenstahl's. Jäger had seen every picture made and too many of Riefenstahl's."[44]

Riefenstahl was to be incognito--she was listed in the passenger manifest as "Lotte Richter" so that her seventeen pieces of luggage, stamped with L. R., would not go astray. In her luggage were three different prints of Olympia, numerous copies of her book, Schönheit im Olympischen Kampf, and other publicity material. Her cover was quickly blown, however, and she became a shipboard celebrity. She was friendly with a set of business people and rich Americans including Mr. and Mrs. Conkey P. Whitehead, large stockholders in Coca-Cola; Mr. Frank H. Powell, president of the Southwestern Portland Cement Company, and his wife; and Frank T. Ryan, youngest son of the New York family of cotton exporters, who had business interests in Berlin. In any situation, Riefenstahl looked for the power brokers. She was quite friendly to Ryan and quickly realized that he might be of some help to her. Having started a map, she marked names beside several large cities. Next to New York she wrote:

> Ernst Oberhumer, important connections in Washington, perhaps road show ... Frank T. Ryan, brother-in-law of President of Chase National Bank, which controls 20th Century Fox.[45]

She would be making similar lists for Chicago and Detroit.

Two members of the German Embassy in Washington, Dr. Tannenberg and Baron von Gienanth, paid their respects and expressed their shock that the trip had been so haphazardly organized. Riefenstahl told von Gienanth that the "Ministry of Economics" had given her eight thousand dollars for the trip that was to last for two months.

> Besides, Goebbels had sent only a brief statement to all the German consulates in the United States, stating that she was travelling privately and was to be approached only if she requested their help.
>
> "Besides, Dr. Goebbels has already washed his hands of me for whatever happens over there," she laughingly rejoined. "He was always against this trip."[46]

Dr. Goebbels' instincts were well founded. The last thing that Riefenstahl needed in America was anything that looked like an endorsement of her trip by the German government. The line was that she was a private citizen and that any red-carpet treatment by German consulates would have been quite out of place. As it turned out, Goebbels was quite right in opposing the trip.

The Europa docked in New York on November 4, 1938, and Riefenstahl was immediately besieged by the press. She made an initial good impression, on some of the journalists at least, and Inez Robb of the Daily News reported, "The child is charming!"[47] Riefenstahl took up residence at the Hotel Pierre. She waded enthusiastically into New York night life and spent an evening at the Stork Club and at El Morocco. She had hopes of meeting Walter Winchell, but she never did. Winchell did, however, mention her in a column, saying that she was "... as pretty as a swastika."[48]

There was a group of people, however, who did not want Riefenstahl to have too good a time at the Stork Club. These individuals were determined that the Olympic film would be boycotted in America. On Monday, November 7, 1938, the Non-Sectarian Anti-Nazi League, claiming a membership of one hundred thousand persons, opened a campaign against Riefenstahl, stating that her film was part of a Nazi campaign "to flood the United States with Nazi doctrines." The league stated that it already had the support of various film distributors and that it was going after the support of the major Hollywood companies and all New York distributors. It should be remembered that Jeremiah T. Mahoney had led the fight against sending an American team to Berlin. Mahoney was narrowly defeated by Avery Brundage. Now the league had enlisted his support.

> ...Mahoney has criticized the Hitler-Riefenstahl films on the grounds that the games themselves were merely Nazi propaganda. "The importance of the games from an athletic standpoint was forgotten," said Mr. Mahoney, speaking as former President of the U.S. Amateur Athletic Union. "The games were for Nazi propaganda."[49]

League officials already claimed the support of many foreign film exporters, including World Pictures, Atlantic Films, Garrison Films, Franco-American Pictures, and Seiden Pictures. These companies may have been small beer to the giant Hollywood companies, but the men involved in the Non-Sectarian Anti-Nazi League were not. The vice presidents included

Mayor F. H. LaGuardia of New York; John Haynes Holmes, pastor of the Community Church, New York; Bishop Francis J. McConnell, presiding bishop of the North Atlantic States of the Methodist Episcopal Church; Clarence H. Low, treasurer of the New York State Democratic Committee; Frank P. Walsh and Rabbi Leon Fram, of Detroit. The president had been Samuel Untermyer, the famous labor lawyer, who had just resigned because of his age but was still politically powerful. Immediately, Riefenstahl was told that there was a boycott movement in effect against her and that difficulties might be awaiting her in New York.

But she had no reason to be dissatisfied with the progress that she was making with the selling of the film. According to Jäger, Riefenstahl first consulted "O. E. Otterson, former director of Western Electric, called, in Germany an anti-Semite."[50] Jäger probably means John E. Otterson, a vice president and general manager in 1927 and 1928 of the Electrical Research Products, Inc., a subsidiary of Western Electric. In 1928, Otterson became a director and president of Paramount pictures, replacing Adolph Zukor, but he was forced out in 1936 in a proxy fight.[51] Because Paramount had maintained its contracts and distributorships in National Socialist Germany, Otterson was highly familiar with the German film industry and in a position to help Riefenstahl in America. Whether Otterson was an anti-Semite is not known. His advice to Riefenstahl was quite sensible:

> The film should first be shown to the men behind the anti-German boycott. If they declared the film contained no propaganda, the matter of a 'release' would be simplified. In this event, he himself would be interested. Since the Hayes Office respected her position as a "private producer" and since one of the three still-active studios in Germany (Paramount) let her understand that they were perhaps interested in buying the film; and since the prospects of a deal with RKO were favorable too--Leni was optimistic.[52]

Riefenstahl became a tourist and visited Radio City Music Hall, which she thought was marvelous. She was certain that Albert Speer would have loved it. She stayed in Harlem for hours to watch the dancing. If one can trust what Jäger recorded, Riefenstahl was fascinated by the Blacks; at the same time, however, she spouted some of Hitler's theories about the Black race. The future author of The Last of the Nuba evidently had some conflicts to work out. She also went to a Black church service the next Sunday, remarking that Julius Streicher would have been amused.

While Riefenstahl was in New York, she contacted the Museum of Modern Art. The correspondence files of the Museum disclose that Riefenstahl was in touch with Iris Barry's husband, John F. Abbott, and that Abbott contacted the German embassy to obtain a copy of the Olympic film for projection.[53] The Rockefeller Foundation had begun funding films in 1935 and, with the help of John Hay Whitney, had set up a fund for the Museum of Modern Art to help get the film library started.[54] Jäger also mentions the "Film Art Museum" and appears to have had the Museum of Modern Art in mind.

Abbott, at a private dinner party, told Riefenstahl that King Vidor, who had just finished Citadel, was on his way home. Having seen Olympia in Paris, he wanted to pay his respects. To Riefenstahl's annoyance, however, King Vidor never showed up. But, all in all, she had no cause to complain about her progress in America. How far the boycott against her would have extended is not known. The Anti-Nazi League was powerful, but three major studios had substantial investments in Germany and might have distributed Olympia in order to get quid pro quo's from the German government. We will never know. Other events rose to the forefront.

On November 7, 1938, a young Jew in Paris named Herschel Grynszpan shot and killed the Third Secretary of the German embassy. The retaliation in Germany was terrible. On the night of November 11, synagogues were burned and Jewish stores all over Germany were looted and destroyed. Because the sound of breaking glass could be heard everywhere, this nationwide pogrom was called Kristallnacht. Jews were rounded up, beaten, tortured, and sent to concentration camps. The pogrom was so awful that different groups among the National Socialists and the regime tended to blame one another for the excesses. In a further cynical gesture, the government ordered the Jews to pay for the destruction of their own property. And the stories that leaked out of Germany did not die down. They grew worse.

Perhaps the events of 1933, which occurred when the

National Socialists took power, were as equally horrendous as Kristallnacht. But now, the world press and world opinion were paying attention. Tolerance for the regime had run out. The effect on American public opinion was cataclysmic. The media, Republican as well as Democrat, heaped abuse on the German government. President Roosevelt recalled the American Ambassador in Berlin, Hugh Wilson, "for consultation." Wilson never returned to his post. Hans Thomsen, the German Chargé d'Affaires in Washington, advised that all secret files in the Washington Embassy be returned to Germany; if the Embassy were seized there would be insufficient time to burn them. Hans Dieckhoff, the Ambassador in Washington, reported to Berlin, "A hurricane is raging here."[55]

On November 11, the German Consul General in New York declared to Riefenstahl:

> Not since the World War has there been such a feeling of animosity in the United States toward Germany. America's attitude toward us is as changeable as the waves. At times it appears as though all hatred has receded and then again it rages like a tempest. A few weeks ago an understanding was within our grasp. Now Berlin has ruined our chances. Our best friends here have forsaken us. Before, we could reassure them that the Jewish question in Germany would be regulated by the Nuernberger laws and that the government would not tolerate any excesses. Now that even the synagogues are burned down we haven't a leg to stand on....[56]

Another high official in the German Consulate cried out:

> Berlin has undone in one day what it took five years to accomplish. It would be better if you went back to Germany. A wave of protest is rising against us.... How can I explain to my American friends why the synagogues are being burned down? Answer me, for God's sake, Fraeulein Riefenstahl![57]

Any hope of getting Olympia shown in America had been destroyed in the ashes of Kristallnacht. Riefenstahl was advised to go back to Germany by Dr. Borchers (the Consul), Heinz Bellers (the representative of the Propaganda Ministry), and Ernst Oberhumer (the Wall Street broker who represented sizable German investments in America). Riefenstahl decided, instead, to keep trying.

She was urged by pro-Germans to speak to important officials at the 1939 New York World's Fair. Hearing this, she must have remembered that she had done herself some good at the Paris Exposition of 1937. She was given an elaborate luncheon by John Hartigan, foreign relations commissioner for the New York World's Fair, who tried to persuade her to get Hitler to change his mind and have Germany participate in the World's Fair. Riefenstahl explained in some detail Hitler's refusal to participate, and Hartigan successfully countered these arguments, persuading Riefenstahl to take photographs and other documents to show to Hitler. Riefenstahl was also greeted by Grover Whalen, the president of the World's Fair.

But the reaction against her and Germany continued to grow. A radio lecture she was to give was postponed--then cancelled. She was supposed to meet William Randolph Hearst, but he could not be reached. Zito, a famous caricaturist and an old friend, would not give her an introduction to Ed Sullivan. A message was cabled from London in secret code that Olympia was banned in England. It appears rather that no distributor wanted to distribute the film in England, which amounts to the same thing.

On November 15, Riefenstahl flew to Washington. She stayed at one of the Vanderbilt family's villas; it had been rented by Ambassador Dieckhoff, who was about to be permanently recalled from Washington. Dieckhoff advised Riefenstahl to go to the Midwest, which, because of its isolationist and pro-German sentiment, was likely to give her a far warmer welcome than the East Coast. He also advised Riefenstahl to see Henry Ford, who admired Hitler and had just stirred up a lot of controversy by accepting a German decoration. After a brief tour of Washington and Mount Vernon, Riefenstahl left for Chicago.

She arrived there on the sixteenth and immediately felt the increased warmth toward her. She checked in at the Drake Hotel and had her first lunch with Avery Brundage. Brundage, an Olympic official, was already acquainted with Klingeberg. Riefenstahl was quickly accepted by a number of prominent Chicagoans, and Mrs. Claire Dux-Swift and Mrs. Henry Bartholemew invited her as "Lotte Richter" to the Women's Athletic Club, which impressed her enormously.[58] She toured the Opera House and decided to rent it for the premiere of the Olympic film. She heard more about the midwestern sympathy toward Germany:

> The polished officials pointed out the propaganda value of German films. Leni's "Triumph of the Will" played 120 times in Chicago to "select audiences." Two small movie houses, "Hansa" and "Kino" played all the German films released in America. An "International Film" exchange was disseminating anti-Semitic propaganda. "There are groups here which count definitely on a revolution."[59]

Riefenstahl was heartened by her reception in Chicago. On November 18, 1938, she was asked to Detroit to meet Henry Ford. Ford was known to be sympathetic to Hitler and Germany. He received Riefenstahl graciously, but she could not use her full powers of persuasion on him; they were never alone together. Also in the room were the German consul Fritz Hailer and Ford's general manager (who was a notorious anti-Semite) E.G. Liebold. Although Ford was gracious, Riefenstahl evidently felt that the interview had not gone particularly well. She did not even ask Ford whether he wanted to see the Olympic film. Liebold took her to dinner at the Yacht Club, and suggested that she contact George W. Trendle, a partner in Paramount in the Detroit area who controlled a chain of large theaters. He also arranged that she, for a specifically reduced price, would have the use of a new Ford sedan.[60]

Riefenstahl returned to Chicago, and at last, Brundage arranged to show Olympia at the Chicago Engineers Club.

> ...Its president, W. A. Mann, had placed the hall at Leni's disposal, at the instigation of the Olympic Committee. A club room was converted into a projection room. Transformers for supplying sufficient current were set up with great difficulty. A transportable screen was fixed according to Leni's strict orders. Besides, the entrepreneurs took precautions in two dimensions: it was to be an ultra-private party. And Leni, a guest, was in no way to conduct the showing with a view toward finding purchasers for the film.[61]

Avery Brundage announced that the film had been accepted by the Olympic Committee. He predicted that the film would be superb. Then Riefenstahl spoke, saying that the audience would be able to verify that the film contained no propaganda but instead represented a bridge between the peoples of the earth, and she hoped that the film would be freely shown in America.

> On the 20th of November, at 4 o'clock, two small, noisy movie projectors rattled away the first reel of a five hour, 25,000 feet view of the Olympics. The entire audience numbered 35 people, seven of them from the consulate.[62]

The showing was a great success. "A few older women cried. The Hitler pictures, the international flags, Richard Strauss' hymn of peace, the negroes [sic], the German officers, the Olympic flame ... all of it moved them."

Brundage wrote to William May Garland in Los Angeles that he had seen the greatest Olympic film ever made; and he expressed hope that Garland would be of the same opinion. The next morning, Riefenstahl telephoned Ambassador Dieckhoff who was about to leave for Germany. She asked him to tell Hitler that she was beginning to have success and that she was leaving for California. Evidently Sonja Henie's manager had offered to buy the film, but Riefenstahl decided not to sell it to him because of bad reports about him from "the Gestapo in New York."[63] She told her travelling companions that she had other Hollywood connections no one even dreamed of and that she must be in Hollywood by the end of the week. With high hopes--and still accompanied by Ernst Jäger and Werner Klingeberg--she headed to California.

Riefenstahl arrived in Hollywood on November 24, 1938, on the Super Chief, evidently expecting a celebrity reception. Her reception was pitifully small, however. She was met by the German consul, Dr. Gyssling; Hubert Stowitts and his brother; and Hans Wolfram. Dr. Gyssling had alienated the film community in Hollywood at the time the film I Was a Captive of Nazi Germany was being produced there; he did this by sending letters on official government stationery to both the authoress and to the players. In the letters, he warned of German reprisals against those participating in pictures "the tendency or effect of which is detrimental to German prestige".[64] Hans Wolfram was the representative from the California Staats-Zeitung, a German-speaking newspaper. He had attended Riefenstahl's press reception at Haus Ruhwald on the eve of the Olympics. Jäger probably was aware that if this motley welcoming committee were representative, Riefenstahl was going to have difficulty in taking Hollywood by storm.

Dr. Gyssling informed Riefenstahl that there had been demonstrations all over Hollywood to protest her presence, including one at the Garden of Allah where she was to stay. Riefenstahl took a look at the Garden of Allah and rejected it on the grounds that it did not provide sufficient security. She stayed instead in the Beverly Hills Hotel, which she greatly enjoyed. She rented a bungalow for three or four weeks; this cost her six hundred dollars.

Stowitts had made some promises. He was art director for Greta Garbo in MGM's The Painted Veil and was going to write to Leopold Stokowski so that Riefenstahl could meet Garbo. This encounter must have sounded promising: perhaps Garbo could do something for her at MGM, Riefenstahl must have thought. She was especially interested in meeting Louis B. Mayer and Joseph Schenck, probably because MGM was anxious to maintain its distribution system in Germany. Stowitts had also promised an invitation to the Disney Studios.

In addition, G. W. van Schmus of the Radio City Music Hall called to make an appointment. At first, Riefenstahl's future must have seemed fairly rosy in California.

But she was shunned--saw no one--even before reading about the surprise that was in store for her. On Tuesday, November 29, 1938, the Hollywood Anti-Nazi League ran the following advertisement in the Hollywood Reporter:

> POST THIS ON YOUR BULLETIN BOARD!
>
> Over A Year Ago
>
> On September 24th, 1937, this LEAGUE called attention to the presence in Hollywood of VITTORIO MUSSOLINI, son of Il Duce, collaborator for Adolf Hitler.
>
> Hollywood demonstrated its unwillingness to entertain emissaries of Fascism.

Today

Leni Riefenstahl, Head of the Nazi Film Industry, has arrived in Hollywood.

THERE IS NO ROOM IN HOLLYWOOD FOR LENI RIEFENSTAHL!

In this moment, when hundreds of thousands of our brethren await certain death, close your doors to all Nazi Agents.

LET THE WORLD KNOW

THERE IS NO ROOM IN HOLLYWOOD FOR NAZI AGENTS!!

SIGN THE PETITION FOR AN ECONOMIC EMBARGO AGAINST GERMANY!

The Hollywood Anti-Nazi League for the Defense of American Democracy[65]

Riefenstahl responded:

> Already in New York I have said that my trip is absolutely private and that I have no official orders to carry out ... I have never held an official position in Germany and could never have been called the head of the Nazi film industry. I am an independent artist. On the strength of my film, "The Blue Light," I was engaged as producer and director for several important documentary films, including two of the Olympic Games.[66]

The Hollywood Anti-Nazi League responded that it was not the league's purpose to attack Riefenstahl personally, but only to expose her as a symbol. This does not alter the fact that the league's tract was not accurate: Riefenstahl certainly was not the head of the Nazi film industry. On the other hand, while Riefenstahl's statements are not exactly untrue, her film did enjoy official status as a Reich-sponsored film. Itemized accounts of her expenses on the American trip appear in Propaganda Ministry files. And certainly, as we have seen, Riefenstahl enjoyed at least semiofficial status on her various trips through Europe to promote the film and could not now credibly abandon that status.

News of the announcement of the Anti-Nazi League was

published all over the world. Riefenstahl was extremely upset. She considered leaving Hollywood then and there. Klingeberg urged her to stay. He reminded her that even if she had not gotten far with official Hollywood, she had made some friends in America.

These friends were the Olympic officials and athletes. The American Olympic Committee had promised to show the picture, and William May Garland, the president of the American Olympic Committee, and his wife had invited Riefenstahl to their Los Angeles home. Riefenstahl decided to stay for a while.

The ban against her grew in strength. A party where she was to meet an important MGM executive was cancelled. Arthur Goebel, the California flyer, arranged a small party at the Coconut Grove, but Riefenstahl was ignored and she left the party angrily. Van Schmus never followed through on his wish to see her. Evidently, he had gotten into some trouble with the league because of his desire to do so. Garbo and Stokowski were not available. _Variety_ ran an article which did not do Riefenstahl any good; it reminded the Hollywood community how the American newsreel companies had been treated in Berlin during the Games:

> Leni Riefenstahl is not expected to get far with efforts to interest American companies in her Olympic films which runs [sic] nearly 20 reels. Aside from the fact that all look askance on the box office potentialities of the subject, the manner in which the American newsreels were taken over the bumps at the Berlin Olympics also is an unfavorable factor....
> The Nazi Olympic Picture record is regarded as a well edited and fairly comprehensive subject by those who have viewed it but industry chieftains fail to see what place it has in the American scene at the present time.[67]

On December 8, 1938, Stowitts and Riefenstahl met Walt Disney, who gave them a three-hour tour of the studio and explained his cartoon techniques.

> "And why not?" she continued. "Disney and I have never met before but our pictures--_Olympia_ and _Snow White_--were the two outstanding successes in

> many outstanding countries. He has the German feeling--he goes so often to the German fables and fairy tales for inspiration.[68]

Riefenstahl said later that Disney was afraid to show her film at the studio because of the strength of the boycott.[69] And Disney was the only producer that she saw.

Having no luck with the film world, Riefenstahl turned to the financial community. But with them she fared no better. She cultivated the influential real estate brothers, Dr. Edwin and Harold Janss, hoping their firm might put up the money for a road show of the picture, but the Janss Brothers were not interested. She again contacted the Portland cement Powells. This, too, was to no avail.

William May Garland, however, was more helpful. Riefenstahl was a guest at a large family dinner. Garland's brother-in-law, Harrison Chandler, son of the _Los Angeles Times_ owner and an acquaintance of Riefenstahl from the Olympics, was present and promised his help. An arrangement was made to show _Olympia_ at the California Club on December 14, 1938.

On the appointed date, the California Club draped one of the club rooms and made it a projection room. Riefenstahl had three versions of the film at her bungalow. The one she chose to show was the one with all shots of Hitler deleted. The original, she felt, was too dangerous, because if the projectionist were too leftist, he might set fire to the film. More than 120 people were at the performance, including Marjorie Gestring, the young diver who had been so popular with the Germans in Berlin, Kenneth Carpenter, the gold medalist in the discus, and the pole vaulters, Bill Graber and Bill Sefton. Johnny Weismuller and Glenn Morris were there, too. The rest were friends and club members. Garland made a short speech asking that no publicity be given either to the California Club or to the parties responsible for the showing.[70]

At first, Riefenstahl felt the showing had been a failure, but the film was better received than she had imagined it would be. Henry McLemore of the _Hollywood Citizen-News_ gave an extremely favorable review that was widely reprinted in contemporary advertisements for the film.

> Los Angeles, Dec. 16-(UP)--Last night I saw the finest motion picture I have ever seen, and you must not dismiss my opinion lightly, because as a man who dates back to John Bunny, Flora Finch, "Broken Blossoms," and "Birth of a Nation," I am qualified to speak as a fairly competent critic.
>
> ...It is not propaganda, but a magnificent filming of the greatest meeting of athletes in the history of the world.... If it is not shown to the youth of this country, the youth of this country will be the loser. From start to finish--and it runs for almost four hours--its only message is the joy and the glory that comes from the development of a superb body.[71]

On December 17, 1938, the Los Angeles Times also reviewed the film enthusiastically.

But if, on the strength of these reviews, Riefenstahl expected the studios to come flocking for a viewing of the film, she must have been sorely disappointed. Nothing happened. The boycott remained in effect. Becoming more and more disillusioned and desperate, Riefenstahl accepted invitations from people she did not even know. She scheduled an unpublicized meeting with Rod Laroque, whom she knew from SOS Eisberg, as well as meetings with Vilma Banky and Sigrid Gurie, but none of these was fruitful.

She began to spend more and more time in Palm Springs where, according to Jäger, she had a lover. A blow-up with Jäger and Klingeberg resulted. Riefenstahl had gone to Palm Springs at a time when there had been an opportunity to go to San Francisco to try to persuade Commissioner George Creel to grant a showing of the film. She wrote a report to Hitler of her troubles in America, and she sent him a telegram:

> Adolf Hitler, Berlin, Reichschancellery. Sending you my Fuehrer most hearty Xmas and New Year greetings from California. Leaving New York January 19, Your Leni Riefenstahl.[72]

After her trip to Palm Springs, Riefenstahl was offered what she felt was another big chance. Winfield Sheehan was a well-known producer and, as Consul Gyssling had told her, a friend of Germany. Maria Jeritza, who was famous in Europe for her singing of Tosca, was married to Sheehan. The

Sheehans held a reception on December 28, 1938. At the reception were Riefenstahl, Klingeberg, and Consul Gyssling. The Sheehans saw Fest der Völker and two reels of Fest der Schönheit. They were terribly impressed, and Jeritza promised to call Louis B. Mayer, Joseph Schenck, and Eleanor Roosevelt(!). Riefenstahl gratefully sent Jeritza flowers.

But still nothing happened. Riefenstahl went to San Francisco. Several World's Fair managers saw the film, but they lost interest when Riefenstahl refused to make any cuts. Riefenstahl went back to Los Angeles and shuttled between there and Palm Springs. Maria Jeritza told her that a meeting with Will Hays could be arranged but that Mrs. Roosevelt was not available. Van Schmus was in trouble because he had even planned to meet Riefenstahl. At Palm Springs, Riefenstahl learned that Will Hays could not meet her after all. She met with some bankers provided by Maria Jeritza, but they were not helpful. The one person who did want to meet her was Samuel Untermyer, the ex-president of the Anti-Nazi League, who wanted to talk to her about the fate of the German Jews. Riefenstahl refused to talk to him.

She had more contacts to make, and she was still hopeful, but her funds had run out and she had no choice but to return home.

> ...Leni's directorial sense told her the climax had been passed with the showing at the California Club. There was nothing left for her but to return to Germany a martyr.

According to Jäger, Jeritza blamed him (immediately before Riefenstahl's departure) for Riefenstahl's failure, charging that since his 1935 trip to Hollywood, he had been active in Berlin as a secret agent and informer for a number of Hollywood studios and that he had been receiving a weekly check to report Riefenstahl's activities to those studios. Riefenstahl believed the story and she fired Jäger. Jäger obviously had no bright future in Germany. He chose to defect to America and that is where he stayed until the fifties.

Jäger's behavior during the trip to America does raise certain questions. When Riefenstahl and Klingeberg returned to Germany, Klingeberg filed a notice of disclaimer for certain expenses run up by Jäger, especially for a trip to Cleveland that Jäger had taken between the third and fifteenth of January, 1939:

> The payment of the above amounts was necessary since Herr Jäger, without the knowledge or the approval of Fräulein Riefenstahl or me, advanced money and spent it. These expenses are not part of the purposes of our trip, and I cannot be responsible for them. Herr Jäger left Los Angeles just when life had become too expensive for the three of us, and we had to be exceptionally careful with the funds left for the trip, which had been extended by fourteen days. Herr Jäger was completely knowledgeable about the financial situation when he left Los Angeles. Neither the raise of the daily allowance to the figure of $25, nor the general outlays for a secretary, nor the trip to Cleveland was necessary. Herr Jäger informed us that he was supposed to have a special assignment regarding the formation of a chain of theaters in the U.S.A. given to him by the director of Tobis Lehmann, and he was to report to Tobis directly. I therefore decline responsibility for the following documents of the Olympia-Film Company pending further clarification.[73]

But the Tobis Company was not assuming responsibility for Jäger either:

> We would be extremely interested in seeing the original text of your submitted statement, according to which Herr Jäger ... "had a special assignment regarding the formation of a chain of theaters in the U.S.A., and that he was to report to Tobis directly." Herr Jäger had no such assignment from us, and never reported to us on a matter of this nature....[74]

It is not known what Jäger was doing in Cleveland; perhaps he was already planning to stay in America and was looking for a job. In any case, Jäger did remain in America, and so he exits from this narrative, sorely missed by this writer.

In spite of all the problems that Riefenstahl and Klingeberg had in America, the two very nearly got the film distributed. Riefenstahl was informed in New York, just before she and Klingberg left for Germany, that British Gaumont wanted to sign a contract to distribute the film in England and in America.[75] It looked, therefore, as if her trip had been a success--even though she had gotten nowhere in Hollywood.

Before the war, however, the film never did get a general release in England or America. This was not because of the failure of Riefenstahl's powers of persuasion but because of the sequence of events in Germany. After Munich and Kristallnacht, and with Hitler screaming abuse at England and America, no one wanted a German product. Hitler had sabotaged her as he was to sabotage many other believers.

The trip raises many interesting questions and issues. For instance, the Hollywood Anti-Nazi League was a Popular Front organization. After the Hitler-Stalin Pact in August of 1939, when many CPUSA members quickly became pro-German, the Hollywood Anti-Nazi League collapsed when its leaders tried to adhere to the new Party line.[76] Under these circumstances, how would Riefenstahl have fared if she had arrived in America a year later?

My guess is that a later arrival time would not have made much difference. Feelings were running too high against Germany for Riefenstahl's film to have been generally appealing as a commercial proposition. But when the film got a limited commercial run in America before the war, it is interesting to note that the run occurred during the period of the Hitler-Stalin Pact.

No easy answers exist as to whether the film should have been boycotted. It certainly did not represent a clear and present public danger to the peace and order of a democratic society; it does not yell "fire" in a crowded theater. The film was propaganda of a kind, since it put the best features of its society on the screen, but Hollywood films were doing the same thing. On the other hand, given the virulent aspects of the regime,--aspects that were becoming more apparent every day--was a film that showed National Socialist Germany as a normal, happy, and healthy society too dangerous to be shown? This is difficult to say. But it should be remembered that many who called for a boycott of Riefenstahl's film later would have their own film work boycotted in ten years. They too would be "symbols."

Olympia did have a commercial run in America before World War II, but the run was not what Riefenstahl had had in mind. In 1940, an entity called the Marathon Film Company released the film in German enclaves in large cities in America.[77] In New York, part one ran at the Eighty-sixth Street Theatre in Yorkville on March 9, 1940. Part two started on March 30. Jay Leyda, film historian, told this writer that he saw the film there and that there were loud cheers for every German victory. The film also ran in Chicago at the Sonotone theater at the end of May 1940.[78] George Pratt of the George Eastman House remembered seeing the film in Chicago, but he had to cross a picket line to do so. Evidently, Riefenstahl did not know that Olympia had been distributed in America before the war,[79] and when Avery Brundage requested a print of Olympia, German Railroads responded on October 17, 1940, that it had never heard of the Marathon Company.[80] It is therefore possible that pirated prints were shown in America, of which the German government had no knowledge. According to the ad for the film in Chicago, Avery Brundage called it, "Unbelievably beautiful, the greatest sport picture ever filmed."[81]

In Riefenstahl's own mind, and in the opinion of the Propaganda Ministry, the trip had been a failure. Riefenstahl had spent about 30,000 RM (duly itemized for Dr. Goebbels) and had achieved few results. The film had been closed out of the following areas: England, along with Canada, New Zealand and Australia; the USA with Panama; and Egypt, Syria, and Palestine. Riefenstahl and the ministry still had high hopes the film would overcome the boycott in these areas, but the worsening international situation made this impossible. In March of 1939, Germany invaded the rest of Czechoslovakia. Up to now, it had at least been able to argue that the areas it annexed were rightfully part of Germany because the inhabitants of these areas were German. But the seizure of the non-German area of Czechoslovakia by brute force was naked aggression and could not be justified. The Olympia film with its message of peace was rapidly becoming an anachronism.

On her return, February 5, 1939, Riefenstahl met with Dr. Goebbels to talk about the future of the Olympia-Film GmbH and to discuss her own plans. Dr. Goebbels reported the meeting as follows:

> 5 February 1939 (Sunday)
>
> In the evening, Leni Riefenstahl reports to me on

> her trip to America. She gives me an exhaustive description, and one that is far from encouraging. We shall get nowhere there. The Jews rule by terror and bribery. But for how much longer?...[82]

Riefenstahl was also there to talk business. She had requested reimbursement for the time she had spent promoting the film in 1938 and 1939, but Dr. Goebbels refused her request for 5,000 RM a month payable from May 1, 1938. Riefenstahl wrote Dr. Goebbels, pressing her claim further:

> Dear Herr Minister: March 6, 1939
>
> In a letter dated October 12, 1938, a copy of which is attached, the Olympia-Film G.m.b.H. made a proposal to the Reich Ministry for Public Enlightenment and Propaganda to remunerate my activity since the completion of my work on the two Olympic films.
>
> On the first of February 1939, in accordance with arrangement, the firm was advised that a payment in the amount of 5,000 RM had been approved, but not from May 1, 1938, as I had proposed, but rather from the first of November 1939.
>
> From this, one assumes that my activity up to this period of time was still within the scope of my contract. This supposition is not quite right, because for the time between April 20, 1938, and February 18, 1939 I have put myself completely at the disposal of the Ministry for tasks that were not foreseen at the termination of the contract. It was a question of trips abroad wished for in the interest of propaganda and exploitation and the trip to America that was necessary for the sale of the film.
>
> By these assignments, not only the possibility of starting a new work was taken from me, but I therefore had unusually high expenses.
>
> Because all of my trips had state status. I took part at the following premieres: Vienna--Graz--Zürich--Baden-Baden (German-French Congress)--Brussels--Paris--Copenhagen--Stockholm--Helsinki--Venice (Biennale)--Rome--Oslo--Lund (University Lecture)--Copenhagen (Second Part and University Lecture)--3 months America--Paris (Lecture German French Society) and Bucharest.
>
> Since in every country these premieres were com-

bined with official receptions and audiences, not only did I have to pay especial attention to my wardrobe, but with consideration for press photos, I had to change it repeatedly. So, according to vouchers, I have spent 28,000 RM for wardrobe alone in this period. My complete expenditures in the last year amounted to 99,000 marks. On this account, the proposed honorarium will in no way provide an indemnification for work already done, but only cover a part of my present assignments, and on this account I would like to ask you to indicate half of the amount as the wardrobe and allowance for representation, since it is a matter of a present repayment for money already disbursed by me, and for which I would like to not to have to pay additional taxes.

In order not to burden further the overhead of the Olympia-Film G.m.b.H., which is busy with the development and exploitation of the remaining materials, I recommend that these wages including February 1939 be paid, and to grant me a share, for my further activity as head of the firm, of 20% of the amount coming to the firm; this only going into effect when Olympia-Film G.m.b.H. has paid back its complete debts.

I hope, most honored Herr Minister, that my recommendation does not seem presumptuous, and I would be very thankful, if you could accept.

When my honorarium seems too high, I ask you to consider that since the summer of 1935 I had to postpone every other assignment, and I therefore worked exclusively for the Olympic films in order to bring them the success that they are having in Germany and abroad.

Yours faithfully, with the warmest regards and

Heil Hitler!
Your

(signed) Leni Riefenstahl[83]

The Propaganda Ministry was not altogether convinced by this letter. It was pointed out that Tobis had quite generously advanced 90,000 RM to Riefenstahl, an amount that would be set against her expenses. In addition, Riefenstahl had taken a lot of friends and colleagues to the premieres, which had substantially added to the costs. Nevertheless, the ministry decided to accept Riefenstahl's recommendation, since the matter of reimbursement for the period of time between May 1, 1938, and February 1939 had not been provided for by her contract.[84]

But other action was taken. If Riefenstahl felt chained to the Propaganda Ministry, the Propaganda Ministry also was not enthusiastic about the relationship. Olympia had been a financial success, and the ministry knew that it would get its money back eventually, but as it saw the situation, it was being put in the position of having to subsidize the extremely expensive short films that the Olympia Company was making. It noted with horror that Olympia-Film had just sold the short film Wildwasser to Bavaria Film for 70,000 RM, a huge sum for that time. It failed to see how the company could stay in business making prohibitively expensive short films, no matter how good the films were. The ministry also knew that Riefenstahl wanted to start work on Penthesilea, not a purpose for which the Olympia-Film GmbH had been established. Since there seems to have been no great interest in subsidizing other Riefenstahl features, the ministry decided to pay Riefenstahl 20 percent of the net proceeds of the film in the future, once all debts had been paid. In addition, it decided to dissolve the Olympia-Film GmbH whose successor in interest would be Riefenstahl-Film GmbH.[85]

A general meeting was held on March 9. In attendance were members of the Propaganda Ministry and Walter Traut and Walter Groskopf of the Olympia-Film GmbH. Judge Pfennig was also present as advisor to the company as well as representative for the Reich Trustee, Dr. Winkler. The discussion focused on the compensation of Riefenstahl as well as on planning a timetable for the dissolution of the company. Riefenstahl wanted to keep the company together--at least until October 1939. A number of jobs still had to be performed, she said, including the preparation of film copies for England and America and the use of remaining material to make training films for the Reich School Film Establishment.[86]

Riefenstahl did wish to keep her staff together but, in truth, there still was much for the Olympia Company to do. Several short films were being made for Tobis, and the company provided footage in its capacity as a sports film archive; it expected to be able to exploit these fields for quite some time. By the time the company wound up, it had produced the following short films: Kraft und Schwung, Der Wurf im Sport, Höchstes Glück der Erde auf dem Rücken der Pferde, Schwimmen und Springen, Wildwasser, and Oster-Skitour in Tirol.[87] The income received from current showings of Olympia were still impressive, and neither the Olympia-Film GmbH nor the Propaganda Ministry were inclined to liquidate the company until the receipts slowed up. The Olympia-Film GmbH and Tobis were confident that the film would be shown in the United Kingdom and in the United States.

On September 1, 1939, World War II began. Germany invaded Poland, and England and France declared war against Germany. At first, this seemed to make little difference to the Olympia Company. Initially, Germany won a brilliant series of victories, and by the end of 1940, many Germans thought the war virtually was over. The Olympia-Film GmbH showed its belief in the inevitability of a German victory in a letter from Walter Groskopf to the Propaganda Ministry dated April 28, 1941. In the letter, Groskopf argued for a delay in liquidating the company on the basis that once the war ended, an American distribution of the film might bring in high receipts, and the receipts, "temporarily stopped by the war," would soon resume. Someone at the Propaganda Ministry was a realist. A large question mark was inscribed near this statement.

Within two months, Hitler invaded Russia, and in December, Germany declared war on America. Although few Germans seemed to be aware of it, their country's doom was now sealed. By the end of 1941, it was apparent that the war would continue for a long while and that receipts from England and America would not be forthcoming for quite some time. Since further windfalls from the Olympic film were unlikely, it was decided to wind up the Olympia-Film GmbH.

But prior to dissolution Dr. Goebbels wanted another contract from the company, this agreement spelling out the property rights to the Olympic film. He was far more careful this time than he had been in December of 1935. He made several changes in the drafts and was particularly careful with clause one, in which he explicitly said that Olympia was Reich property.

Berlin, October 10, 1941

Contract

Between the Reich Ministry for Peoples' Enlightenment and Propaganda, the Party of the First Part, and Riefenstahl Film G.m.b.H., the Party of the Second Part.

The Olympia-Film G.m.b.H., which has been in liquidation since January 1, 1940, will, on the instruction of the Reich Ministry for Peoples' Enlightenment and Propaganda, be dissolved in the next few weeks.

Reference is made to the contract between Fräulein Leni Riefenstahl and the Reich ministry for Peoples' Enlightenment and Propaganda with relation to the formation of an Olympia-Film organization. In order, however, further to exploit the Olympic films, the following arrangement is made between the Reich, represented by the Reich Ministry for Peoples Enlightenment and Propaganda, and the Riefenstahl Film G.m.b.H.:

1. The Olympic films are Reich property. The exploitation and administration of the Olympic films for the Reich will be taken over by the Riefenstahl Film G.m.b.H., in whose custody the negatives will also be kept.
2. With the financial exploitation of the films, after the deduction of all expenses and taxes, 20% of the remaining net proceeds are to be paid to Fräulein Riefenstahl.
3. Administrative expenses are not to be charged. The Riefenstahl Film G.m.b.H. represents the interests in the exploitation of the Olympic films at the order of the Reich for nothing. However, direct expenses in connection with new starts of the film, conservation of negatives or the preparation of a metal copy for the purpose of long storage, as soon as this procedure is carried out promisingly, as well as costs incurred as a result of special orders through the Reich Ministry for Peoples' Enlightenment and Propaganda or the Reich Chancellery, will be deducted from the receipts.
4. The Riefenstahl Film G.m.b.H. has the obligation to provide a quarterly report to the Reich Ministry for Peoples' Enlightenment and Propaganda of its activities.
5. This contract takes effect on the date of the dissolution of the Olympia-Film G.m.b.H., Berlin.

Reich Ministry for Peoples' Enlightenment and Propaganda	Riefenstahl Film G.m.b.H.
(Signed) Dr. Ott	(Signed) Groskopf[88]

On January 9, 1942, as the Russian army was handing the Wehrmacht its first major defeat in the Battle for Moscow, the Olympia-Film GmbH was dissolved.[89] Its successor in interest was to be the Riefenstahl-Film GmbH. The Olympic film was now Reich property.

Most of Riefenstahl's team went to war. Looking chic in a tailored uniform complete with boots and a pistol, Riefenstahl herself went to Poland with a camera team. She had intended to cover the campaign but became sickened by what she saw and returned to Germany. Even Riefenstahl could find very little beauty in this particular struggle. Guzzi Lantschner, Heinz von Jaworsky, Walter Frentz, Sepp Allgeier, Albert Kling, and Wilhelm Siem were all active in propaganda companies filming the invasion of Poland. Jaworsky was chief cameramen for Feuertaufe, and the others got cameramen's credits for Feldzug in Polen. Hans Ertl became a lieutenant in a propaganda company and was active in the French and Russian campaigns. Frentz also became prominent as Hitler's chief film cameraman; he was attached to his headquarters.[90]

Some Olympia cameramen died in the war; others survived. Eberhard von der Heyden died on Crete. Wolf Hart and Hans Gottschalk went down with the Bismarck.[91] Willy Zielke, however, lived. He had been thrown back into an insane asylum immediately after finishing his work on Olympia; there he stayed until 1942. Riefenstahl got him out to help on Tiefland, but he was too sick and exhausted to work and he went home. Ironically Zielke's state of health--he was too ill to be drafted--may be the reason he is alive today.

During the War, Olympia continued to be shown. It had runs in Switzerland, in Scandinavia, and in the occupied territories, such as France and Holland. The film brought in some money, but not much. It was screened in Japan in July of 1942. A lunatic SS officer suggested that the film be shown to the captive Russian population with a foreword saying that the Russian people, too, could have participated at the wonderful 1936 Olympics if they had not been slaves to the perversions of communism.[92] Since the National Socialists were systematically starving the Russian civilians in the occupied areas, it is doubtful whether this propaganda would have been particularly effective. No doubt the Russians would have been more than happy to be in a warm theater--no matter what was playing.

As the war went on, Olympia stopped running. Tobis itself was in the process of being amalgamated in the Cautio Treuhand, the huge trust that would be running the whole motion-picture industry in Germany. In any case, by 1943, Olympia was an old film. Its commercial possibilities had been exploited. The situation worsened. It became clear that Germany was going to lose the war, so the Propaganda Ministry preferred to show mindless entertainment films, or such inspirational ones as Kolberg. Riefenstahl did nothing to promote the film. She was busy working on Tiefland and (if Heinrich von Jaworsky is correct) waiting for the allies to win the war.

And then, it was over. Hitler was dead, Germany in ruins. But Riefenstahl still had her health. She was relatively young; and, she still had the negatives of Olympia. What would the future of the film be?

OLYMPIA SINCE THE WAR

The subsequent history of the Olympic film has in some ways become symbolic of the efforts of Europe and America to lay the ghost of National Socialism to rest. Since the war, Riefenstahl has maintained that the film was not a National Socialist one, and that she was an innocent film maker caught in a certain time and place. Others are not so sure. But in the meantime, the Olympic film has assumed a life of its own quite apart from what its adherents or detractors may say about it. The film has been recut so many times that seeing the full version shown in 1938 is nearly impossible. Most persons have only seen a scratched 16mm print borrowed from a local library, but even under these conditions the film survives and manages to make an impression. This chapter will recount the history of the film's return to respectability.

In England, a country with little reason to let bygones be bygones with regard to Hitler, and the only country where

Olympia did not get some kind of showing before the war, the change of heart came quite quickly in 1948. The Olympic spirit flourished in Britain even under awful post-war conditions, and there was great interest in the film, as well as the wish to get some ideas for the proposed British Olympic film.

The British were lucky. They had excellent prints of both the long and short version. The long English language version the German embassy had was seized at the beginning of the war, and the film was then turned over to the Army Kinema Corporation. It was shown to the press in February of 1948 and got generally good reviews, although one newspaper called it "... a brilliant and intermittently repulsive work."[93] Other papers said the victory ceremonies and the flag raisings went on far too long, but the British critics were generally respectful. Interestingly, the BBC obtained its own copy of the film to train announcers.[94] Evidently the BBC was impressed by the effectiveness of the narration in the film.

During these years, the legal status of Olympia, as with other German films produced in the Third Reich, was nonexistent. All copyright protection had been forfeited, and the films could be used by anyone having an interest in them. In 1948, the Westport International Company got hold of a long English nitrate version of Olympia at the Library of Congress. Westport chopped it up to make a shorter film called Kings of the Olympics. The film almost completely concentrated on the American victories. Ironically it seems far more chauvinistic than did the original film. At first, the Westport people made some effort to recut the film, but after initial attempts, Westport paid Riefenstahl the backhanded compliment of including the sequences with no changes at all. The original nitrate film and the material cut up by the Westport International group still remain in the Library of Congress nitrate vaults at Suitland, Maryland--evidence of the trivializing of a great film.

There is evidence that the Cinémathèque Française has some material from Olympia, but it is not clear how much. Another repository of film in France, the Centre Nationale de la Cinématographie, has part one of the French version, Les Dieux du Stade, but it is not known whether this version is part of the spoils of war. So Olympia remained known, and it was shown to select audiences quite soon after the war. As almost always happens with films that for one reason or another are difficult to see, its reputation began to soar. The Museum of Modern Art had a print, although a very bad one, and it circulated the diving and marathon sequences widely to film clubs. Adding to Olympia's reputation, in 1948 the International Olympic Committee finally delivered to Riefenstahl the Olympic Gold Medal that had been awarded to her in 1939, thus giving the impression that the Olympic film could have not been propaganda.

In these same years, Riefenstahl herself was not enjoying the same quick return to respectability as the Olympic film. She had been held for interrogation by both the American and French authorities and was in jail intermittently until 1948. According to her own statements, she lost all property to the French Army of Occupation, and it was only after 1948 that she could begin a number of lawsuits to get the negatives of the Olympic film returned to her. Also according to her, she was cleared of any direct or implied wrongdoing in the National Socialist period by all courts and denazification tribunals and, on this basis, she was able to get the Olympic film returned to her.

The results of the American Seventh Army interrogation declared Riefenstahl to be a Nazi sympathizer; her comments, therefore, should be taken with at least a grain of salt. This writer has also seen none of the French evidence or findings on Riefenstahl, which if they exist, should be interesting reading. During Riefenstahl's denazification, Ernst Jäger wrote an extremely eloquent and handsome statutory declaration on her behalf.[95] He pointed out that Riefenstahl was certainly no National Socialist and that in many ways she had defied the regime. He described her as being politically blind, but he also said that this fault was shared by others, too, who buried themselves in artistic and intellectual pursuits. (This was a grateful gesture on Jäger's part, and one that seems to have been spontaneous.)

In the late fifties, Riefenstahl returned to something like respectability, and the Olympic film, at least in expurgated versions, began to be seen again. The British producer Norman Swallow put fifty minutes of Olympia on BBC-1 in 1957. In December of 1957, the films were seen for the first time in Germany since the war. When shown to film clubs at the Titania-Palast in Berlin and at the Studio für Filmkunst in Bremen, they were received enthusiastically. As a result of these showings, Riefenstahl decided to get the films released for public viewing in West Germany.

Getting these films approved for release proved to be far from easy. In the 1950's, West Germany feared a recurrence of fascist tendencies. The government was worried that a look at swastikas or Adolf Hitler might somehow stimulate a new wave of enthusiasm for National Socialism. The first time that Hitler's face appeared on a magazine cover in the Federal Republic after the war, the event received international coverage, with special attention paid to the reaction of Germans, who were extremely sensitive to criticism directed at the new Federal Republic. Since Riefenstahl had been one of the best-known celebrities of the former regime, it is not surprising that her films were not easily approved for showing in West Germany.

A few words on the censorship system in the Federal Republic of Germany are in order. In 1949, after the Allies relinquished censorship control, the West German government established an organization based on the American Breen Office, a self-censorship authority known as the *Freiwillige Selbstkontrolle der Filmwirtschaft* (FSK). This organization decided which films would be released for viewing to the general public, as well as which films could be seen by children. This organization is still officially the main censorship authority in the Federal Republic. However, there is another authority --called the Filmbewertungsstelle (FBW)--that in an interesting way imposes a sort of positive censorship. If the FSK is the stick of the system, the FBW is the carrot. It can award films of special merit or artistic value with the rating "valuable" or "especially valuable." This special rating entitles the film to a considerable rebate on the entertainment tax that normally must be paid on every film shown in the Federal Republic. Obviously, the rating is one that is much coveted. In theory, the two organizations are independent. In fact, they are interrelated, and until 1971 a release from the FSK was a prerequisite for submission to the FBW.

To get *Olympia* released by the FSK as well as to get a rating for the film from the FBW, Riefenstahl worked up extensive defenses of *Olympia*, supported by affidavits from Frederick A. Mainz and Hans Ertl, letters of support from Carl Diem and Ritter von Halt--everyone maintaining that the film was nonpolitical and a document celebrating the glory of the Olympic spirit. Riefenstahl submitted a number of the best reviews of the film. In Appendixes C and D, the author has included the text of two of the most complete defenses, "A Report on the Production of the Olympic Film," and "The Foundation of the Appeal against the Decision of the Committee of Review of January 30, 1958." These defenses give a good idea of Riefenstahl's main arguments. The appeal from the FBW decision is especially interesting because it describes the German unease about the visual style of the film after the war, as well as Riefenstahl's defense of this style as nonpolitical.

Riefenstahl's defense is a mixture of excellent arguments, omissions of fact, and highly inaccurate statements. Her argument that Dr. Goebbels tried to get rid of her seems adequately supported by the record. But some of her other points in "A Report on the Production of the Olympic Film" should be mentioned:

- A proof that the Games were non-political is shown by the IOC's decision of June 8, 1939 to hold the Winter Games in Garmisch-Partenkirchen once again, as well as the award on the same date of the Olympic medal of honor to Leni Riefenstahl.

This, in fact is more accurately a reflection on the conservative politics of the members of the IOC than it is an indication that the Games were nonpolitical.

- There was full Jewish participation in the Games.

As most books on the subject have pointed out, with the exception of a few token Jews forced upon the National Socialists, Jewish participation was far from complete.

- Even after the Games, Dr. Lewald and Dr. Diem were not attacked by the regime.

After the Games were over, Dr. Lewald was asked to resign as president of the Organization Committee, and his place was taken by that worthy Olympian, Field Marshal Walter von Reichenau.

- The Olympic film was not sponsored by a government organization, either before or after its creation.

The author believes that the preceding material renders this statement at least questionable.

- The government had nothing to do with the financing of the film, which was solely financed by Tobis.

This seems an especially shaky allegation in light of the abundant material in Coblentz, described by Hans Barkhausen, as well as in chapter I.

It should also be pointed out that the witnesses backing Riefenstahl's claim were not too solid. Ritter von Halt was, after all, a National Socialist. Dr. Diem was a fine man, and no one denied his dedication to sport, but his protests that the 1936 Olympic Games were nonpolitical, an "oasis" in the horror of National Socialism, clash rather oddly with his statement written exultantly at a time the Germans were attaining victory after victory in the first stages of World War II:

> How much of that which constitutes the new German ideology and German strength is an inheritance from ancient Sparta![96]

After the war, Diem unceasingly tried to defend the 1936 Games as non-political, never admitting to what extent he had been used by the Nazis as a figurehead. His defense of Riefenstahl was partially a defense of himself.

However, Riefenstahl was successful in obtaining distribution for the film. One can see how shrewd her defense was. To refuse Olympia a release after all the glowing endorsements by Ritter Von Halt and Dr. Diem, not to mention the support of major international figures in international sport like Avery Brundage, would be tantamount to saying that the major figures in the Olympic movement were either lying, or closet fascists (which, after all, was the argument the East Germans had been making for years). Her position was more powerful than it first seemed.

On January 8, 1958, Fest der Schönheit was released for general viewing, and on February 5, 1958, Fest der Völker was also released by the FSK. The film, with judicious cuts, could be seen in Germany. Riefenstahl was not so successful with the FBW, however. The film was refused a rating by the Committee of Review, and on April 19, 1958, Riefenstahl filed an appeal (see Appendix D). It does not appear that she ever got a special rating for the film, but she was free to exploit the film in Germany.

Even with the FSK's approval of the film's release, Riefenstahl's troubles were far from over. It has been mentioned previously that films produced by the Reich between 1933 and 1945 were considered to have lost all copyright protection. They could be used by anyone who wanted to use them. The documentary film The Rise and Fall of the Third Reich, narrated by William L. Shirer, is a case in point; the film was a compilation of films acquired from numerous archival sources. The producers did not have to pay for the use of the film or get permission to use it, and many other films documenting the Third Reich were produced equally as inexpensively. However, in 1963, as a conciliatory gesture to the Federal Republic of Germany, the American government once again turned over the ownership rights of certain German films to the West German government. The films included documentaries and newsreels formerly owned as property of the Reich. In the usual German fashion, a government-sponsored corporation was established to control these films and exploit them commercially. The corporation was called the Transit-Film GmbH. If an American film maker now wants to use part of a wartime German newsreel, he must (theoretically at least) contact Transit-Film for permission to use the film. Then he must pay a fee for the footage.

In 1963, Transit began to look through the materials of Cautio Treuhand. It found that the signing over to the Reich of rights for the Olympic film--as well as the other Propaganda Ministry documents--which I have alluded to in chapters one and five conclusively established that Olympia was a film produced by the Third Reich; Riefenstahl therefore, was not the legal owner of the film.

This meant that Olympia became the property of Transit-Film and not the property of Leni Riefenstahl-Produktion. Riefenstahl must have been shocked, for several reasons, not the least being the possible blow to her reputation and the loss of income from the exploitation of the film. She took the position that these papers were a legal fiction, established on her behalf for tax or other purposes. Transit believed otherwise, and it looked as though a legal case was brewing. However, there were equally compelling reasons for settling the case out of court. Even if Riefenstahl's legal position were correct, the publicity from the court case would not have done her any good. And Transit, too, might have had substantial problems in proving its allegations. Most witnesses were dead, and Transit may also not have wanted problems or publicity. In any case, the parties came to the following agreement, which is observed to this day:

AGREEMENT

Between
Transit-Film Corporation by its legal representative, Frankfurt (Main), Hochstrasse 17, hereafter called Transit
and
Frau Leni Riefenstahl, Munich 13, Tengstrasse 20, (hereafter called LR for short)

Conditions:

Preliminary Remarks:

A. L.R. within the framework of the firm 'Olympiade-Film-GmbH, later in Olympia-Film GmbH--made both films about the Olympic Games of 1936 in Berlin; Fest der Völker and Fest der Schönheit in various language versions, as well as other sports films. She alone created these films as director, artistic group leader and head of production of the firm. Her interest was in the hands of her and her brother Heinz. Up to now LR was of the opinion that she was the single holder of all copyright and commercial rights in the Olympic film.

On the other hand, Transit, to which is assigned the job of the commercial exploitation of all films that were the property of the former German Reich, has uncovered documents that, in the opinion of Transit, lead to the overwhelming conclusion that the copyright and commercial rights in the Olympic film belonged to the German Reich, and that LR and her brother only held their interest in the Olympia-Film GmbH as trustees.

LR states that these documents were unknown to her up to now, and that these documents could only have formal significance: she refers to the possibility that the trusteeship might have been established for tax or some other reasons that can no longer be solidly established, on her behalf. For this reason, however, the real legal position and the real legal ownership of the Olympic film have not changed.

Transit, on the other hand, refers to the discovered documents from which it is clearly established that the German Reich became the possessors of the copyright and commercial rights.

B. In the interest of a calm further exploitation of the Olympic films, the parties make the following agreement:

1. Transit transfers the exploitation of the Olympic film of 1936 including all related short films as well as the archive materials to LR.

   LR is empowered hereby to designate herself at the closing of the agreement as possessor of the commercial rights in the film.

2. The net proceeds from exploitation, thus the remaining proceeds after the deduction of all expenses, will be shared between LR and Transit in the proportion of 70-30.

   LR is thereby empowered to deduct the usually classified costs and certainly costs of copies, censure and marketing up to 15% as well as the value-added tax.

3. LR will render an account half-yearly, starting with June 30, 1964, of her commercial activities.

4. No division of the commercial proceeds will take place for compensation that LR receives for contracts in connection with the projection of the Olympic films.

5. For the time until December 31, 1963 it is hereby agreed that eventual mutual claims

against each other are held cancelled, and all proceeds obtained up to December 31, 1963 belong to LR.

6. After 30 years from the taking effect of this agreement, the commercial rights return to Transit film.

7. Both parties pledge to keep the contents of this agreement secret as to third persons who are not a party to these proceedings.

Munich, the Frankfurt (Main), the 16 of January, 1964

Transit-Film GmbH

(signed) Dr. Mooshake Dr. Söhmel[97]

The reputation of the Olympic film since has been one of semirespectability, rather like that of a criminal who has reformed and become a pillar of the community--a small doubt always remains. Olympia has been firmly established as an art film. It shows up regularly at the retrospective houses, at college campuses, on educational television, appropriately shorn of most of the shots of swastikas, SS men, Julius Streicher, Dr. Goebbels, and Hitler. Riefenstahl's name sometimes appears in connection with some episode in the history of the Third Reich. By and large, however, Olympia escapes most accusations. In a large part, the excellence of the film, its apparent lack of bias and, in addition, the campaign waged by Riefenstahl and her supporters, have had the desired effect. But in spite of the kind words and acclaim for the film, still there are people who are not inclined to forgive or forget. Olympia was to be shown in February 1983, during the Olympic Week in Lausanne, Switzerland. The rabbi in Lausanne filed an official protest against the showing. He claimed that the film was shot at the order of the National Socialist regime and that therefore it, "was at the service of National Socialist propaganda."[98] Olympia was not shown.

In spite of occasional controversy, the film survives. The reels turn, the arc light flickers. Once again, framed against a brilliant Baltic sky, Erwin Huber tosses an iron ball; Jesse Owens soars in slow motion to his world's record in the broad jump; Dick Degener defies gravity in the diving sequence. On the screen, these are timeless images, seemingly unconnected to the historical events that gave birth to these images half a century ago.

NOTES

1. "Festliche Münchener Olympia-Film-Premiere," Licht Bild Bühne, 28 April 1938.

2. "Heute: Olympia-Film in Wien," Licht Bild Bühne, 28 April 1938.

3. Licht Bild Bühne, 2 May 1938.

4. Bavaria Tonwoche 19/1938 (newsreel).

5. Völkischer Beobachter, 3 May 1938.

6. "Olympia-Film bestand internationale Feuertaufe," Film-Kurier, 11 May 1938, p. 1.

7. "Telegramm an Leni Riefenstahl aus Griechenland," Film-Kurier, 14 June 1938, p. 3.

8. "Leni Riefenstahl und Sascha Guitry sprechen über Filmkunst," Film-Kurier, 20 June 1938; William L. Shirer, The Collapse of the Third Republic (New York: Simon & Schuster, 1969), p. 385n, citing Documents on German Foreign Policy, 1918-1945. Washington, D.C. Series D., Vol II, pp. 978-979; Paul Farmer, Vichy: Political Dilemma (New York: Columbia University Press, 1955), p. 188.

9. "Brusseler Start im Beisein des Königs," Film-Kurier, 24 June 1938, p. 1.

10. Jäger, "Hitler's Girlfriend," part V, 26 May 1939, p. 5.

11. "Festliche Olympia-Premiere in Belgrad," Film-Kurier, 24 June 1938, p. 2.

12. "Leni Riefenstahl à Paris," Le Figaro, 1 July 1938, p. 4; "Au Normandie: Les Dieux du Stade," Le Figaro, 6 July 1938; Le Matin, 3 July 1938.

13. "Paris vom Olympiafilm begeistert," Licht Bild Bühne, 7 July 1938, p. 2.

14. "Pressestimmen aus Frankreich über den Olympiafilm 1936," a typewritten list compiled by Riefenstahl, a carbon copy of which she sent to the author.

15. "Paris vom Olympiafilm begeistert," Licht Bild Bühne, 7 July 1938, p. 2.

16. RMVP, BA, R55/503, p. 221.

17. Riefenstahl, "Ein Bericht über die Herstellung der Olympia-Filme," p. 5.

18. RMVP, Bundesarchiv, R55/503, p. 221.

19. "Olympia-Film wird italienisch synchronisiert," Film-Kurier, 29 July 1938, p. 2.

20. "Skandinavien-Reise von Leni Riefenstahl," Film-Kurier, 3 August 1938, p. 2.

21. "Olympia film-Erfolg in Dänemark," Film-Kurier, 3

August 1938, p. 2.

22. "Leni Riefenstahl in Stockholm und Helsingfors," _Film-Kurier_, 6 August 1938, p. 2.

23. Ibid.

24. "Triumphaler Erfolg des Olympia-Films," _Film-Kurier_, 27 August 1938, p. 1; "Triumph des Olympia-Films in Venedig," _Licht Bild Bühne_, 27 August 1938, p. 1.

25. "Telegramme aus Venedig," _Film-Kurier_, 27 August 1938, p. 1.

26. "Grosser Erfolg des deutschen Filmschaffens," _Film-Kurier_, 27 August 1938, p. 1.

27. _New York Times_, 1 September 1938, p. 7; 2 September 1938, p. 21; 4 September 1938, p. 2.

28. Shirer, _The Rise and Fall of the Third Reich_, p. 377.

29. _Film-Kurier_, 27 September 1938, p. 1.

30. Richard M. Griffiths, _Fellow Travellers of the Right_ (London: Constable & Co., 1980), p. 292.

31. "Ausserordentlicher Erfolg des Olympia-Films in Rom," _Licht Bild Bühne_, 1 October 1938, p. 3.

32. "Leni Riefenstahl beim norwegischen König," _Film-Kurier_, 13 October 1938, p. 1; "Olympia-Film der Tobis in Anwesenheit Königs in Oslo gestartet," _Film-Kurier_, 14 October 1938, p. 1.

33. "Leni Riefenstahl vor den Studenten von Lund," _Film-Kurier_, 18 October 1938, p. 1; "Leni Riefenstahls Erfolg Kopenhagen," _Film-Kurier_, 19 October 1938, p. 1.

34. "Wardour Street Gossip by 'Tatler'," _Daily Film Renter_ (London), 29 October 1938.

35. "Bericht über die Reise nach London zwecks Placierung des Olympia-Films," RMVP, BA, R55/1327, pp. 334-336.

36. "Nix Nazi Olympix," _Variety_, 2 November 1938, p. 12.

37. "Wardour Street Gossip by 'Tatler'," _Daily Film Renter_, 1 November 1938.

38. Dilys Powell, "Films of the Week," _Times_, 13 April 1947.

39. Seventh Army Interrogation, p. 3.

40. RMVP, BA, R55/1328, p. 75.

41. Jäger, "Hitler's Girlfriend," 2 June 1939, part VI, p. 10.

42. Bill Henry, _Los Angeles Times_, 10 August 1936, (part 2), p. 13.

43. Berlin Document Center; Klaus Ullrich, _Olympia_

und die Deutschen, ([Berlin]: Gesellschaft zur Förderung des Olympischen Gedankens in der DDR [1961]), pp. 87-88, citing Mario Segni, "Operazione O. R.: I nazi a Roma," Vie Nouve, 15, No. 33, 20 August 1960, pp. 16-17.

44. Jäger, "Hitler's Girlfriend," part VI, p. 10.

45. Jäger, "Hitler's Girlfriend," 9 June 1939, part VII, p. 14.

46. Jäger, "Hitler's Girlfriend," part VI, p. 10.

47. Ibid.

48. "Walter Winchell on Broadway," Daily Mirror, 9 November 1938, p. 10.

49. "Anti-Nazis Protest Riefenstahl's Visit to Circulate Olympic Film," Motion Picture Herald, 12 November 1938, p. 19.

50. Jäger, "Hitler's Girlfriend," part VI, p. 11.

51. New York Times, 11 August 1964, p. 33.

52. Jäger, "Hitler's Girlfriend," part VI, p. 11.

53. Baron V. E. von Gienanth, Attaché to the German Embassy in Washington, to John E. Abbott, 20 December 1938, Museum of Modern Art Correspondence files.

54. Russell Lynes, Good Old Modern (New York: Atheneum, 1973), p. 111.

55. Shirer, The Rise and Fall of the Third Reich, p. 433 fn.

56. Jäger, "Hitler's Girlfriend," part VII, p. 13.

57. Jäger, "Hitler's Girlfriend," part VI, p. 11.

58. Jäger, "Hitler's Girlfriend," part VII, p. 14. Claire Dux was a quite famous Polish lyric soprano who had sung often in Berlin, where she had been married to Hans Albers. She sang with the Chicago Civic Opera and she married the food magnate Charles H. Swift in 1926.

59. Ibid.

60. Ibid., Acc. 285/Box 2197/Folder 949, Archives and Research Library, Henry Ford Museum, Dearborn, Michigan.

61. Jäger, "Hitler's Girlfriend," part VII, p. 14.

62. Ibid.

63. Ibid.

64. Cunningham, "Hitler makes U.S. Olympic Films advertise Germany," p. 15.

65. Hollywood Reporter, 29 November 1938, p. 5.

66. Jäger, "Hitler's Girlfriend," part IX, 23 June 1939, p. 13.

67. "Leni Riefenstahl Still Getting Business' Brushoff," Variety, 7 December 1938, pp. 1, 55.

68. Jäger, "Hitler's Girlfriend," part IX, p. 13.

69. Letter from Riefenstahl's secretary quoting Riefenstahl to author dated 16 September 1981.

70. Jäger, "Hitler's Girlfriend," part X, 10 July, 1939, p. 13.

71. Henry M'Lemore, "Henry Goes to Bat on Berlin Olympic Film--No Propaganda," Hollywood Citizen News, 17 December 1938.

72. Jäger, "Hitler's Girlfriend," part XI, 17 July 1939, p. 15.

73. RMVP, PA, R55/1328, p. 51.

74. Ibid., p. 53.

75. Leni Riefenstahl, interview with author (this particular comment was not transcribed).

76. William C. O'Neill, A Better World (New York: Simon and Schuster, 1982), p. 213, citing Leo C. Rosten, Hollywood: the Movie Colony, the Movie Makers (New York: Harcourt, Brace and Co., 1941).

77. Avery Brundage Collection, Applied Life Studies Library, University of Illinois, Urbana, Illinois.

78. Chicago Daily News, 29 May 1940.

79. Letter from Riefenstahl's secretary dated 16 September 1981.

80. Avery Brundage Collection.

81. Chicago Daily News, 29 May 1940.

82. Goebbels, Joseph, The Goebbels Diaries 1939-1941, trans. and ed. Fred Taylor (New York: G. P. Putnam's Sons, 1983), p. 9.

83. RMVP, BA, R55/1327, pp. 258-260.

84. Report to the Minister dated 16 March 1939, RMVP, BA, R55/1328, pp. 6-10.

85. Ibid.

86. RMVP, BA, R55/1327, p. 272.

87. RMVP, BA, R55/1328, pp. 9-10.

88. RMVP, BA, R55/1327, pp. 137-138.

89. Ibid., p. 19.

90. Hans Barkhausen, Filmpropaganda für Deutschland im Ersten und Zweiten Weltkrieg (Hildesheim and New York: Olms Presse, 1982), pp. 215, 216, 219, 240.

91. Javorsky, interview with author, interview with Gordon Hitchens, p. 128.

92. "Olympiade Film von L. Riefenstahl, Einsatz in den ehemaligen sowjetischen Gebieten," 1942. RMVP, BA, R55/1293.

93. News Chronicle (London), 7 February 1948.

94. Jack Davis, "Release this Olympic Film," Sunday Graphic (London), 1 February 1948.

95. Ernst Jäger, "Eidesstattliche Versicherung," 31 July 1948, sent by Leni Riefenstahl to author.

96. Kruger, _Die Olympischen Spiele 1936 und die Weltmeinung_, p. 12, citing Carl Diem, _Der Olympische Gedanke im neuen Europa_ (Berlin: 1942), p. 7.

97. Cautio Treuhand, R 109 I, vol. 2163, BA. According to a letter from Transit signed by W. Trimmel and dated 4 July 1983, this agreement is still in effect.

98. "Olympia-Film Verbannt," _Rhein-Zeitung_ (Coblenz), 16 February 1983.

• CHAPTER VI •

CONCLUSION

Regardless of Frau Riefenstahl's protestations and the natural inclination of most people to forget the past, Olympia is profoundly implicated with the National Socialist regime. It was financed by the Party. Every effort was made by the regime to insure that the film would be a success after its release. The Propaganda Ministry financed Riefenstahl's various jaunts all over Europe and the United States. German ambassadors and consular officials smoothed her way wherever she went, and she was clearly aware of this.

In an effort to show her independence from the regime, Riefenstahl has maintained that Olympia was in reality a sort of shoestring production. For instance, she says that she did not have an army of cameramen, but only some thirty-odd, and of those only Ertl, Frentz, Lantschner, Neubert, Scheib and Zielke turned out to be first-rate. However, she omits mentioning the hundreds of workers, such as the cafeteria and household crew at Haus Ruhwald, the drivers, the assistants, the prop men, and the stage managers; they, also, were at her disposal. In addition she could call upon various government and party units when she needed to. Dancing schools cooperated in providing nudes for the prologue; the German Navy lent its support at Kiel--and these are only two examples. Without the German government behind her, Riefenstahl certainly would not have had access to the newsreel footage shot by private companies at the Olympic Games. Her resources were immense, and the regime provided them.

But the film is most deeply and dangerously implicated with the regime in its depiction of National Socialist Germany itself. Both the Propaganda Ministry and Riefenstahl stated that the goal of the film was to show the Olympic Games in the framework of the New Germany. It is this aspect of the film that needs, most seriously, to be examined.

THE OLYMPIC FILM AS NATIONAL SOCIALIST PROPAGANDA

The author considers the Olympic film to be National Socialist propaganda. But there have been countless definitions of the word propaganda, none of which have been totally successful.[1] The most common definition denotes one group trying deliberately and consciously to change the ideas of another group. If we assume that definition as well as Riefenstahl's version of the facts, then Riefenstahl's arguments are correct. Such a definition of propaganda would exclude her film as propaganda. She has always denied that she was deliberately trying to instill National Socialist ideology in anyone. As we have seen, this position is questionable, but even assuming it to be true, this makes her no less a propagandist.

For my own purposes, I wish to quote extensively Jacques Ellul's _Propaganda: The Formation of Men's Attitudes_,[2] which includes a far broader notion of the word. Ellul argues that man in a technological society is surrounded by multiple forms of propaganda, many of which are not official. He makes a distinction between political propaganda and what he calls sociological propaganda. Political propaganda is propaganda as it is usually defined--that is, an attempt by government or another group to influence the goals of the public. But Ellul, on the other hand, describes sociological propaganda as "the penetration of an ideology by means of the sociological context."[3]

> Sociological propaganda springs up simultaneously; it is not the result of deliberate propaganda action. No propagandists deliberately use this method, though many practice it unwittingly, and tend in this direction without realizing it. For example, when an American producer makes a film, he has certain definite ideas he wants to express, which are not intended to be propaganda. Rather, the propaganda element is

> in the American way of life with which he is permeated and which he expresses in his film without realizing it. We see here the force of expansion of a vigorous society, which is totalitarian in the sense of the integration of the individual, and which leads to involuntary behavior.
>
> Sociological propaganda expresses itself in many different ways--in advertising, in the movies (commercial and non-political films), in technology in general, in education, in the Reader's Digest; and in social service, case work, and settlement houses. All these influences are in basic accord with each other and lead spontaneously in the same direction; one hesitates to call this propaganda. Such influences, which mold behavior, seem a far cry from Hitler's great propaganda setup. Unintentional (at least in the first stage), non-political, organized along spontaneous patterns and rhythms, the activities we have lumped together (from a concept that might be judged arbitrary or artificial) are not considered propaganda by either sociologists or the average public.
>
> And yet with deeper and more objective analysis, what does one find? These influences are expressed through the same media as propaganda. They are really directed by those who make propaganda. To me this fact seems essential.... Such activities are propaganda to the extent that the combination of advertising, public relations, social welfare, and so on produces a certain general conception of society, a particular way of life."[4]

Ellul has provided a powerful mechanism with which one can classify many of the artifacts of popular culture as propaganda. He gives us a tool we can use to categorize a film like the Howard Hawks-Christian Nyby The Thing from Another World as anti-communist propaganda. This holds true for the film even though its subject matter is not communism and the film was certainly not made at the order of any government agency. Hawks or Nyby might indignantly (and correctly) state that the film was not intended to be propaganda. Their denial makes no difference. What they have produced is unconscious propaganda. In Ellul's view, not only do we all submit to propaganda, but we unconsciously make it ourselves. In this sense, Riefenstahl's film is National Socialist propaganda. It is also sociological propaganda and I would now like to discuss why I believe this.

In maintaining that the Olympic film is National Socialist propaganda, one must keep in mind long-term propaganda goals and short-term problems of the regime. Supporters of the film have been extremely naive about the National Socialists. They have decided that the film was not a propaganda instrument because it did not mindlessly display a string of German victories and crudely disparage the athletes of other nations. This explanation does not give the National Socialists much credit either for shrewdness or for duplicity.

Historically, the National Socialists were always ready to repress their true aims in the interest of practical politics. When it suited them, they could profess themselves as peace-loving. When it was to their advantage, they could pretend fairness to the Jews. When it seemed necessary, they could even dispense with their most deeply held belief, anti-Marxism, and sign a nonaggression pact with Soviet Russia. It is no wonder that some experts have said that National Socialism really had no ideology outside Führer worship. So, if the Olympic film seems unbiased and a tribute to the Olympic movement, this illusion in no way runs counter to the propaganda aims of the National Socialist regime in the middle thirties. Rather it supports them.

The Olympic film reflects several of the long-term propaganda goals of Germany in the mid-thirties. First, it must be remembered that the Olympics were held at a time (1935-1937) when Germany was waging a peace offensive (see Chapter I), and wanted to show itself to Europe and the world as "liberal." The National Socialists saw that the Olympic Games were a marvelous way to further this aim. To show the extent to which they were willing to go, one need only point to the Propaganda Ministry directives to German newspapers regarding press treatment of black athletes.

No doubt the National Socialists were truly revulsed at the victories of the American black athletes. After Jesse Owens' and Ralph Metcalfe's wins, <u>Der Angriff</u> ran its famous polemic against "black auxiliaries." In his diary, Dr. Goebbels said that Owens' victory was a day of shame for the white race. The point is, however, this revulsion is not reflected in public policy. On August 3, 1936, the Propaganda Ministry told the German press:

> The race question should be completely disregarded. Negroes are American citizens and must be treated as such. That does not exclude the fact that stating a negro [sic] to be a winner could be repeated in a secondary position.[5]

And later on, the Propaganda Ministry insisted that Owens be well treated in German papers. Upon his return to America, Owens had defended Hitler and stated that it was bad taste for journalists to attack Germany's man of the hour.[6] As a result, on January 18, 1937, Herr Berndt ordered:

> Jesse Owens has been repeatedly attacked and his behavior treated critically or ironically in the German press. Such criticism does not have a favorable effect in foreign countries, because the impression is produced that Germany was forced to have consideration for its guests during the Olympic Games. Now, however, it unveils its true nature. In addition, Jesse Owens is supposed to have remained loyal to Germany throughout, and for instance, flatly declined a Jewish offer to work against Germany.[7]

The German press was also directed to report the Games in a scrupulously fair manner. On August 12, 1936, the Propaganda Ministry cautioned the German newspapers against reporting the winning of bronze medals by German athletes in large headlines, while reporting on the winning of silver and gold medals by foreign athletes in small print.[8] The papers also were told to stop hiding the fact that the German soccer team had been defeated by the Norwegians.[9] An article entitled "Sport and Race" was suppressed by the Ministry on the grounds that it would annoy foreigners,[10] and the German press was enjoined against rejoicing too much over German victories or talking too much about them.[11] The Propaganda Ministry went so far as to stop all point lists. This refers to the common practice of giving a nation three points for each gold medal, two for each silver medal, one for each bronze medal, and then adding up the points to see which nation "wins." Germany was far ahead in points, and at first the Propaganda Ministry said the practice was perfectly all right, but it soon changed its policy, and on August 6, 1936, the Propaganda Ministry ordered:

> The tabulation of point lists for the Olympic events must henceforth be forbidden, because they establish bad feeling, and the International Committee has already complained officially. Newspapers with point lists will be confiscated. Also, the comparison of numbers of gold, silver and bronze medals should better be discontinued, or in any case, cautiously handled, since otherwise, from this, further difficulties might also arise. The axiom is that it is not nations that compete, but persons.[12]

It would be naive to think that the National Socialists would allow the media to be anything but totally unpartisan and unbiased in reporting the Olympics.

In light of this position, Riefenstahl's treatment of the Games seems to fulfill the major propaganda aims of the regime. At least, it does not run counter to them in any major way. The film seems to have treated the athletes fairly. I knew very little about the 1936 Olympics when I first saw the film, and I had the strong impression that America would have "won" the Olympics, had points for medals in the different events been tallied. In truth, however, Germany won quite handily, a fact that is not reflected in the film--all of this very much in line with Propaganda Ministry directives.

Riefenstahl has said that she was attacked for including too much footage of black athletes--Owens and Metcalfe for example. Perhaps for Dr. Goebbels' taste, there was too much footage, but its presence does not alter the fact that treating the black athletes fairly was official National Socialist policy.

Another major goal of the National Socialists was to depict the friendliness and good will of Germany. The film reflects this propaganda aim in several ways. In its fairness to all nations, the film disarms criticism. The author is aware that this comment, as well as several of the preceding ones, puts Leni Riefenstahl in something of a double bind. If she had made a racist, chauvinistic film, then she would clearly have been making a National Socialist film. But by making a film that does not reflect racism or nationalism, she is still making a National Socialist film. To be fair, it must be remembered that artists and writers who produce sociological propaganda may be entirely unaware that they are doing so. Intent may be a very important part of the definition of political propaganda. It is not so critical in a definition of sociological propaganda.

The film shows the friendliness and good will of Germany in another way: its treatment of Hitler. Ernst Jäger had said that if Triumph des Willens was designed to show Hitler as a god, then Olympia was designed to show Hitler as a friendly, smiling sports lover--the man next door. Riefenstahl may not have had this specific intention in mind, but the finished film certainly reflects its accomplishment. The long German version, especially, features numerous shots of Hitler and his entourage cheering and laughing at victories, and appearing saddened by defeat. The effectiveness of this approach can be seen in a quote from a Hungarian newspaper:

> I saw the film and I saw the Chancellor. This Führer is more than a diplomat, he is more than a statesman, he is more than the all-powerful Chancellor of a people of 75 million. This Führer is a man. A man with warm inner feelings, with a warm heart, because a man who can so unself-consciously pay homage to beauty, who can applaud a symbolic victory of sport, who finds such a happy joy in youth--he is the true Führer, the true man, who does not have only intelligence, but also soul![13]

Herman Weigel describes Hitler in this film as "ein rechter Spassvogel."[14] The description is not inaccurate, nor is it accidental.

The Olympia film made excellent propaganda in yet another way--the simple fact of its existence. A nation's technology and accomplishments provide another form of propaganda. Like the airship Hindenburg, the Autobahns, and the Olympic Games themselves, the Olympic film was a huge propaganda accomplishment for the regime.

The German newspapers delighted in pointing out that the 1932 Olympics had been held in Los Angeles, the film capital of the world. In spite of this major opportunity, the newspapers went on to say, no Olympic film had come out of these Games. In noting this fact, the Germans were hinting that the grasping, materialistic film merchants in Hollywood had not had sufficient idealism or intelligence to recognize the importance of an Olympic film. Film-Kurier stated in April 1936:

> In the USA, new records in newsreel coverage were established. It was reported how many thousand meters from the competitions on the West coast would be shown in New York.... An artistic, permanent production covering the noble meeting of nations came to nothing. Naturally Hollywood and others had calculated to the last dollar what the foreign influx of the film industry would have cost the studios in interrupted labor ... $250,000 was established.[15]

The German press mocked the sole monument (outside of the newsreels) that Hollywood produced, The Runner from Marathon with Victor de Kova.[16] In contrast, Germany had displayed the imagination and foresight to pour a huge amount of money and talent into the production of an Olympic film, a film which amazed and pleased the world. If the Olympic Games themselves had been a propaganda coup, so was the Olympic film, and it reached far more people than the Games had. By its very existence, people were forced to admire the nation that produced it.

In the same vein, Frank Maraun said in his criticism of the film:

> A triumph of the documentary film. In Los Angeles the Americans tried, at the time, to produce a film of the Olympic Games. They filmed a great deal, but the film was never seen. It was a failure. In Germany, the place of cultivation and the stronghold of the documentary film, it has succeeded in a most convincing manner. It had to succeed here because Germany had created, for the 11th Olympic Games in Berlin, such a grandly perceived, symbolic framework which from the outset lifted the event out of the sphere of a mere sports report for the creatively reproducing camera and because here we already have a tradition of not only copying reality with the film but also revealing the idea which animates and illumi-

> nates. This is not only an action of the film, it is a result of National Socialism, which is penetrating the total life of the nation into its most detailed ramifications, with its idea-based directional force and which has accustomed us to see reality and idea together. Only in the ideological structure of National Socialism could this great documentary film have come into being as an artistic achievement. Indeed it had never existed previously.[17]

So Olympia qualifies as propaganda for the regime on this level as well.

In addition, Olympia may not be as unbiased as it first appears. A certain bias is discernible in three main categories.

First, the original German version contained much National Socialist material that was not seen by foreign viewers of the film. German victories in the hammer throw, the javelin, and the shot put were shown as special cause for National Socialist celebration. Hitler, especially in part one, was felt as an almost continual presence. So the German version, through a glorification of the National Socialist leaders, had a certain propaganda goal and was engineered with this goal in mind.

Second, the use of slow motion, reaction shots, and emphatic music gave some emphasis to German victories. In addition, even when they did not win, German athletes could be emphasized by means of editing footage. In the 100-yard dash, though numerous preliminary heats were run, Riefenstahl chose the one in which the German, Erich Borchmeyer, was victorious. In the discus, she showed Willi Schroeder as one of the final contestants, although he was out of the serious competition quite early. The decathlon was portrayed so that the only serious competition for the Americans was the German Erwin Huber.

Third, evidence exists that the nations friendly with Germany got better coverage than the nations Germany disliked. For instance, Japan had signed an anti-comintern pact with Germany in November of 1936, and Japanese victories got extensive coverage. Italy, Britain, and the United States were also well treated. On the other hand, not one Czech victory was either mentioned or shown.

From these points, one can make a case that the film is unfair. To do so, however, is to miss the point. The film is dangerous _because_ of its apparent fairness, not in spite of it. If the film had been transparently unfair or racist, it could be dismissed as another typical piece of Nazi stupidity. To the extent the above charges are true, the film would not have the credibility that made it such a brilliant propaganda weapon.

The film is alluring. If one could erase the knowledge of the subsequent horrors, it would be almost impossible to see the film and not be conned into believing that living in National Socialist Germany might not be so bad after all. Hitler's Germany of 1936 seems like a normal community--more than that, an exceptionally healthy and happy one. If the film gives this effect now, one can only guess at the effect the film had before World War II and Auschwitz. It promotes Germany and, in addition, makes fascism appear dangerously attractive. _Olympia_ shows a country that apparently has overcome the fragmentation inherent in a modern capitalist society and has achieved a oneness with native community, a _Volksgemeinschaft_. The film suggests that through sheer will and heroicism, not through politics or community effort, man can transcend his limitations. It shows a Germany that has fulfilled itself, a country that wants only to share peace with the other nations of the world.

Fascist impulses were felt in almost every European country in the late thirties. _Olympia_ spoke directly to these impulses and reached millions of European people directly in ways the original Olympics had not.

Carl Diem called the Berlin Olympics an "oasis" from the horrors of the National Socialist regime, but his is a false analogy. An oasis is not manmade, its waters are real, not illusory, and it does not deceive. Perhaps neither Carl Diem nor Leni Riefenstahl meant to deceive anyone, but the fact remains that the Olympic Games and the film portraying them were the cruelest of deceits. Both held out the promise of peace during a time when Germany had already set its course for war. If an analogy is needed either for the 1936 Olympic Games or for Leni Riefenstahl's film about them, an apt classical analogy would be the Trojan Horse.

Olympia was as culturally embedded in the time and

place in which it was made as any fossil is embedded in the soil in which it once lived. This work shows clearly that Olympia was intimately connected with the National Socialist regime, receiving from this regime its financing and promotion throughout the world. Riefenstahl may have been promised complete freedom to make the film as she wished, but the reason that she was permitted such freedom related directly to her friendship with Adolf Hitler. The records in the Bundesarchiv show that, for the most part, relations between Dr. Goebbels and Riefenstahl were such that they could at least work together in a reasonably amicable way. In the last six months of 1936 an open feud existed between them. For obvious reasons, Riefenstahl emphasized this feud as evidence of her distance from the party. But National Socialist Germany was, as H. R. Trevor-Roper called it, a satrapy, and warfare between prominent party figures was common. Dr. Goebbels carried on feuds with both Field Marshal Goering and Alfred Rosenberg; even so, their devotion to National Socialism is not in doubt.

I have also maintained in the dissertation from which this work is derived that the aesthetics of Olympia are very much of their time and place and show a strong relationship to a neoclassical tradition and romantic tradition, carried on in a trivialized manner in National Socialist art. The neoclassical style and the Romantic style were also popular in Weimar Germany, and the use of these styles by Riefenstahl is a continuation of her ongoing aesthetic approach rather than a major interruption of it. This reading tends to be in line with a growing number of interpretations, some of them Marxist, which see National Socialism as the logical continuation of trends already apparent in Weimar society. In any case, Olympia is very much in keeping with the irrational mystical tendencies discernible in German ideology since the beginning of the nineteenth century.

Largely because of Riefenstahl's desire to idealize the images in Olympia, the film sometimes comes perilously close to being kitsch. Romantic art has often fallen into this trap because of its excessive sentimentality. And in Olympia, with the soft focus, the quasi-religious iconography and Windt's pounding music, the images in the film in part seem overdone. One example of almost classical bad taste is the living postcard. Yet this is precisely what we are given in the prologue as Myron's Discobolus "becomes" Erwin Huber with his loincloth and, that ugliest of all haircuts, the Berliner Schnitt. The transition is saved only because of the strength of Willy Zielke's photography and because of the importance of the idea behind the transition. However, parts of the "morning mood" sequence, in which Windt's music blares over the soundtrack while we are presented with the pale behinds of naked athletes romping in the water, are impossible to salvage. The shots seem affected and silly.

This desire to superimpose meaning on the shot is probably the most old-fashioned aspect of Olympia. The current fashion is an attempt by directors to be more objective, which gives us more room to interpret the film ourselves. Riefenstahl's style gives us very little room to do this.

There is obviously a Bazinian issue here. Because of her reliance on editing and her lack of interest in the long take, Riefenstahl is often cited as a director whose style is in conflict with André Bazin's philosophy of sound film. But the contrast has been oversimplified. Riefenstahl used long takes in Olympia--in the gymnastics footage and in the 1500-meter run. It is true that Riefenstahl favored a narrow depth of field, which Bazin, at least during one phase of his career, felt was not the high road of cinema. But Bazin himself did not remain true to these aesthetic beliefs. What he seems to have consistently had as his objective was what he called "the illusion of objective presentation,"[18] and it seems to me that Bazin always remained true to this aesthetic aim. It was why he was so much enamored of the Italian neorealists, and it would appear that it is precisely this objective presentation, this wish for Latin clarity, that is lacking in Riefenstahl's subjective, idealistic, and highly German film.

Although it was a documentary film, and I believe that Olympia would fit most definitions of a documentary film, how much of the world does it show? The Berlin Olympics were themselves a kind of theatrical ritual, cut off totally from the realities of existence in Germany. They were perhaps National Socialist Germany's largest and most successful Thingtheater. Riefenstahl photographed much of this material in a romantic, mystical way; then she took the material and made a construct of it to show a mythical and metaphysical world order evolving out of the Olympic Games themselves. She may even claim to have demonstrated some notion of Platonic realism by showing the realities behind the mere appearance of things, but in much of the film at least, the objective reality is smothered under layers of superimposed meaning achieved through music, sound, photographic style, and editing. For this reason, the aesthetics of Olympia seem somewhat dated; perhaps no one would make a film in quite this style again.

Whatever the defects in style, Olympia is a great film and an important one. Olympia was a film that took chances. It experimented with montage in extremely interesting ways, although in ways quite different from those used by the great Russian directors. It is also significant because Riefenstahl showed an inclination to experiment with the sound track and to let sound and music be, at times, the organizing force rather than merely the image. This interest in the sound track was shared by two other films of the same period, Walt Disney's Fantasia and Sergei Eisenstein's Alexander Nevsky. All three films displayed the same ambitiousness, and in a way all three suffer from the same faults. But each reveals its director's interest in synesthaesia--the combination of sight, sound, and the other senses to produce film art of greater intensity than what was known before. Writing about Penthesilea, Riefenstahl stated:

> Film will become art only when--by the means that are possible only in film--it creates the artistic experience that no other art form can give us: the harmonious fusion of optical, acoustical, rhythmical and architectonic factors--then film will become the king of all arts.[19]

But Penthesilea was never made. Disney's film was a disappointment at the box office, and Eisenstein's experiments came to an end when Ivan the Terrible was shelved. On the level of commercial film, these very tentative experiments have never been resumed, which I believe has been a terrible loss.

With all its faults, with its tendency to kitsch, with its pretentiousness, Riefenstahl's Olympia still seems to be one of those works that becomes larger than its subject. It is as German as Wagner's Der Ring des Nibelungen, and in its way, as epic. Initially a documentary film on the Olympic Games, it became instead a cosmology. In the words of the critic Herman Weigel, Olympia is Riefenstahl's greatest and maddest work.

NOTES

1. George N. Gordon, Persuasion: The Theory and Practice of Manipulative Communication (New York: Hastings House, 1971), citing Michael Choukas, Propaganda Comes of Age (Washington, D.C.: Public Affairs Press, 1965), pp. 13-18.

2. Jacques Ellul, Propaganda: The Formation of Men's Attitudes, trans. Konrad Kellen and Jean Lerner (New York: Alfred A. Knopf, Vintage Books, 1973).

3. Ibid., p. 63.

4. Ibid., pp. 64-65.

5. BA Sammlung Sänger, 3 August 1936, Zsg. 102, vol. 3, p. 3.

6. Louis Effner, "Owens, Back, Gets Hearty Reception," New York Times, 25 August 1936, p. 25.

7. BA, Sammlung Sänger, 18 January 1937, vol. 4, p. 44.

8. BA, Sammlung Traub, 12 August 1936, Zsg. 110, vol. 2, p. 105.

9. Ibid., 13 August, p. 111.

10. Ibid., 13 August, p. 111.

11. BA, Sammlung Sänger, 3 August 1936, p. 3.

12. Ibid., 6 August 1936, p. 10.

13. "Ungarisches Presselob für den Olympia film," Licht Bild Bühne, 7 October 1938, p. 2, citing Eugen Piday in Pesti Ujsag.

14. Herman Weigel, "Randbemerkungen zum Thema," Film-Kritik, no. 188, August 1972, p. 430.

15. "Das Olympische Filmwerk in den ersten Vorbereitungen," Film-Kurier, 22 April 1936, p. 1.

16. Paramount's Million Dollar Legs (1932) with W. C. Fields and Jack Oakie, and Walt Disney's Barnyard Olympics (1932) do not go far in disproving Germany's argument.

17. Frank Maraun, "Triumph des Dokumentarfilms," Der deutsche Film, no. 11, May 1938, trans. in Film Culture, no. 56-7, Spring 1973, p. 192.

18. André Bazin, "The Evolution of the Language of Cinema," What Is Cinema, trans. and ed. Hugh Gray (Berkeley, Los Angeles and London: University of California Press, 1967), p. 37.

19. Riefenstahl, "Why Am I Filming 'Penthesilea'?" Film Culture, p. 197.

• APPENDIX A •

CONTRACT

For the Production of an Olympic Film

§1

To Fräulein Leni Riefenstahl in Berlin-Wilmersdorf Hindenburgstrasse 97 will be conferred the production of a Summer Olympic Film. The said person will direct the overall administration and production of this film.

§2

The cost of the production of the film is estimated at 1.5 million Reichsmarks and will be paid out to Fräulein Riefenstahl in the following amounts:

On November 15, 1935	RM 300,000
On April 1, 1936	RM 700,000
On November 1, 1936	RM 200,000
On January 1, 1937	RM 300,000

§3

Out of the amount of 1.5 million Reichsmarks (§ 2) Fräulein Riefenstahl will receive for her work exclusive of her outlays (for travel, expenses, autos, etc.) a personal renumeration of 250,000 RM.

§4

Fräulein Riefenstahl is obligated to the Reichsministerium für Aufklärung und Propaganda to keep and submit substantiated accounts of the employment of the 1,500,000 RM.

§5

Fräulein Riefenstahl is alone responsible for the artistic creation and the organizational execution of the Olympic film.

§6

The Reichsministerium für Volksaufklärung und Propaganda insures as was the case of the production Triumph of the Will, that the German newsreel companies, Ufa, Tobis-Melo and Fox, will subordinate themselves to Fräulein Riefenstahl and are to arrange for all material shot for the Olympia film to be placed at her disposal in the following ways:

(a) Finished archive material on hand up to a license fee that may not be higher than 3 RM.
(b) Newly taken and scrap material free of charge.
(c) A lavender copy of every newsreel that appears in a theater will be produced at Fräulein Riefenstahl's expense.

§7

The cost for the seal of the contract will be undertaken by Fräulein Riefenstahl.

The Reich Minister für
Volksaufklärung und Propaganda__________________

• APPENDIX B •

AGREEMENT

Between

the Olympiade-Film G.m.b.H. represented by Miss Leni Riefenstahl, hereafter called "G.m.b.H." of Berlin Neukoelln, Harzerstrasse

and

"Firma"

the following contract referring to the coverage of events of the Olympic Summer Games is made.

I.

This agreement includes all events as mentioned in the official time-schedule of the Organization Committee for the 11th Olympic Games, as well as all shots which may be taken in connection with these games from 8 a.m. of August 1st, 1936. This refers especially to shots taken (e.g.) of the official festival in the Berlin "Lustgarten" at 12 o'c; the run of the torch-bearer on this date; the drive of the Leader (Mr. Hitler) and the Olympic Committee through the triumphal-road, etc. Further this agreement includes all shots taken in the Olympic Village before and during the games and all shots taken of the training work of Olympic contestants.

This agreement does not include, however, the torch run from Athens up to the gates of Berlin; furthermore it does not include any governmental or other official receptions on occasion of the games, e.g., art events, sail-flying contests, the meeting of the international youth associations in their tent camps, etc.

II.

The Minister for Popular Enlightenment and Propaganda has put Miss Leni Riefenstahl, manager of the Olympiade-film G.m.b.H., in charge of the management of the German news reel companies in the same manner as this was done before on the occasion of the filming of the Party-Day-Film "Triumph des Willens."

At the same time the reel companies are held to put the total of their positive and negative material--with the exception of the cut original negative of the censored newsreels--at the disposal of the "G.m.b.H." without pay. In addition hereto the reel companies are obliged to furnish at cost price one lavender print as well as one black and white print of each newsreel released in the theatres.

Furthermore the reel companies have to deliver to the "G.m.b.H." at cost price a first-class lavender print of all footage delivered to foreign countries.

The reel companies are obliged to treat the negative as carefully as possible to draw a black and white print from the complete negative (i.e., from all shots taken by them) and to do the cutting on the positive print. The cost for this positive print as well as any additional expenses arising from the cutting job on the positive print are being borne by the "G.m.b.H." This does not include Emelka News Reel Company, because it is their habit to do the cutting on the positive print.

The total of the material as mentioned herein has to be delivered directly and in first class condition to the "G.m.b.H." until August 25, 1936 at the latest.

III.

The "G.m.b.H." has been appointed by the Olympic Committee as the Central organization for all filming made during the Olympic Games. Therefore, "G.m.b.H." grants to all film companies cooperating at the Olympic Summer Games the necessary letters of authority; assign the requested operation space (as far as possible) and hold the reel companies to keep strictly to the orders issued by them (G.m.b.H.).

"G.m.b.H." will furnish the reel companies with the fixed program schedules as soon as they themselves get hold of such information from the Olympic Committee and will, instead and on behalf of the Olympic Committee, give all information necessary for the taking of pictures to the reel companies.

In order to guarantee a concordant cooperation between the reel companies and "G.m.b.H." the following details must be submitted:

a) The names and number of cameramen and their help, number and details of the motor cars and sound cars used;

b) Their requests regarding the individual sporting events. "G.m.b.H." will try their utmost to fulfill all requests, provided that the consent of the Olympic Committee can be obtained. In case that the allotted space does not suffice for the activities of all reel companies, and, provided that these companies do not come to an agreement between themselves, the manager of the "G.m.b.H.", Miss Leni Riefenstahl, will act as arbiter.

c) The reel companies are also held to assign a representative who has to attend the direction conferences. These conferences will be held as necessity arises, but surely once a day, and the reel companies are bound to act strictly in accordance with any decisions taken at these conferences, as to avoid differences with the Olympic Committee. The "G.m.b.H." asks that express attention be paid to the fact that the Olympic Committee is entitled to expell any cameraman or operator regardless of whether he be a member of "G.m.b.H." or another company--from further activity if he does not comply strictly with the orders issued by the Olympic Committee.

d) Furthermore the reel companies have, if so requested, to put at the disposal of "G.m.b.H." any of their cameramen who are not busy on work for the Olympic Reels.

IV.

"G.m.b.H." is not allowed to use any of the newsreel shots for purposes other than that in the Olympiade-Film.

On the other hand the reel companies are bound to use any of their prints--be it by themselves or through the medium of third parties--only and exclusively for projection of the usual newsreels. The "Firma" is under no condition allowed to use or have used any of their shots in such a manner that by compilation of several newsreels or sequences thereof another film is obtained; the only permitted use of their coverage is to compile the usual newsreels which are screened together with program pictures. It is not allowed to use any Olympic newsreel shots for the compilation of program pictures, educationals, etc. "G.m.b.H." reserve to themselves all copyrights for the total Olympic coverage of the reel companies and grant solely permission that this coverage is used for the usual projection (screening) within the usual newsreel.

The length of these newsreel films to be screened in Germany, is not to exceed 250 metres and "Firma" is only allowed to compile newsreels within a four-day period, respectively twice a week. "Firma" is however, at liberty to subdivide the allowed weekly total quantity of 500 metres. The length of newsreels exported to foreign countries is not to exceed 400 metres or 800 metres per week. [This ambiguity is unexplained in the provisions of the agreement.]

These quantities refer only to films covering events as stipulated in No. I of this contract.

"Firma" is expressly bound to force any foreign parties handling these reels--especially those parties handling the lavender prints abroad--to comply strictly with all conditions as specified under No. IV.

V.

Concerning all events connected with the Olympic Games and not included in this contract (such as the torch race run from Athens up to the gates of Berlin, international youth meets, etc.) the following is ordered:

a) "G.m.b.H." reserve to themselves the right to request delivery of certain films of these events. In the case of such a request, the conditions for its use are equal to those specified under No. II of this agreement.

b) To such shots No. III of this contract cannot be applied. If necessary the reel companies have to obtain themselves all required identification papers, letters of authority, etc., etc.

c) No. IV of this agreement refers to such shots only if "G.m.b.H." should request delivery of same.

VI.

The original negative of the cut (finished) newsreels which the company does not need any more (provided same has not been delivered to foreign countries) has to be submitted to "G.m.b.H." until September 15, 1936, at the latest. "G.m.b.H." will pay [for it] to "Firma" the cost price of the dupe negative which has to be kept in the records of "Firma."

• APPENDIX C •

A REPORT ON THE PRODUCTION OF THE OLYMPIC FILMS
(according to authentic documents and supporting evidence)
By Leni Riefenstahl*

On the occasion of the re-showing of the Olympic film on the Olympic Games in Berlin for 1936, it appears necessary, in order to avoid prejudice, publicly to present the facts about matters which are not generally known.

1. The Olympic Games are a festival of the International Olympic Committee, that alone has responsibility--never, however, the nations in which the Games take place, according to the rules of the IOC.

The technical and organizational leadership was followed through by the Organization Committee for the XI Olympiade Berlin of 1936. The President of the Committee was Herr Dr. Lewald (non-Aryan), the Secretary-General was Herr Professor Carl Diem, who was dismissed from all his German positions after the seizure of power. This Organization Committee was not German, but rather an international institution.

The Propaganda Ministry or other National Socialist Party-or state authority had neither an influence on the Olympic Games nor on the production or creation of the Olympic films.

2. The Olympic Games were carried out in an orderly manner and without damaging Olympic neutrality. A clear proof is the fact that on June 8, 1939 in London at the meeting it was decided to again bestow the Olympic winter Games upon Germany (Garmisch-Partenkirchen), which would not have happened if the Berlin Games had been misused. If anything had happened in Berlin that could have been detrimental to Olympic neutrality or dedication, at least one or another member would have been induced to abstain from voting or to vote against a renewed transfer of the Games to Germany.

3. At the same meeting, the Olympic gold medal was awarded to Leni Riefenstahl in recognition of her impeccable creation of the Olympic

*In the author's copy, Leni Riefenstahl's name on the title page is handwritten.

films by the International Olympic Committee on the proposal of their President Brundage (USA), and the French Secretary of the Navy Pietri (thus not by any chance by German instigation). The War prevented its transmission, but it took place in an orderly fashion in 1948 with appropriate transfer of ownership.

4. The Organization Committee could operate in all circumstances without influence. So Jewish participants took part, not only in foreign teams, but on the German teams as well. Here one should mention the brothers Ball in ice hockey and the fencer Helene Mayer, who won the silver medal. Dr. C. Diem has confirmed that the eligibility was not later barred to these non-Aryan German participants. Nor did the non-Aryan president of the Olympic Committee, Herr Dr. Lewald, and Herr Professor Dr. Carl Diem undergo any attack whatever until the collapse of the regime. Also in this area the agreement with the IOC was observed.

5. Among the duties of the Organization Committee was the reporting of the Games in every form that was not placed under the supervision of the Propaganda Ministry. In this capacity, Frau Riefenstahl was given the assignment of the documentary film. The Propaganda Ministry had nothing to do with this decision, and also its later objections have not been considered.

6. Frau Leni Riefenstahl had also obtained filming rights from the Organization Committee, and had committed herself to observe all conditions placed upon her without objection.

7. The widely disseminated assumption that the Olympic film was produced or sponsored by a Party or government authority does not agree with the facts. The opposite was the case.

8. Dr. Goebbels and the men of the film section on his ministry boycotted Leni Riefenstahl's works with every means at their disposal, as much as they could. Many declarations under oath of foreigners and Germans who were not National Socialists affirm this in all respects. These declarations were examined for years by the Allied services and German denazification tribunals with the result that Leni Riefenstahl was completely rehabilitated by <u>all</u> authorities and also by the normally constituted courts of justice, and therefore her Olympic films as well, which had been seized as war booty, were again returned to her.

9. Leni Riefenstahl has written no memoirs, in spite of the highest offers from publishing houses and magazines, in contrast to almost all others. These memoirs could have completely removed the burden of publicity as well as the courts from her. She reasoned that it would only be worthwhile when she could write the whole truth without regard for any now living person. She wanted to avoid this, in order to devote herself only to her artistic task. If, however, the prejudice stemming from ignorance of the true circumstances be so great that

further creative work from L.R. should be seriously endangered, then she will publicly render a report of her life.

10. Here, only a few incidents should be made public for the first time that deal exclusively with the work on the Olympic film.

11. L.R. never tried to be put in charge of the Olympic film. On the contrary, she transferred this assignment to her male colleague and teacher, Dr. Arnold Fanck, because it seemed too difficult and carried so much responsibility, exactly as she had transferred the assignment to produce the Party Day film Triumph des Willens to the recognized director Walter Ruttmann. In both cases, it was impossible for her to avoid Hitler's categorical decision. The extensive investigations of the courts and denazification tribunals produced the proof that the aforegoing in fact took place in this manner.

12. In creation of both films, however, L.R. kept her complete artistic and economic freedom. Only after Hitler had told her that she could produce the Party Day film Triumph des Willens as well as the Olympic films Fest der Völker and Fest der Schönheit without any influence from Party or State authorities, did L.R. promise, since she now understood that any evasion after this exceptional compromise of Hitler was impossible. These unique conditions, to be able to create freely, could only be attained because she would not have made the films without Hitler's promise. Although Hitler prized L.R. very highly as an artist, under no circumstances did he want to grant this. Only in this way can it be understood that until the world premiere of her films, neither Hitler, Dr. Goebbels or other personalities of the Party or State officials saw only one scene of the film beforehand. L.R. attained this not through "protection" as generally assumed, but exclusively through her refusal to compromise.

13. Because of this independence of mind, L.R. not only incurred the wrath of Dr. Goebbels and his Propaganda Ministry, but also that of the highest Party functionaries. Also many colleagues in the film industry, who could know nothing about what was really happening, and have no idea through what sacrifices and dangers L.R. purchased her artistic independence, envied her freedom. It is from this, as well as in the hatred of the men of the Propaganda Ministry against L.R. that the roots of the countless, most evil slanders led to the result that L.R. had to spend three years in prisons and camps before a possibility was given to her for rehabilitation.

14. All slanders against L.R. had to be retracted legally, and under no circumstances could even one of the untrue declarations and libels be maintained as true.

15. Also the Party Day film Triumph des Willens is to be regarded as a documentary film and not as a propaganda film, since this film not only received the first prize at the Venice Biennale in 1935 from an international jury, but also the special honors that France allowed the

film to receive. The French Prime Minister Daladier personally bestowed the gold medal and the Diplôme de Grand Prix of the French Republic to L.R. personally at the Paris International Exposition of 1937 for the Party Day film Triumph des Willens. Award and gold medal in the possession of L.R.

16. Because of the wish of L.R. to proceed with the Olympic film in her private firm, unimaginable difficulties were presented against this work, since the Propaganda Ministry unanimously boycotted her work on the Olympic film. This was evidenced by the following measures:

17. The German newsreel camera personnel, who were the most valuable for this documentary shooting, since they were the most practiced, were not at L.R.'s disposition for her work. The newsreels appeared with their own special reports especially copiously, because Dr. Goebbels believed in this way, he could destroy the financial success of the Olympic film.

18. It is untrue when it is maintained that a huge army of cameramen were placed at L.R.'s disposal. It is rather true that after the cancellation of the newsreel camera personnel, and since most of the good camera personnel had fixed contracts with Ufa, Tobis, Bavaria and other large firms, only a few very good cameramen were at L.R.'s disposal. With the exception of Willy Zielke, who photographed the prologue of the Olympic film, and who was a brilliant artist, L.R. had only six cameramen of surpassing ability at her disposal, who had to carry the major burden of shooting the film. These were Hans Ertl, Walter Frentz, Guzzi Lantschner, Kurt Neubert and Hans Scheib. Beside these, there were 24 other cameramen; however, a large part of these were amateurs, who were to make shots of the public on 16mm film, as well as assistants and beginners.

19. It is untrue as maintained, that unlimited means were placed at L.R.'s disposal, and that the film is supposed to have devoured over 5 million.

What the magazine Der Spiegel wrote is rather true published in May 1952 in number 22/52. p. 75:

"The production of my two Olympic films, each one running the length of an evening, including foreign dubbing and versions, as well as twelve other sport films and Kulturfilme, as well as to the creation of a former great sport film archive amounted to 2.2 million RM."

As can be proved at any time, my Olympic film received a total gate of 7 to 8 million RM.

This amount does not include what was made on the film abroad after the War. I can point out in this regard that my film has been shown in the USA since 1948 under the title Kings of the Olympics.

20. The Olympia-Film G.m.b.H., whose only partner and only di-

rector was L.R., concluded a distribution contract months before the beginning of the Olympic Games, with the former General Director of Tobis-Filmkunst, Herr Friedrich A. Mainz. This contract contained a guarantee of 750,000 RM. Because of this distribution contract, Herr Direcktor Friedrich A. Mainz later had to justify himself before the men of the Propaganda Ministry. In a letter that he wrote on June 19, 1950 to Frau Dr. Widerer in Munich, can be read inter alia:

> I was the former production head of Tobis and the sole director of Tobis-Cinema A.G. The discussions over the contract were carried out and concluded between the legal advisor and myself. In this matter, Herr Dr. Scheuermann told me that all parts of the Olympic film G.m.b.H. were supposed to belong to Frau Leni Riefenstahl.
>
> During the production of the films, that were only finished after around 1½ years, I was eliminated from Tobis on May 3, 1937. The former Propaganda Ministry, and the Reich Film Chamber acting through its agents, President Dr. Lehnich and the Bürgermeister Dr. Max Winkler, made representations to me to the effect that I had damaged Tobis because of the inadvisable guarantee of 750,000 RM--and that this deal would conclude with a great loss for Tobis. At that time, I offered to bear the loss myself if the profits from the Olympic film were assigned to me. This offer was refused. Later I discovered from Herr Bürgermeister Winkler, from Frau Riefenstahl and my former co-workers of Tobis, that both Olympic films had done a huge business, and many millions had been made on the films. I satisfied myself that both in Germany and abroad, the film met with a resounding commercial success. Herr Bürgermeister Winkler perceived belatedly that the contract concluded by me had obtained exceptionally satisfactory results. Tobis got back the guarantee of 750,000 RM paid out by it soon after the premiere of the film.

21. Even richer in information is the following, each extract from the

Statement Under Oath

of Friedrich A. Mainz from the records of the Courts and denazification tribunals of April 15, 1948:

> ...a few days after the beginning of the Olympic Games, Frau Riefenstahl was forbidden to enter the stadium in Berlin by Dr. Goebbels, because a witch hunt without bounds was instigated against her by the Propaganda Ministry of the NSDAP, the SA and the SS leadership. The press chief of Tobis and the functionary of the Propaganda Ministry senior Civil Servant Räther told me that Frau Riefenstahl was supposed to be unendurable, and was rejected by the controlling functionaries of the Party. In spite of this, Frau Riefenstahl worked with demoniac energy and threw herself into her task. The witch hunt against Frau

> Riefenstahl, which emanated principally from the Propaganda Ministry, grew wider and wider. Another person told me that Frau Riefenstahl was supposed to be half Jewish, had earlier had traffic with Jews, was supposed to have, the same as before, Jewish relationships and to be politically undependable. It was prophesized to me that Frau Riefenstahl would never finish her Olympic film.... In spite of the great success of the Olympic film, Frau Riefenstahl was also later persecuted by Dr. Goebbels and the Party authorities through dirty tricks and vile gossip, with the result that she had to break off work on Tiefland again and again, so it could not be finished before the end of the war.... Frau Riefenstahl tenaciously refused to become a member of the NSDAP and its organizations. She also refused every honorary office and State title.... (I affirm the correctness of the aforegoing under oath. Friedrich A. Mainz.)

22. A few of the most unbelievable steps taken against L.R. were the following:

Shortly before the opening ceremonies of the Olympic Games in Berlin, SS men attempted to remove the only sound camera that was fixed in place in the stadium. The sound men and camera personnel resisted in vain. As the protest of L.R. was also useless, nothing else remained except to guard the camera herself, which meant that she had to stay standing there until the end of the opening ceremonies and could not carry out her assigned work.

On the fifth day of the Games in the stadium, it came to an open scandal between Dr. Goebbels and L.R. The origin was that L.R. had had a quarrel with a German referee because, in spite of previous agreements by the Olympic contestants, he wanted to remove her camera personnel by force from the interior of the stadium. This was a violation of the agreement and seriously detrimental to the work, since the athletic events were not repeatable and so irretrievably lost for the film. As L.R. vehemently fought for the positions of her camera personnel, the referee complained to Dr. Goebbels. Upon this matter later, Riefenstahl was immediately recalled from her work. Goebbels made such a violent scene with her in the stadium that it caused a sensation. Goebbels tried to provoke a scandal to prove that a woman was unsuitable for such work (A witness to this scene was among others Herr Ritter von Halt).

L.R. was forced to ask the referee's pardon. In any case, the important shots of the hammer throwing on this day were totally lost.

In order to get at least these shots of the German Olympic victors, L.R. assigned the cameraman Hans Ertl with his assistant Bertl Höcht to get the lacking shots at a sports festival in Nuremberg. They were prevented by force from making these shots by the then chief of the Reich Film Chamber, Herr Hans Weidemann. As Hans Ertl in his declaration under oath stated on 8.29.48, he was simply pulled out of bed by the SS and ordered together with his assistant

Höcht to make the very same shots under Weidemann's authority. On Ertl's protest that he was engaged to shoot film for Riefenstahl's Olympic film, Weidemann answered that that was all the same to him, and bestowed on Frau Riefenstahl the quotation from Götz. Further, Ertl declared in his statement under oath: "Thus and similar appeared the 'protection' that Frau Riefenstahl and her staff of workers could enjoy from the highest Party circles."

In September 1936, after the ending of the Olympics, Herr Minister-Councillor Berndt by order of Dr. Goebbels officially told the German press in the assembly room of the Propaganda Ministry that it was officially forbidden in word or in picture to report about Leni Riefenstahl and her Olympic film. This press ban against L.R. remained in effect for 1 1/2 years and was only lifted two months before the world premiere of the films, since they were already finished and a further boycott was pointless.

In October of 1936, L.R. was told by State Secretary Hanke of the Propaganda Ministry that she was immediately to fire her press chief Ernst Jäger, who was married to a Jewess and expelled from the Reischsschrifttumskammer. Aside from this, it was imparted to her that Dr. Goebbels did not want her to show too many victorious black athletes in the Olympic film.

In spite of the risk involved, L.R. refused to fill these demands. This had the result that Dr. Goebbels gave the order to the Film Kredit Bank, which was maintained by his ministry, to stop all further credit to the Olympiafilm G.m.b.H. With this, the war between Dr. Goebbels and L.R. reached its highest point.

23. There was no longer any possibility for L.R. except to clarify the situation through a personal consultation with Hitler, to whom L.R. had not spoken alone for a period of 1 1/2 years. However, Dr. Goebbels succeeded in preventing every discussion with Hitler for another two months, so long that L.R. experienced a total collapse of her health. Only in December of 1936, with the support of Hitler's adjutant Fritz Wiedemann did L.R. succeed in speaking to Hitler.

This occasion established that Hitler had absolutely no idea of what was going on and at first did not want to believe her. Only when she laid the supporting evidence before him which made everything obvious, for instance, the press ban against L.R., the blocking of credits, the abduction of cameramen under duress by the SS, etc., Hitler became very stirred up and considerate. As then L.R. explained that she could not continue to work in Germany under such conditions, Hitler said that she would receive a decision in a few days.

It has never become known what Hitler arranged with Goebbels in this matter. But 5 days after this conference, L.R. was told by the adjutant of the Reich Chancellery that a new arrangement had been struck with Dr. Goebbels, by which she would have no more difficulties with the Propaganda Ministry, since she and her firm from now on would only formally be under the control of this ministry.

From this moment on, L.R. was in fact totally removed from the influence of the Propaganda Ministry. This certainly had the result that she could work undisturbed from then until the beginning of the war; however at the same time, because of this decision, a new wave of envy and mistrust by her colleagues came about. A whispering campaign maintained that such a privileged position meant that L.R. was Hitler's mistress. This was all too happily believed, and these libels spread further and further. So these wicked rumors have penetrated deeper and deeper, so that by this means, the fate of L.R. took a tragic turn even until today, and has most strongly limited her creative power.

24. While L.R. was in the Geyer Laboratories in Berlin-Neukölln, quite self-absorbed in cutting the Olympic film, the fantastic reports appeared about her everywhere in the foreign press, about which she then had no awareness. So the serious Swiss weekly magazine Die Weltwoche (Zürich) wrote a three page article with the headline, "The Fallen Angel of the Third Reich," France-Soir (Paris) wrote, "The Pompadour of the Third Reich," the Times (USA) wrote "Hitler's Girl Friend," etc.

Although after the war through the investigations of the courts and denazification tribunals, through many declarations made under oath, it was established that not one word of this story, invented by journalists, was true, it is still disseminated after twenty years, although errant fantasy. This poisoning of the well can no longer be redressed, and is the root cause why L.R. must again and again overcome new prejudice.

Since in the above mentioned articles, Dr. Goebbels was quite disparaged and attacked, he attempted to refute these foreign articles, which accused him of having publically slapped L.R.'s face because she was a Jewess, in the following manner: he ordered posed photographs made of Hitler, L.R. and himself. These had the following consequences:

L.R. was notified that on the next day in the garden of her house, into which she had not yet even moved, photographs of Hitler, Goebbels and her would be made. In fact, Dr. Goebbels arrived with a huge bouquet of roses, presented it to L.R. At that time, L.R. could not yet have an inkling that because of the harmless photographs, taken without her assistance or wish, she would enter into the greatest misery. During the time of her imprisonment, the French headquarters of the Army of Occupation, on the basis of these pictures, took all of her property, both real and personal, and she never got it back. On this account, L.R. had to live in the greatest poverty when she got her freedom back three years after the end of the war, so that she had put in a claim for legal aid in order to follow through the many trials that she had to conduct for her rehabilitation.

25. After the finishing of the Olympic film in February, 1938, there were again difficulties with Dr. Goebbels. First the world premiere was again and again postponed, so that the finished film had to remain sitting for two months. Then the last obstacle came, the cen-

sorship. L.R. knew that there was a dangerous hurdle here, since censorship was under the authority of Dr. Goebbels, and the censor's cuts would radically change the form of the Olympic film. To escape this, since L.R., with reason, was afraid for her 'black athletes,' she let her copy be cut to bits again and again, and made up excuses until the premiere so that she succeeded in the seemingly impossible task of showing both Olympic films uncensored at the premiere. In addition, neither Hitler nor Dr. Goebbels had seen a meter of this film before the premiere. After the great success of this premiere, at which the foreign press was in attendance, it was no longer possible for Dr. Goebbels to demand a cut version.

26. Five months after the German premiere, the Tobis distribution had already received 4,210,290 RM in receipts, a unique, unrivalled event. The receipts in foreign currency amounted to more than from all other German films put together. It is moreover remarkable that a financial success was not expected from the complete film enterprise, especially because before this Olympic film it was still not granted by anyone, and the film people could not imagine, that a plotless film about track and field, and so on, could enthrall the public. In addition, above all because the film would only be released two years after the Olympic Games. Everyone had assumed that after so long a waiting time, the film could no longer evoke any present interest. On this ground, Ufa had also turned down a distribution contract, not least also because on the ground that it was informed about the boycott of the Propaganda Ministry against L.R. and her films.

27. In the commercial exploitation of the films, neither in Germany nor abroad did any German Party authority support the distribution of the film. Complete costs of premieres in several European cities were the result of the invitation and at the expense of foreign buyers, if possible supported through subsidies from the distribution firm.

28. In Hollywood, L.R. was the personal guest of Walt Disney, who congratulated her on her first prize at the Biennale in Venice, where his film Snow White was the strongest competition for the Olympic film. Also the Kings of Norway, Denmark, Rumania and Belgium, Prime Minister Spaak and other personalities honored L.R. through their presence at these premieres of the Olympic films as well as through personal audiences. This would have been impossible if the films had contained National Socialist propaganda.

29. Without one exception, the complete foreign press, in addition to the recognition of the artistic and athletic worth of the Olympic films, called special attention above all to the great objectivity of this film. Although the film ran in all countries and in the same version as in the German original version, it was never said that in this film was contained propaganda for Germany or National Socialism.

30. The distribution of the Olympic gold medal to L.R. for the Olympic films should make the film tabu for those who by hook or crook

want to see politics in this film, where there are none present. In addition, there were none in the original version. The words of Herr Professor Dr. Carl Diem, the Secretary-General of the Olympic Games in Berlin are to be welcomed. He writes: "It appears desirable to us on this account, in this film not to carry on the justified criticism of the Nazi reign of terror, but rather to honor the Olympic Games as a respected oasis."

• APPENDIX D •

FILMBEWERTUNGSSTELLE
The Foundation of the Appeal Against the Decision of the Committee of Review of January 30, 1958

In re: Olympic Film-Berlin 1936

Part I	Fest der Völker	Control No. 4208
Part II	Fest der Schönheit	Control No. 4209

1. The refusal of certification by the Committee of Review of the FBW (Filmbewertungsstelle) for the above two films is based on false assumptions:

The Committee maintains:

"After its completion, the Olympic film was released with the agreement of the highest authorities of the National Socialist regime and was exploited in connection with National Socialist propaganda."

It is rather true:
The Olympic film was neither during its preparation nor after its completion supported or produced through any authority of the National Socialist regime. It was neither exploited in Germany nor abroad in connection with National Socialist propaganda. The opposite was the case.

Herr Minister Dr. Goebbels and the men of his propaganda Ministry attempted with all means at their disposal to prevent the completion of the Olympic film. Enclosure 1 (Page 19A) contains a collection of these proceedings on the basis of legal material and statements under oath.

The world artistic success of the Olympic films (see enclosure-international prizes and comments of the foreign press) are solely the result of the artistic creation of this film. It was created without any exercise of influence from a third party on L.R. Until the premiere of this film, no person from the government or the regime had seen even one section of the film.

Also in the original version, the Olympic film had no scenes that glorified the National Socialist regime. Nowhere in this film were there SS-or SA parades or other National Socialist rallies. Not once was the arrival of Hitler in the stadium, that was extensively shown in all foreign and German newsreels, shown in the Olympic film. This is also testified to by the fact that abroad, for example in America, France, England and other nations, only the original version was shown. This would, at least after the war, be unthinkable if the film, as the FBW maintains, were full of National Socialist atmosphere.

Out of the original version, only the following scenes were removed: (only in Germany)

a) The formal declaration of the opening of the Olympic Games by Hitler (as prescribed by the IOC for every statesman).
b) The Olympic oath (a prescribed ceremony by the IOC at the opening ceremonies) removed because of the swastika flag.
c) Two German victory ceremonies because of the swastika flags.
d) Short cameo shots showing Hitler and other personalities of the former regime as spectators.
e) Long shots and near shots of the public in the stadium, saluting with the raised right arm. 86 meters were removed from part I, in part II, 1 1/2 meters (von Tschammer Und Osten).

2. The Committee of Review maintains:

The conception and style of the Olympic film bear traits that have been borrowed from the arsenal of National Socialist ideological propaganda.

<u>It is rather true</u>

If this position were true, then the following would be impossible:

a) Award of the Olympic gold medal
No Olympic film has been granted this rare award of the International Olympic Committee since. The conditions are that the Olympic film must be free of any political tone and must be artistically valuable as well as valuable as a document of sport. How can it be reconciled that the Committee of Review can deny the Olympic film certification, when the film has obtained the supreme award of honor from the most competent authority?

b) First Prize at the Venice Biennale as the best film in the world, selected by an international panel.

c) Award of the Grand Prix and the Gold Medal of the French Nation at the International Exposition in Paris.

c) Award of the Polar Prize from Sweden.

e) The extraordinary ovations that L.R. received from heads of state as the film was shown abroad. As for instance, through audiences with the King of Norway, Denmark, Rumania, Belgium, Prime Minister Spaak, and others.

f) The notices that appeared in foreign newspapers by important critics about the Olympic film are insurpassable in their raves about the film. These notices are at random:

So writes the French paper, Liberté, (Paris), "A film that has the effect of enobling all who see it." The very objective Neue Zürcher Zeitung writes: "...there has come a film which shows itself to be in the vanguard of films, a record of a unique kind...." L'Ordre (Paris): "It is more and better than a film and even than a play..." and the great paper Los Angeles Times: "...a triumph for the camera and an epic poem of the screen."
Citizens News (Hollywood):
"...Last night I saw the best film that I have ever seen.... It is not propaganda but a magnificent filming of the greatest meeting of athletes.... It is superb, and should be shown wherever there is a projection screen and a lover of sport."

If the judgment that FBW brings against the Olympic film were correct, then at least one or the other critic would have written something about it. But the fact is that neither before nor since the war has anyone at all written that the Olympic film contains National Socialist tendencies. In addition, the opponents of the former regime have unanimously admitted that this film, that reports on the only Olympic Games that have ever taken place on German soil, has not been equalled up to now.

3. The Committee of Review maintains:

"...Never before was athletic competition so blatantly misused for an ideological-political alibi as 1936 in Berlin."

See documents: Testimonials and letter to the FBW from Herr Professor Dr. Carl Diem.

4. The Board of Certification stated:

That the film is full of echoes of formerly used title or propaganda maxims like "Glaube und Schönheit", and of slogans like Kampfgeist, Das Letzte hergeben, bis zum Sieg, and that these are identical with the never-say-die jargon of National Socialist propaganda.

The answer to this is:

All of the above cited slogans do not appear in the Olympic film. However, even if the narrator chose similar expressions for the rendering of the Games, these are very much in the same vein of expression as used by all sports reporters in the world. In the Olympic film, a great many disciplines were narrated in an objective, terse fashion. However, this was not always possible, because the film would have become monotonous. The gradation of reportage from objective to passionate enthusiasm is a question of artistic creation.

5. The Committee of Review writes:

"It is therefore not surprising that this film was awarded the title of State Film 1937/38 by the National Socialist Regime."

The reply to this:

If the FBW maintains the award of this prize as negative, why then do they ignore the award of all the great international prizes? It was certainly understandable that the Olympic film has to get the German State Prize for 1938, because the international press had already written ten days before that the Olympic film had attained a unique success in the history of film. If the Olympic film has miscarried, or had not been recognized internationally, then it never would have received the State Prize. A proof is that the Winter Olympic film from Garmisch-Partenkirchen that was produced with the support of Dr. Goebbels and the Propaganda Ministry, unceremoniously disappeared. This film was made by the leader of the film section of the Propaganda Ministry, Herr Hans Weidemann, with the same camera personnel that were at my disposal. In spite of very beautiful shots, in spite of all the promotion that this film got through the Propaganda Ministry, every success remained denied to it.

6. The Board of Certification writes:

"With its stylized means, the film aims at an excessive heroicism, not only of the athletes, but of humanity generally. The stylizing of the human form does not reflect human reality, but a false one, oriented by ideology for a determined political purpose.

To this the answer is:

Never before in an Olympic film was the athlete shown so naturally as in the Olympic film of 1936. Every human emotion was recorded by the camera. Grief, joy, doubt, tension, hope. We see man as he is, not stylized and heroicised. Since these shots, taken during competition, certainly could not have been recorded except in every weather and light condition, such a stylizing of shots would have been technically impossible.

Only at the beginning of the first part in the prologue did I have the possibility of making stylized shots. Here the stylizing was an artistic necessity, since the film begins in Greek antiquity. The Greek temples and statues, that lead us to the roots of the Olympic

Games, which lead from Myron's Discobolus to living human beings, and the figures of the maidens, from whose gestures the Olympic flame is born, could only be stylized and shown in montage and backlight. The montages were necessary here because the whole scene is plotless, so the shots had to flow into one another, to be enhanced into a picture-poem. Shots that were back lighted were necessary above all, because the classic forms of the maidens, that I certainly could not show clothed, would have appeared erotic if they were photographed with frontal or side lighting. Only through backlighting and especially artistic camera placement was it possible to photograph the maidens so that the effect was pure and unerotic in spite of their nakedness. That this was successful is indicated by the fact that even the censorship of the Vatican did not object to these shots. Sculptors and painters often portray athletes unclothed. Is it then so misguided that the film artist attempt it as well?

On the subject of the prologue, I would like to mention a very typical statement from the review of the serious Parisian newspaper, L'Ordre:

"From the beginning and without the least forfeiture of athletic truth, she instills a moral and artistic character into her work, in which is embodied the glory of Greece."

7. The Committee of the FBW reproaches me for using too many steam and smoke clouds, which have nothing to do with the Olympic Games.

Factually, the following is to be established:

The smoke that the Olympic torches and Olympic fire produce are inseparable from the Olympic Games. So is the steam from the Finnish sauna, that certainly was to be found in the Olympic Village. Also the ground fog in the Olympic Village, that in fact was there during the run through the woods and the morning training of the athletes, was in immediate connection with the Olympic Games. I can assure the Committee that the camera people used no smoke rockets for these shots, but rather reported to me very happily that they had had the luck to capture shots that were full of mood. It is certain that they never thought, as the Review Board now accuses us, "to want to instill in the viewer a pseudo-mystical spirit, that became a special goal of National Socialist propaganda." These just enumerated shots have a running time of not even two minutes.

Artificial fog was used by us only with the Greek statues, in order to avoid the dry character of Kulturfilm photography. Moreover, it would have been extremely difficult to get the spectators to forget the museum in which most of these statues had to be photographed. These shots also have a running of time of not quite 50 meters--1 1/2 minutes of running time.

Nature shots having nothing to do with the Olympic Games, as the FBW maintains, are not in the film. Once there is a shot of the moon intercut, in order to make the transition in the pole vault from day shots to night shots.

8. The Certification Committee writes:
"From the standpoint of today, it is a question of an extremely out-of-date form of sports reporting..."

This opinion contradicts the judgment of the German AND international professionals and critics of film. I refer to the enclosed supporting documents of the *Olympia* press book, where especially the newest notices from December, 1947 (pages 1-4) are significant.

One would scarcely ascribe a pro-Nazi attitude to the *Berliner Telegraf*. But even this paper is objective and writes on December 8, 1957 about the Olympic film:
"...In the Titania-Palast the opportunity was presented to see this film, which has never been equalled in the area of film technique or athletics..." Also in the German reviews, it was again and again emphasized that the Olympic film of 1936 far surpassed the other Olympic films in the areas of art, film technique and athletics.

"...the far too frequent slow motion", criticizes the FBW about one section of the shots of the Olympic film.

It is precisely these shots that give the film its artistic worth. They were employed according to laws of art and rhythm. Never before or since has this principle of individually various shot tempi been employed, because it is extremely difficult, artistically and technically. It would be going too far afield to try to explain these more exactly. Let it be said here that the shots are no normal slow motion shots, but rather every shot is shot in a different tempo, thereby creating a heightening of the experience in the spectator. For months before the beginning of the Olympic Games, I practiced with three of my camera personnel, who were specialized for this task. Without this technique, and without this empathy for rhythm, the film never would have produced this effect. Many important film critics recognized this immediately. So the Swedish newspaper *Svenska Dagbladet*-Stockholm (page 7 in Olympic press book):
"...a factual report that is raised to the value of a poem. This gigantic visual series in fact points the direction to a new world of film and to a new means of expressing film aesthetics, that up to now has scarcely been seen by the directors of genius in feature films. This visual symphony soars in the freest flight, and above all, this film is a wonderfully instructive demonstration of filmic rhythm, composed and cut with the same musicality as by one who writes a musical score...."

9. Also, the Committee of the FBW criticizes the "often too small framing."

In fact, no Olympic film up to now has had near so many close ups and half close ups as the 1936 one. It would be easy to show this by counting the close ups. It would also be possible that the projectionist forgot to set the frame correctly, which happens quite frequently. In such a case, 25% of the frame of the picture could be cut off by the incorrect framing.

The Olympic film can be projected onto a very large screen without the least loss of sharpness or graphic power.

10. "The simple stringing together of athletic events is meanwhile recognized as a deficiency...", writes the FBW.

What film critic or professional maintains this? There is nothing more difficult in the art of editing than editing the sequences together as in this concentrated form, without unimportant trimming. Nothing in this film was arbitrarily cut. This seemingly simple stringing together is an artistic construction, joined together by picture and sound transitions. Any shift of a single sequence to a different place would destroy the architecture.

11. <u>The reportage</u>

With an objective appraisal of the two parts of the Olympic film, it is ascertainable that the greatest part of all athletic competitions were narrated in a terse, objective form. When by way of comparison, the reporting of all the other Olympic films are drawn upon, it is then first conspicuous that the other films use narration almost without pause. The first part of the Olympic film contains 1200 meters--more than a third--where absolutely nothing is said. From the opening of the film until the end of the opening ceremonies alone, 600 meters of film have run (20 min.) without a spoken word. All technical events, and there were many, had brief and objective texts. Only in the running events, and there only in part, was it necessary to communicate the great passion of the spectators over to the film by means of the narrator.

The proof that the mode of expression and the modulation of the speaker has nothing to do with National Socialism, as maintained by the FBW, is shown by the fact that the English, French and Italian broadcasters, who were able to improvise freely in the foreign versions of the Olympic film, were carried away by the images to the same enthusiasm. They quite resemble in words and modulation the German speaker.

In the first part of the Olympic film, the members of the FBW will establish by a more exact observation, that the affected objections with regard to the reportage are nowhere correct. Only in the second part of the Olympic film, on dramatic grounds was it necessary, and especially in two sports disciplines, to give a very passionate narration to contrast with the very lyrical sequences that had gone directly before. Among the lyric sequences I mean "Olympic Village," "Gymnastics," "Sailing," "Fencing," "Mass gymnastics," "Polo," and "Diving" in the swimming stadium, as well as the closing ceremonies. In order to make this film not only an "aesthetic" film, and in order not to lose all tension, it was necessary, where any possibility was given, to support the dramatic elements of the reportage. The reportage, which disturbed the members, comes only with the decathlon and the rowing events in Grünau.

From an athletic point of view, the decathlon is regarded as one of the most important events. From the filmic point of view, it is one of the most thankless and most difficult to show. For this reason, the decathlon had never been shown in an Olympic film up to then. It is a thankless task for film on this ground; that one can show no direct struggle, since it is a question of attaining a victory on points which must be added up from ten competitions. To boot comes the fact that each of these single exercises is less interesting than the same event already shown being contested by the specialists, who naturally are superior to the athletes in the decathlon. It is quite another experience to watch Jesse Owens in the 100 meter run as a decathlon contestant. I did not want to omit showing that the decathlon athlete is, however, in reality the most perfect athlete. In order to avoid a repetition of track and field events, I placed the decathlon in the second part of the Olympic film, although this part contains no track and field events. That alone was not sufficient to make the decathlon in film terms the event that it is. The making of the film was made all the more difficult because the American Glenn Morris had absolutely no serious opponent--he was far too superior. In order to give this competition, which was in itself no dramatic, a certain tension, the speaker had to replace what the picture did not furnish. Otherwise, I would have had to abandon the whole decathlon, which would have meant a lessening of documentary and sports value. I had to make a compromise here. Perhaps from this problem, the members of the FBW can weigh the difficulties that must be solved in the creation of an Olympic film.

With the rowing in Grünau, the problem was different. Because of the rainy weather, we only got gray, dull shots. In addition, the Germans won five medals in rowing, the sensation of the Olympics. However, in order to avoid repetition, I could only show one German victory. As a result of this, the speaker had to attempt in a short report (1 1/2 minutes) to express what the spectators in Grünau experienced. Only those who were there and experienced the human storm of emotion know that the narrator in his reporting only expressed what the spectators cheered and experienced.

After the German athletes won 36 gold medals, and thereby for the first time in the history of the Olympic Games pushed the otherwise unbeatable American Olympic team into second place, it should be permitted once in the two Olympic films to address the national feelings of the German spectator.

Why does the FBW pick out just those sentences from the two Olympic films in which national feeling resonates, while it apparently does not notice that I did not even show German victories, in contrast to those of other nations? As a matter of tact, I left the achievements of German athletes in the background. For instance, the German gymnasts won five gold medals. Although the Olympic film shows them in the picture, it mentions neither their names nor their victories.

I took great pains to show the greatest athletic successes from all nations--a difficult, almost unsolvable task. This is also a reason why the most ideal solution was to join the athletic contests directly to one another.

12. The Committee of the FBW writes:

"This stimulating effect is ultimately achieved through an intrusive and purposive symphonic score which blares into the ears of the spectator almost unceasingly.... As a matter of fact, since the music temporarily comes to a halt in the first half of the second part, it suggests that even the author of the film has had the feeling that the effects are laid on too thick."

In fact the following should be established:

The first part has a length of 3,184 meters--2 hours running time. In this area around 2,000 meters are completely without music, thus 2/3 of the film. An ideal proportion, for if the film were completely without music, in the course of time the realistic sounds would become unendurable for the ears. The proposition of the members of the FBW that the music is almost unceasing and blaring is in fact false.

The Olympic Hymn, that is heard in the film repeatedly, was composed by Richard Strauss; the Olympic fanfares were composed by von Egk; at the victory ceremonies, the national hymns (at that time) of the victorious nations (with the exception of Germany) were used; the rest of the film is purely background music and was by Herbert Windt.

In order to facilitate the correctness of my declaration at the review, I will enumerate all the sequences of the first part without music: Discus-men, discus-women, javelin-women, women's hurdles, hammer throw, all 100 meter runs, high jump-women, shot put-men, 800 meter run, pole vault-night, 100 meter relay-men, 100 meter relay-women, 400 meter relay-men.

The first act has background music, because there is no speech, and the film can not run silently. Otherwise, music is used only as a background for: Hop, step and jump, men's javelin, pole vault-day, the marathon and the end of the film.

Contrary to the statement of the FBW, the second part contains much more music than the first part. This is because, as the title of the film says, above all the beauty of the Olympic Games is being shown.

13. The Committee of the FBW maintains:

The points of view, which have been abolished, which glorify the National Socialist regime should be taken out of the film.

As already declared in paragraph 1, there were never, even in the original version, scenes which glorified the regime.

14. <u>The Committee of the FBW further maintains:</u>

"That in the submitted version, there are still too many shots remaining which show swastika flags or the representatives of National Socialist regime (Hitler, Göring, Frau Goebbels, von Tschammer und Osten) or uniformed SA and SS men (the close-ups of SS men in uniform are completely unnecessary)."

<u>These statements of the FBW are incorrect:</u>

Neither Hitler, Göring nor Frau Goebbels were in the version that the Committee saw. It was the same copy that was shown beforehand to the FSK (Filmselbstkontrolle) for review, and from which after many weeks, all shots of Hitler, Göring, Goebbels, etc. were removed. We never had a shot of Frau Goebbels. These shots had already been removed from the film when the film was shown in the film clubs in Berlin and Bremen. Since I possess absolutely no second copy of the complete version, there is no possibility of error. Also an SS man in close-up or half close-up is unknown to me. Maybe someone confused an usher with an SS man. Also I have never seen uniformed SS men in the film. Only in the marathon can SA men be seen in the shadows. They were used to keep the public from the course in order to protect the runners.

Swastika flags were only shown before the German victories. I had already cut all these from this copy before the review of the FSK. In spite of the 36 gold medals that German athletes won, not one single German victory ceremony is to be seen. Now they can be seen only once in the film alongside the English flags, since otherwise the victory of the English relay team could not have been shown. This would be extremely unfortunate, because this was the only gold medal that the English won in track and field. Otherwise, the swastika banner is only visible once or twice for a very short time, as it was not possible to cut it out on technical grounds.

In part II of the Olympic film, the swastika banner is clearly visible only one time, in the march past of all the other flags in the closing ceremony. For technical reasons, here also, the flag could not be cut out. In the event, however, that the short moment in which the flag is visible causes offense, then I would be ready to attempt to block out the swastika by a trick procedure.

I would also like to remark that the salute with the raised arm is the 'Olympic Greeting' that was taken from ancient times and was used before 1936. (See supporting document: photo with Olympic greeting from the 1924 Olympic Games in Paris.)

In closing, I would like to mention the following events that in any circumstances would be unthinkable, if the Olympic film embodied the spirit of the National Socialist period:

1. Only last year the English Ministry of Education inquired through the Foreign Ministry in Bonn (Herr Dr. Rowas) about the possibility of buying copies of both Olympic films for English schools

and Institutes of Culture.
2. Parisian television want to broadcast both Olympic films in France.
3. The German critics who wrote reviews on the occasion of the showing of the Olympic films in Berlin and Bremen at the end of the last year, said unanimously that the Olympic film today is by far the best of the Olympic films, and Telegraf-Berlin said that it was unequalled in the area of film techniques and athletics.
4. I request the members to read carefully the two American reviews, copies of which I included. These reviews were written in a time in which America was in the throes of the strongest wave of hatred against National Socialist Germany--that is, a few months after the frightful Kristallnacht. One must be aware of the mood at that time in America in order to be able to grasp completely the value of these American reviews of the Olympic film. If the film had contained even the slightest glimmer of National Socialist atmosphere (it was shown in the original version as everywhere else), then it would have been unthinkable that such then great papers as the Los Angeles Times and the Hollywood Citizen News could have written such fantastic reviews, which have never been equalled by a German film up to now. It should certainly be possible that the same objectivity should be available to men of a German governing body, as that found by the American journalists at that time, when everything that came out of Germany was (correctly) held in disrepute.

   But the real mainspring of the film, that came about from the upholding of the Olympic idea and the idea of athletic competition, was stronger than hate and political prejudice.
5. One cannot simply make the statement that all foreign newspapers and critics, who in 1938-39 wrote so unusually good reviews about the Olympic films, were supposed to be pro-Nazi. It is generally known that the Swiss press, for instance, never took a pro-Nazi position, and one could never take newspapers like the Neue Zürcher Zeitung, Berner Tageblatt, or Neue Basler Zeitung as pro-Nazi. In my supporting documents we found notices that were partly written by Jewish critics and opponents of the Nazi regime. They would certainly not allow it to be said that they had written their notices in "National Socialist terminology," as the FBW states in its list of reasons.

Therefore, I would like once again to refer to the words that Herr Professor Dr. Carl Diem wrote to the Filmbewertungsstelle on March 5:

"It appears desirable to us on this account in this film, not to carry on the justified criticism of the Nazi reign of terror, but rather to honor the Olympic Games as a respected oasis."

I close with these words, and ask the men of the High Committee to consider objectively the Olympic film as an athletic and artistic document, and not to deny it the same recognition that has been given it in foreign countries, Germany, and by opponents of the Nazi regime.

Munich, April 19, 1958

(signed) Leni Riefenstahl

• APPENDIX E •

OLYMPIA. Der Film Von Den XI. Olympischen Spielen, Berlin 1936

Gewidmet Dem Wiederbergründer Der Olympischen Spiele, BARON PIERRE DE COUBERTIN, Zur Ehre Und Zum Ruhme Der Jugend Der Welt

Gesamtleitung und Kunstlerische Gestaltung: LENI RIEFENSTAHL

Musik: HERBERT WINDT

Herstellungsleitung: WALTER TRAUT, Walter Groskopf

Die Aufnahmen Für Den Prolog Machte: WILLY ZIELKE

An Der Kamera: HANS ERTL, WALTER FRENTZ, GUZZI LANTSCHNER, KURT NEUBERT, HANS SCHEIB, Andor Von Barsy, Wilfried Basse, Josef Dietze, E. Epkens, Von Friedl, Hans Gottschalk, Richard Groschopp, W. Hameister, Wolf Hart, Hasso Hartnagel, Prof. Walter Hege, E. V. D. Heyden, Albert Höcht, Paul Holzki, W. Hundhausen, H. Von Jaworsky, Von Kaweczynski, H. Kebelmann, S. Ketterer, Albert Kling, Ernst Kunstmann, Leo de Laforgue, Lagorio, E. Lamberti, Otto Lantschner, Waldemar Lemke, Georg Lemki, C. A. Linke, E. Nitzschemann, Albert Schattmann, Wilhelm Schmidt, Hugo Schulze, L. Schwedler, Alfred Siegert, W. Siehm, Dr. Ernst Sorge, H. Von Stwolinski, Karl Vass

Die Wochenschauen: FOX-PARAMOUNT-TOBIS MELO-UFA: Stellten Ihr Gesamtes Material Zur Verfüngung

Die Fackellauf-Trickaufnahmen Wurden Von Der ARBEITSGEMEINSCHAFT SVEND HOLDAN Durchgeführt

Technische Mitarbeit: RUDOLF SCHAAD

Die Leitung Der Tonaufnahmen Lag In Händen Von Tonmeister: SIEGFRIED SCHULZE

Tonschnittmeister: MAX MICHEL, JOHANNES LUDKE-ARNFRIED HEYNE-GUZZI LANTSCHNER; Assistenten: Wolfgang Brüning-Otto Lantschner

Sprecher: DR. PAUL LAVEN-ROLF WERNICKE, Henri Nannen und Johannes Pagels

Sportliche Beratung: DIPL. SPORTL. JOSEF SCHMÜCKER

Aufnahmeleiter: ARTHUR KIEKEBUSCH-RUDOLF FICHTNER-KONSTANTIN BOENISCH

Filmtechnische Bauten: ARCHITEKT ROBERT HERLTH

An Der Musikalischen Synchronisation Waren Beteilight: DER KITTELSCHE CHOR UNTER LEITUNG VON PROF. KITTEL; DAS PHILHARMONISCHE ORCHESTER; DIE LEIBSTANDARTE UNTER LEITUNG VON OBERMUSIKMEISTER MÜLLER-JOHN; DAS UFA-SINFONIE-ORCHESTER UND DAS TOFI-ORCHESTER

Leitung Der Foto-Abteilung Und Bildpropaganda: ROLF LANTIN

Die Durchführung Der Filmarbeiten Wurde Durch Das INTERNATIONALE OLYMPISCHE KOMITEE Und Durch Das OLYMPISCHE KOMITEE Unterstützt Verleih: TOBIS, FILMKUNST G.M.B.H. Weltvertrieb: TOBIS, CINEMA FILM A.G. K o p i e: KARL GEYER

• SOURCES CONSULTED •

BOOKS

Barkhausen, Hans. Filmpropaganda für Deutschland im ersten und zweiten Weltkrieg. Hildesheim and New York: Olms Presse, 1982.

Barnouw, Erik. Documentary. New York: Oxford University Press, 1974.

Bazin, André. What Is Cinema? 2 vols. Edited and translated by Hugh Gray. Berkeley and Los Angeles: University of California Press, 1967.

Berliner Illustrierte Zeitung. Olympia-Sonderheft. [Berlin, 1936].

Bohlen, Friedrich. Die XI Olympischen Spiele Berlin 1936: Instrument der innen- und aussenpolitischen Propaganda und Systemsicherung des fastischen Regimes. Cologne: Pahl-Rugenstein Verlag, 1979.

Butler, Eliza Marion. The Tyranny of Greece over Germany. Cambridge: Cambridge University Press, 1935.

Butler, Rohan D'O. The Roots of National Socialism. New York: E. P. Dutton and Co., Inc., 1942.

Christmann, Sepp, and Huber, Erwin. Lauf, Sprung und Wurf. Berlin: Weidmann Verlagsbuchhandlung, 1941.

Cigaretten-Bilderdienst. Die Olympischen Spiele 1936. 2 vols. Hamburg: Altona Behrenfeld, 1936.

Copleston, Frederick. A History of Philosophy. The Bellarmine Series 18. Vol. 7: Fichte to Nietzsche. Westminster, Md.: The Newman Press, 1963.

Craig, Gordon A. The Germans. New York: G. P. Putnam's Sons, 1982.

Curtius, Ernst. Olympia. Berlin: Atlantis Verlag, 1935.

de Jonge, Alex. The Weimar Chronicle: Prelude to Hitler. New York and London: Paddington Press, Ltd.

Dewey, John. German Philosophy and Politics. New York: G. P. Putnam's Sons, 1942.

Diem, Carl. Sport. Leipzig and Berlin: B. G. Leubner, 1920.

Dorfles, Gillo. Kitsch: The World of Bad Taste. New York: Universe Books, 1969.

Dyhrenfurth, Günter Oscar. Baltoro, ein Himalaya-Buch. Basel: B. Schwabe and Co., [1939].

Ellul, Jacques. Propaganda: The Formation of Men's Attitudes. Translated by Konrad Kellen and Jean Lerner. New York: Alfred A. Knopf, 1965; Vintage Books, 1972.

Ertl, Hans. Meine wilden dreissiger Jahre. Munich: F. A. Herbig Verlagsbuchhandlung, 1982.

Ford, Charles. Leni Riefenstahl. Translated to German by Antoinette Gittinger. Munich: Wilhelm Heyne Verlag, 1982.

Friedrich, Werner P. An Outline-History of German Literature. New York: Barnes and Noble, 1948.

Fromm, Bella. Blood and Banquets. New York and London: Harper Brothers, 1942.

Gay, Peter. Weimar Culture: The Outsider as Insider. London: Secker and Warburg, 1968.

Goebbels, Joseph. The Goebbels Diaries 1939-1941. Translated and edited by Fred Taylor. New York: G. P. Putnam's Sons, 1983.

Griffiths, Richard. Fellow Travellers of the Right. London: Constable and Company Ltd., 1980.

Grunberger, Richard. The 12-Year Reich: A Social History of Nazi Germany 1933-1945. Published previously in England under the title A Social History of the Third Reich. New York: Ballantine Books, Inc., 1972.

Halkett, G. R. The Dear Monster. London: Jonathan Cape, Ltd., 1939.

Haus der Kunst, Munich. Die Dreissinger Jahre: Schauplatz Deutschland. Munich: Haus der Kunst, 1977.

Hinz, Berthold. Art in the Third Reich. New York: Pantheon Books, 1979.

Hitler, Adolf. Hitlers Tischgespräche im Führerhauptquartier. 3rd ed. Edited by Dr. Henry Picker. Stuttgart: Seewald Verlag, 1976.

_______. Reden und Proklamationen, 1932-1945. Edited by Max Domarus. Wiesbaden: Löwit, 1973.

_______. Secret Conversations. New York: Farrar, Straus and Young, 1953.

Hölderlin, Johann Christian Friedrich. Selected Verse. Edited and translated by Michael Hamburger. The Penguin Poets Series, D. 54. Baltimore, Md.: Penguin Books, 1961.

_______. Selected Poems of Friedrich Hölderlin. Translated by J. B. Leishman. London: The Hogarth Press, 1964.

Holmes, Judith. Olympiad 1936: Blaze of Glory for Hitler's Reich. New York: Ballantine Books, 1971.

International Council for Philosophy and Humanistic Studies. The Third Reich. New York: Howard Fertig, 1975.

Johnson, William O. All That Glitters Is Not Gold. New York: G. P. Putnam's Sons, 1972.

Kracauer, Siegfried. From Caligari to Hitler. Princeton, N.J.: Princeton University Press, 1947.

Kruger, Arnd. Die Olympische Spiele 1936 und die Weltmeinung. Berlin, Munich and Frankfurt am Main: Verlag Bartels und Wernitz KG, 1973.

Mandell, Richard D. The Nazi Olympics. New York: Macmillan Co., 1971.

McClatchie, Stanley. Sieh: Das Herz Europas. Berlin: Verlag Heinrich Hoffman, 1937.

Mann, Thomas. Doctor Faustus. Translated by H. T. Lowe-Porter. New York: Alfred A. Knopf, 1948.

Merker, Reinhard. Die bildenden Künste im nationalsozialismus. Cologne: DuMont Buchverlag, 1983.

Mosse, George L. The Crisis of German Ideology. New York: The Universal Library, Grosset and Dunlap, 1964.

Noyce, Wilfred. Scholar Mountaineers: Pioneers of Parnassus. New York: Roy Publishers, 1950.

Organisationskomitee für die XI Olympiade, Berlin 1936. XI Olympiade Berlin 1936: Amtlicher Bericht. 2 vols. Berlin: W. Limpert, [1937].

_______. The Olympic Games, Berlin 1936: Official Report. Translated from German. 2 vols. Berlin: Wilhelm Limpert, [1937].

Reichsrundfunk G.m.b.H. Olympia-Weltsender. Berlin: Deutscher Verlag für Politik und Wirtschaft, 193-.

Riefenstahl, Leni. XI Olympiade, Berlin. Official photographs of the Olympic Games made under the direction of Leni Riefenstahl. 67 photographs 9 x 11 inches in album 15 x 17 inches. Personal dedication to Adolf Hitler on flyleaf. Located in Library of Congress, Prints and Photographs Section.

_______. [Ernst Jäger, ghostwriter]. Hinter den Kulissen der Reichparteitagfilms. Munich: Zentralverlag der NSDAP, 1935.

_______. Schönheit im Olympischen Kampf. Berlin: Im deutschen Verlag, 1937.

Shirer, William L. Berlin Diary. New York: Alfred A. Knopf, 1941.

_______. The Collapse of the Third Republic. New York: Simon and Schuster, 1969.

_______. The Rise and Fall of the Third Reich. New York: Simon and Schuster, 1960.

Stern, Fritz. The Politics of Cultural Despair. Berkeley and Los Angeles: University of California Press, 1961.

Taylor, Robert R. The Word in Stone. Berkeley, Los Angeles and London: The University of California Press, 1974.

Thomas, Hans Alex. Die deutsche Tonfilmmusik von den Anfangen bis 1956. Gütersloh C. Bertelsmann Verlag, 1962.

Tobis Cinema Film A. G. Olympia: Fest der Völker: Erster Film von den Olympischen Spielen Berlin 1936. Erstes Presseheft. [Berlin: 1938].

_______. Olympia: Fest der Schönheit: Zweiter film von den Olympischen Spielen Berlin 1936. Zweites Presseheft. [Berlin: 1938].

Ullrich, Klaus. Olympia und die Deutschen. [Berlin]: Gesellschaft zur Förderung des Olympischen Gedenkens in der DDR, 1961.

Vaughan, William. German Romantic Painting. New Haven and London: Yale University Press, 1980.

Wallechinsky, David. The Complete Book of the Olympics. New York: Penguin Books, 1984.

Wolff, Paul. Dr. Paul Wolff's Leica Sports Shots. New York: William Morrow and Co., 1937.

Zielke, Willy. Einführung in die Akt-Fotographie. Düsseldorf: Wilhelm Knapp Verlag, 1961.

NEWSPAPERS

"Am Telefon: Leni Riefenstahl." Film-Kurier, 17 October 1935.

"Gestaltung des Olympia-Films." Völkische Beobachter (Berlin), 10 December 1935.

"Vom Olympia-Winter zum Olympia-Filmwerk." Film-Kurier, 1 February 1936.

"Leni Riefenstahls Rombesuch: Mussolinis Interesse am Dokumentfilm." Film-Kurier, 27 February 1936, pp. 1-2.

"Das Olympische Filmwerk in den ersten Vorbereitungen." Film-Kurier, 27 April 1936.

"Leni Riefenstahl sammelt Motive." Film-Kurier, 13 May 1936, p. 3.

"Der Olympia-Film wird angekurbelt." 12 Uhr (Berlin), 14 May 1936.

"Filmgeographie von Grünau." Film-Kurier, 5 June 1936, pp. 1-2.

"Kiel im Olympia-Film." Film-Kurier, 8 June 1936, p. 1.

"Für den Prolog des Olympiafilms." Licht Bild Bühne, 9 June 1936, p. 1.

"Leni Riefenstahl bei der Olympia-Auswahl der Segler in Kiel." Licht Bild Bühne, 9 June 1936.

"Rund um Leni Riefenstahls Olympiafilm: Hans Ertl." Film-Kurier, 11 June 1936, p. 3.

"Filmvorbereitungen für Olympia-Kiel." 12 Uhr, 12 June 1936.

"500000 Meter Olympia Film." Nachtausgabe (Berlin), 12 June 1936.

"Olympiade in der Zeitlupe: Kurt Neubert bei Leni Riefenstahl." Licht Bild Bühne, 12 June 1936, p. 1.

"Kampf, Schönheit, Olympische Idee." Film-Kurier, 26 June 1936, p. 1.

"Vom Werden des Olympia-Films: Schnappschusse." Licht Bild Bühne, 26 June 1936, p. 1.

"Nah genug herankommen: Das Problem der Olympia-Operateure." Film-Kurier, 30 June 1936, pp. 1-2.

"Drei Filmautos begleiten den Fackellauf der Olympiade." Der Film, 4 July 1936, p. 1.

"Rund um Leni Riefenstahls Olympiafilm: Walter Frentz." Film-Kurier, 10 July 1936, p. 3.

"Täglich 15000 meter Olympia-Film: Geyer-Werke vor Riesenaufgabe." Film-Kurier, 13 July 1936, p. 1.

"Vor Leni Riefenstahls Olympia-Film-Schlacht." 8 Ufa Abendblatt (Berlin), 14 July 1936.

[Jäger, Ernst]. "Fackellauf durch Griechenland." Sonderdruck aus dem Film-Kurier. July, 1936.

"Telegramm aus Athen." Film-Kurier, 22 July 1936, p. 1.

"Leni tanzt in Delphi." Film-Kurier, 23 July 1936.

"Olympiade-Film--Erster representätiver Tonfilm des Sports." Licht Bild Bühne, 23 July 1936.

"In- und auslandische Presse bei Leni Riefenstahl." Licht Bild Bühne, 30 July 1936, p. 1.

Birchall, Frederick T. "11th Olympics Open Today in Gay and Crowded Berlin." New York Times, 1 August 1936, p. 6.

"Haus Ruhwald, Hauptquartier des Olympia-Filmstabs: Leni Riefenstahl und 300 Mitarbeiter startbereit." Film-Kurier, 1 August 1936, p. 7.

"Immer schussbereit--Eine Schulter-Filmkamera: Keine verwackelten Bilder." Deutsche allgemeine Zeitung, 1 August 1936.

"Geyer konstruiert neue Kopiermaschine für Bild und Ton." Film-Kurier, 1 August 1936, pp. 5-6.

"Das 'Riefenstahl-Filmheer' steht bereit." Licht Bild Bühne, 1 August 1936, p. 4.

Birchall, Frederick T. "100,000 Hail Hitler as the Olympics Open." New York Times, 2 August 1936, sec. 1, p. 33.

[Jäger, Ernst]. "Die Kamera kämpft mit." (On several days entitled "Und die Kamera kampft mit.) Film-Kurier, 3-17 August 1936.

Part 1. "Die ersten beiden Olympia-Tage," 3 August 1936, pp. 1-2.
Part 2. "Die Hundert Meter," 4 August 1936, pp. 3-4.
Part 3. 5 August 1936, p. 3.
Part 4. 6 August 1936, p. 3.
Part 5. "Lachendes Olympia." 7 August 1936, p. 3.
Part 6. "Eine Woche Aufnahmeschlacht." 8 August 1936, p. 3.
Part 7. "Marathon-Sonntag." 10 August 1936, p. 3.
Part 8. "Meisterstücke von Marine und Film." 11 August 1936, p. 3.
Part 9. "M.a.M." 12 August 1936, p. 3.
Part 10. "Ein Hirn ohne Ruhe." 13 August 1936, p. 3.
Part 11. "Dritter Tag vor Schluss." 14 August 1936, p. 3.
Part 12. "Lachendes Olympia II." 15 August 1936, p. 3.
Part 13. "Letzter Schnappschuss." 17 August 1936, p. 3.

"Reels Get Wider Latitude in Shooting the Olympics." Motion Picture Daily, 5 August 1936, pp. 1-2.

"Olympia-Halbzeit." Licht Bild Bühne, 8 August 1936, p. 1.

"Grosskampf bei Geyer." Film-Kurier, 8 August 1936, pp. 1-2.

Cunningham, James P. "Hitler Makes U.S. Olympic Films Advertise Germany." Motion Picture Herald, 8 August 1936, pp. 13-15.

Henry, Bill. Los Angeles Times, 10 August 1936, sec. 2, p. 13.

"Ein Kapitel Marathonlauf: Film bei Kontrolle 5." Licht Bild Bühne, 10 August 1936, pp. 1-2.

"Nachtaufnahmen zum Olympia-Film." Licht Bild Bühne, 10 August 1936.

"Olympia-Filmarbeit nach dem 16. August." Licht Bild Bühne, 14 August 1936, p. 11.

Birchall, Frederick T. "Humble Old Lady and the Führer Get Biggest Kick from Olympics." New York Times, 14 August 1936, p. 20.

"Nächtliche Nahaufnahmen." Film-Kurier, 15 August 1936, p. 6.

"In Grünau: 21 Kameras trotz Regen." Film-Kurier, 15 August 1936, p. 1.

Birchall, Frederick T. "Olympics Leave Glow in the Reich." New York Times, 16 August 1936, sec. 4, p. 5.

Birchall, Frederick T. "Games in Berlin Close Amid Pomp." New York Times, 17 August 1936, p. 11.

"Kurt Neubert--mit dem Zeitlupen 'Tank.'" Film-Kurier, 18 August 1936, p. 3.

"Hans Scheib--Der Mann mit der langen Brennweite." Film-Kurier, 19 August 1936, p. 3.

Effner, Louis. "Owens, Back, Gets Hearty Reception." New York Times, 25 August 1936, p. 25.

"Filmburg auf der Nehrung hinter Stacheldraht." Preussische Zeitung, 27 September 1936.

Tolischus, Otto D. "Reich Shows Uses of Its Materials." New York Times, 9 May 1937, p. 33.

Philip, P. J. "Paris Exposition Is Inaugurated: Most of Buildings Uncompleted." New York Times, 25 May 1937, p. 29.

"Besuch bei Leni Riefenstahl." Film-Kurier, 2 June 1937, p. 2.

"La Disgrâce de Leni Riefenstahl." Paris Soir, 14 June 1937, p. 1.

"Lügen über Leni Riefenstahl." Film-Kurier, 16 June 1937, p. 1.

"Ovationen unter dem Eiffelturm: Leni Riefenstahl in Paris--Prof. Dr. Lehnich sprach im 'Ciné--Photo--Phono.'" Film-Kurier, 3 July 1937, p. 2.

"Leni Riefenstahls Rede in Paris." Film-Kurier, 5 July 1937, p. 2.

"Parteitag-Film in Paris: Begeisterte Aufnahme von Triumph des Willens." Film-Kurier, 5 July 1937, p. 1.

"Leni Riefenstahls Ansprache in Paris." Licht Bild Bühne, 6 July 1937, p. 4.

"Der Olympia-Vorfilm: Immer wieder Interesse in Paris." Film-Kurier, 7 September 1937, pp. 3-4.

"Herbert Windt der Komponist heroischer Filme." Film-Kurier, 19 November 1937, p. 4.

Riefenstahl, Leni. "Kraft und Schönheit der Jugend mögen filmische Form gefunden haben." Film-Kurier, 31 December 1937.

"Philharmoniker spielen Filmmusik." Film-Kurier, 10 January 1938, p. 3.

"Zwei Filme von Willy Zielke wurden gezeigt." Film-Kurier, 4 February 1938, p. 2.

"Leni Riefenstahl zum 10. April." *Film-Kurier*, 9 April 1938, p. 3.

"Olympia-Film startet am Geburtstag des Führers." *Film-Kurier*, 11 April 1938, p. 1.

"Schönheit im Olympischen Kampf." *Licht Bild Bühne*, 12 April 1938, p. 1.

"Geleitwort des Reichssportführers zum Olympia-Film." *Licht Bild Bühne*, 14 April 1938, p. 1.

"Kurs auf die Premiere des Olympia-films." *Film-Kurier*, 14 April 1938, p. 1.

Schnauk, Wilhelm. "Wie entstand der Olympiafilm?" *Licht Bild Bühne*, 14 April 1938, p. 1.

"Begeisterte Aufnahme des Olympiafilms." *Film-Kurier*, 21 April 1938, p. 1.

"Die Ehrengäste der Olympia Aufführung." *Licht Bild Bühne*, 21 April 1938, pp. 1-2.

"Der Sieg einer Filmdichtung." *Licht Bild Bühne*, 21 April 1938, pp. 1-2.

"Weltpresse über den Olympia-film." *Film-Kurier*, 22 April 1938, p. 1.

"Der Reichssportführer über den Olympia-Film." *Licht Bild Bühne*, 22 April 1938, p. 1.

"Im Geiste Olympias: Herbert Windts Musik zum *Fest der Völker*." *Film-Kurier*, 23 April 1938, p. 2.

"Musik der Woche." *Licht Bild Bühne*, 23 April 1938, p. 4.

"Festliche Münchner Olympia-Film-Premiere." *Licht Bild Bühne*, 28 April 1938.

"Gestern Abend in Zürich: Olympia-Film bestand internationale Feuertaufe." *Film-Kurier*, 11 May 1938, p. 1.

"Olympia Fest der Schönheit." *Film-Kurier*, 13 May 1938, p. 2.

"Fest der Schönheit: Der 2. Teil des Olympiafilms im Ufa-Palast am Zoo." *Licht Bild Bühne*, 3 June 1938, pp. 1-2.

"Fest der Schönheit: Ufa Palast am Zoo." *Film-Kurier*, 3 June 1938, p. 2.

"Herbert Windts Musik-Olympia: 'Fest der Schönheit'--musikalisches Volkstum im Film. Film-Kurier, 4 June 1938, p. 6.

"Telegramm an Leni Riefenstahl aus Griechenland." Film-Kurier, 14 June 1938, p. 3.

"Man hört und liesst." Film-Kurier, 16 June 1938, pp. 2, 3.

"Leni Riefenstahl und Sascha Guitry sprechen über Filmkunst." Film-Kurier, 20 June 1938, p. 1.

"Brusseler Start im Beisein des Königs." Film-Kurier, 24 June 1938, p. 1.

"Festliche Olympia-Premier in Belgrad." Film-Kurier, 24 June 1938, p. 2.

"Leni Riefenstahl à Paris." Le Figaro, 1 July 1938, p. 4.

"Au Normandie: Les Dieux du Stade." Le Figaro, 6 July 1938.

"Paris vom Olympiafilm begeistert." Licht Bild Bühne, 7 July 1938, p. 2.

"Stockholmer Erfolg des Olympia-Films." Licht Bild Bühne, 8 July 1938, p. 3.

"Olympia-Film wird italienisch synchronisiert." Film-Kurier, 21 July 1938, p. 2.

"Skandinavien-Reise von Leni Riefenstahl." Film-Kurier, 1 August 1938, p. 1.

"Olympiafilm-Erfolg in Dänemark." Film-Kurier, 3 August 1938, p. 2.

"Leni Riefenstahl in Stockholm und Helsingfors." Film-Kurier, 6 August 1938, p. 3.

"Finnlands Presse äussert sich begeistert über den Olympia-Film." Film-Kurier, 16 August 1938, p. 3.

"Heute startet am Lido der Olympia-Film der Tobis." Film-Kurier, 26 August 1938, p. 3.

"Grosser Abend am Lido: Triumphaler Erfolg des Olympia Films." Film-Kurier, 27 August 1938, p. 1.

"In Anwesenheit Leni Riefenstahls: Triumph des Olympia-Films in Venedig." Licht Bild Bühne, 27 August 1938, p. 1.

"Telegramme aus Venedig." Film-Kurier, 27 August 1938, p. 1.

"Olympia-Film 2. Teil und 'Urlaub auf Ehrenwort' am Lido erfolgreich." Film-Kurier, 31 August 1938, p. 1.

"Preisverteilung am Lido: Grosser Erfolg des deutschen Filmschaffens." Film-Kurier, 1 September 1938, p. 1.

"Telegramme des Reichsfilmkammerpräsidenten aus Venedig." Film-Kurier, 2 September 1938, p. 1.

"Die polnische Presse: 'Leni Riefenstahl Film trägt den Stempel des Genies." Film-Kurier, 17 September 1938, p. 1.

"Ausserordentlicher Erfolg des Olympia-Films in Rom." Licht Bild Bühne, 1 October 1938, p. 3.

"Ungarisches Presselob für den Olympiafilm." Licht Bild Bühne, 7 October 1938, p. 2.

"Leni Riefenstahl beim norwegischen König." Film-Kurier, 13 October 1938, p. 1.

"Olympia-Film der Tobis in Anwesenheit des König in Oslo gestartet." Film-Kurier, 14 October 1938, p. 1.

"Leni Riefenstahl vor den Studenten von Lund." Film-Kurier, 18 October 1938, p. 1.

"Leni Riefenstahls Erfolg in Kobenhagen." Film-Kurier, 19 October 1938, p. 1.

"Triumph des Olympia-films in Skandinavien." Licht Bild Bühne, 28 October 1938, p. 4.

"Wardour Street Gossip by 'Tatler.'" The Daily Film Renter (London), 29 October 1938.

"Wardour Street Gossip by "Tatler.'" The Daily Film Renter, 1 November 1938.

"Nix Nazi Olympix." Variety, 2 November 1938, p. 12.

Winchell, Walter. "Walter Winchell on Broadway." Daily Mirror, 9 November 1938, p. 6.

"Anti-Nazis Protest Riefenstahl's Visit to Circulate Olympic Film." Motion Picture Herald, 12 November 1938, p. 19.

"Post This on your Bulletin Board!" Hollywood Reporter, 29 November 1938, p. 5.

M'Lemore, Henry. "Henry Goes to Bat on Berlin Olympic Film--No Propaganda." Hollywood Citizen News, 17 December 1938.

"'XI Olympiad' Thrilling Record of Great Games." Los Angeles Times, 17 December 1938.

"Leni Riefenstahl Still Getting Film Business Brushoff." Variety, 6 December 1938, pp. 155.

Jäger, Ernst. "How Leni Riefenstahl Became Hitler's Girlfriend." 11 Parts. Hollywood Tribune, 28 April-17 July 1939.

Part 1. 28 April 1939
Part 2. 5 May 1939
Part 3. 12 May 1939
Part 4. 19 May 1939
Part 5. 26 May 1939
Part 6. 2 June 1939
Part 7. 9 June 1939
Part 8. 16 June 1939
Part 9. 23 June 1939
Part 10. 10 July 1939
Part 11. 17 July 1939

Powell, Dilys. "Films of the Week." Times, 13 April 1947.

Davis, Jack. "Release this Olympic Film." Sunday Graphic (London), 1 February 1948.

News Chronicle (London), 7 February 1948.

"Leni Riefenstahl haut auf." Film-Woche, 5 April 1952, p. 14.

Stueck, Hans. "Leni Riefenstahl Returns to the Olympics." New York Times, 23 August 1972, p. 31.

"Olympia-Film verbannt." Rhein-Zeitung (Coblentz), 16 February 1983.

INTERVIEWS

Riefenstahl, Leni. Munich. Interview, 23 May 1983.

Von Jaworsky, Heinz [Henry Javorsky]. Holliswood, New York. Interview, 7 July 1983.

Zielke, Willy. Bad Pyrmont (German Federal Republic). Interview, 17-18 May 1983.

ARTICLES IN MAGAZINES, JOURNALS, AND BOOKS

Barkhausen, Hans. "Footnote to the History of Riefenstahl's Olympia." Film Quarterly 28 (Fall 1974): 8-17.

Corliss, Richard. "Leni Riefenstahl, a Bibliography." Film Heritage 5 no. 1 (Fall 1969): 27-36.

Delahaye, Michel. "Leni and the Wolf." Cahiers du Cinéma in English, no. 5, pp. 49-55.

Eisner, Lotte. "Kitsch in the Cinema." Dorfles, Gillo, ed., Kitsch: The World of Bad Taste. New York: Universe Books, 1969.

Flanner, Janet [Genêt]. "Berlin Letter." New Yorker, 1 August 1936, p. 40.

Goelz, Erwin [Frank Maraun]. "Triumph des Dokumentarfilms." Der deutsche Film 2 (May 1938): 317.

Gronostay, Walter. "Deutsche Filmmusiker: Herbert Windt." Der deutsche Film 1 (1937): 316.

Hitchens, Gordon. "Leni Riefenstahl Interviewed by Gordon Hitchens, October 11, 1971, Munich." Film Culture 56-57 (Spring 1973): 94-121.

________; Bond, Kirk; and Hanhardt, John. "Interview with Henry Jaworsky by Gordon Hitchens, Kirk Bond and John Hanhardt." Film Culture 56-57 (Spring 1973): 122-61.

Hoelterhoff, Manuela. "Art of the Third Reich: Documents of Oppression." Art Forum 14 no. 4 (December 1975): 55-62.

Kramer, Jane. "Letter from West Germany." New Yorker, 19 December 1983, pp. 102-120.

Laven, Paul. "Neue Sprechkunst beim Olympia-film: Der Sprecher als 'Star.'" Tobis Cinema Film A.G., Olympia: Fest der Völker: Erstes Presseheft. [Berlin: 1938], p. 61.

Laven, Paul. "Ein Welterlebnis in Bildern." Kölnische illustrierte Zeitung, 17 February 1938.

Mannheim, L. Andrew. "Leni: Maligned Genius of the Nazis?" Modern Photography, February 1974, pp. 88-95, 112-19.

Müller, Hedwig, and Servos, Norbert. "From Isadora Duncan to Leni Riefenstahl." Ballett International. April 1972, pp. 15-23.

Riefenstahl, Leni. "Why Am I Filming 'Penthesilea'?" translated by John Hanhardt. Film Culture, no. 56-57 (Spring 1973); 192-215.

Sontag, Susan. "Fascinating Fascism." New York Review of Books, 6 February 1975, pp. 23-30.

von Tschammer und Osten, Hans von. "Ein Hoheslied menschlicher Leibeskraft und Lebensbejahung." Olympia: Fest der Völker: Erstes Presseheft, p. 11.

Vaughan, Dai. "Berlin versus Tokyo." Sight and Sound, 46 no. 4 (Autumn 1977): 210-215.

Weigel, Herman. "Interview mit Leni Riefenstahl." Film-Kritic 188 (August 1972): 397-410.

______. "Randbemerkungen zum Thema." Film-Kritik, 188 (August 1972): 426-433.

Windt, Herbert. "Warum Musik im Film?" Jahrbuch der deutschen Musik. Leipzig: Walter Tiemann, 1943, pp. 182-3.

Zielke, Willy. "Die Überblende." Der deutsche Film, 2 (1937): 74-77.

"Die Arbeit am Olympia-Film." Der deutsche Film 2 (1938): 252-54.

"Gibt es einen deutschen Kamerastil?" Der deutsche Film 2 (1938): 176-77.

"Im Geist von Olympia." Tobis Cinema Film A. G. Olympia: Fest der Völker: Erstes Presseheft, pp. 39-41.

"Leni Riefenstahl." Der deutsche Film 1 (1936): 40-1.

"Musikalische Pionierleistungen beim Olympia-Film." Tobis Cinema Film A. G. Olympia: Fest der Völker: Erstes Presseheft, pp. 57-60.

"Neue Klassik: Geist und Gesetz der Olympia-Filme." Tobis Cinema Film A. G. Olympia: Fest der Völker: Erstes Pressenheft, p. 65.

"Olympia: Ein deutscher Film." Stuttgarter illustrierte Zeitung, 23 February 1938.

"Olympia: Fest der Völker." Illustrierte Film-Kurier 2792 (1938).

"Olympia: Fest der Schönheit." Illustrierte Film-Kurier 2794 (1938).

"Der Olympia-Prolog: Leni Riefenstahl schönste Film Dichtung." Tobis Cinema Film A. G. Olympia: Fest der Völker: Erstes Presseheft, pp. 43-7.

"Sommer-Olympia-Film in Front!" Der deutsche Film 1 (July 1936): 38-40.

DISSERTATIONS AND PAPERS

Garafola, Lynn. "The Odyssey of Hubert Stowitts." New York 1983. (Typewritten)

Wallace, P. A. "An Historical Study of the Career of Leni Riefenstahl from 1928 to 1933." Ph.D. dissertation, University of Southern California, 1975.

ARCHIVAL SOURCES

Berkeley, California. University of California. Bancroft Library. Paget-Fredericks Collection.

Berlin, German Federal Republic. Berlin Documents Center.

Champaign-Urbana, Illinois. University of Illinois. Applied Life Studies Library. Avery Brundage Collection.

Coblentz, German Federal Republic. Bundesarchiv.
- R2. Reichsfinanzministerium, Vols. 4754, 4766 fol. 1, 4788, 4789, 4808, Anh. 26, fol. 1.
- R18. Reichsministerium des Innern, vols. 5609, 5614, 5680.
- R55. Reichsministerium für Volksaufklärung und Propaganda. Vols. 69, 503, 1327, 28.
- R56. Reichsministerium für Volksaufklärung und Propaganda. VI/9, fol. 1-427.
- R 109 I Cautio Treuhand.
- NL 118. Nachlass Goebbels. Tagebucher
- Zsg 101. Sammlung Brammer
- Zsg 102. Sammlung Sänger
- Zsg 110. Sammlung Traub.

Dearborn, Michigan. Henry Ford Museum--Archives and Research Library.

Frankfurt am Main, German Federal Republic (presently). Deutsches Institut für Filmkunde. Olympia file.

Potsdam, German Democratic Republic. Archiv für den wissenschaftlichen Film.

Washington, D.C. Library of Congress.

Washington, D.C. National Archives. Captured German Documents Section.

UNPUBLISHED MATERIALS

Riefenstahl, Leni. "Die Arbeit am Olympiafilm." (This is an 11-page typewritten document, signed by Leni Riefenstahl, which is the same material published in the official report of the Olympic Games.)

[________.] "Begründung des Einspruchs gegen die Entscheidung des Bewertungsausschusses vom 30 Januar 1958." (Typewritten, 12 pages).

[________.] "Ein Bericht über die Herstellung der Olympia-Filme (nach authentischen Dokumenten und Unterlagen.)" (Typewritten, signed "von Leni Riefenstahl" in her handwriting, 10 pages.)

[________.] "Pressestimmen aus Belgien über den Olympiafilm 1936." (Typewritten, sent to author by Leni Riefenstahl, 2 pages.)

[________.] "Pressestimmen aus Frankreich über den Olympiafilm 1936." (Typewritten, sent to author by Leni Riefenstahl, 6 pages.)

[________.] "Pressesstimmen aus Ungarn über den Olympiafilm 1936." (Typewritten, sent to author by Leni Riefenstahl, 4 pages.)

[________.] Über die Herstellung der Olympia-Filme." (This manuscript was sent to the author from Leni Riefenstahl.)

FILMS

Bavaria Tonwoche 19/1938. Potsdam. Archiv für den wissenschaftlichen Film, NP09389.

Behind the Scenes of the Film About the Olympic Games. Library of Congress, FAA 9677.

The Call of the Olympic Bell. German Railroads Information Office, 1936. Library of Congress, FAA 1171.

Compulsory Gymnastic Exercises for the XI Olympic Games in Berlin, Library of Congress, FAA, 1193.

Die XI Olympiade Berlin 1936. Bayer Leverkusen Produktion 1936. Library of Congress, FRA 5437-5441.

XI Olympiade Berlin 1936: Moderner Fünfkampf. Heeres-Filmstelle 1936.

Gebt mir vier Jahre Zeit. Tobis-Bavaria Archives. Library of Congress, FBA 6738.

Jugend der Welt. Bundesarchiv, Coblentz.

Kings of the Olympics. Westport International Films Inc., 1948. Library of Congress, FEB 3470-76.

Der Mensch. Bundesarchiv, Coblentz.

Olympia: Fest der Völker, Fest der Schönheit. English version, copyright by Leni Riefenstahl-Produktion, 1975. Library of Congress, FCA 7662-7664; FDA 2514-2515.

Olympia: Fest der Völker, Fest der Schönheit. Original German version, copy sent from Bundesarchiv in 1968. Library of Congress, FBA 7556-7564.

Olympia: Fest der Völker, Fest der Schönheit. Version returned from Reid H. Ray. Produced Olympia-Film G.m.b.H. Library of Congress, FPA 755-778.

Olympiade 1936: Kameraleute bei der Arbeit. Potsdam. Archiv für den wissenschaftlichen film NP 15780.

Olympia-Vorbereitung in Deutschland. Ufa Kulturfilm. Library of Congress, FBA 2194.

Olympic Games of 1936. Library of Congress, FBB 4194.

Olympic Games 1936: Opening Ceremony, August 1, 1936. German Railroads Information Office, 1936. Library of Congress, FAA 2023-27.

Olympic Games 1936. German Railroads Information Office. Library of Congress, FAA 2023-2027.

Olympic Sidelights. R.D.V. Boehner Film, Dresden 1936. Library of Congress, FAA 2006.

Olympische Reiterkämpfe. Heeresfilmstelle, 1936, series no. 228. Library of Congress, copy 1, FBB 351-52; copy 2, FAA 2001-2005.

Olympische Spiele Berlin 1936. Olympia Film G.m.b.H.--RWU, 1940. Series no. 245. Library of Congress, FAA 2020-22.

Ostmark Wochenschau [April, 1938] Potsdam. Archiv für den wissenschaftlichen Film, NP 09546.

La seconda Parti del Film dell Olympiade di Berlino. Olympia-Film G.m.b.H., Washington D.C. National Archive, 242 MID 2183.

Das Stahltier. Coblentz. Bundesarchiv.

Wege zum Kraft und Schönheit. Ufa 1925. Coblentz. Bundesarchiv. (Bundesarchiv copy has English titles and is entitled *The Golden Road to Beauty*.)

• INDEX •